LANGUAGE AND LITERACY SERIES

Dorothy S. Strickland and Celia Genishi, SERIES EDITORS

ADVISORY BOARD: RICHARD ALLINGTON, DONNA ALVERMANN, KATHRYN AU,
EDWARD CHITTENDON, BERNICE CULLINAN, COLETTE DAIUTE,
ANNE HAAS DYSON, CAROLE EDELSKY, JANET EMIG,
SHIRLEY BRICE HEATH, CONNIE JUEL, SUSAN LYTLE

D1445151

tinued)

THE BEST
FOR OUR CHILDREN

Critical Perspectives on Literacy for Latino Students

Edited by
MARÍA DE LA LUZ REYES
and
JOHN J. HALCÓN

TEACHERS
COLLEGE
PRESS

Teachers College, Columbia University
New York and London

Published by Teachers College Press, 1234 Amsterdam Avenue, New York, NY 10027

Library of Congress Cataloging-in-Publication Data

The best for our children : critical perspectives on literacy for Latino children / edited by María de la Luz Reyes and John J. Halcón.
    p. cm.—(Language and literacy series)
  Includes bibliographical references and index.
   ISBN 0-8077-4007-1 (cloth: alk. paper)—ISBN 0-8077-4006-3 (pbk. : alk. paper)
    1. Hispanic Americans—Education—Social aspects. 2. Literacy—Social aspects—United States. 3. Language arts—Social aspects—United States. 4. Bilingualism—Social aspects—United States. I. Reyes, María de la Luz. II. Halcón, John J. III. Language and literacy series (New York, N.Y.)
LC2672.4.B48 2001
370.117'5—dc21   00-056375

ISBN 0-8077-4006-3 (paper)
ISBN 0-8077-4007-1 (cloth)

Printed on acid-free paper
Manufactured in the United States of America

08 07 06 05 04 03 02 01   8 7 6 5 4 3 2 1

In memory of our parents:
Isabel G. Reyes
José Saavedra Halcón and Lucila Fuentes Halcón
who nurtured our bilingual and bicultural identities.

Also for Juan and Vanessa Halcón
who hold the promise that biliteracy
will continue into the next generation.

Contents

PART I:
SOCIOCULTURAL, SOCIOHISTORICAL, AND SOCIOPOLITICAL CONTEXT OF LITERACY

PART II:
BILITERACY, HYBRIDITY, AND OTHER LITERACIES

PART III:
READING THE WORD BY READING THE WORLD

Foreword

When it comes to the education of Latino students in the United States, almost everyone has had a say. Educators, researchers, and policy makers have offered all manner of solutions for the massive educational problems faced by Latinos in our schools. These have included English-only programs, quick-exit bilingual education, no bilingual education, retention in grade until students develop English literacy, ESL programs for parents so that they speak only English to their children, and many other proposals. A common feature of many of these proposals has been a focus on the "problem" of Spanish, in spite of the fact that a growing body of research suggests that, for young people who speak Spanish, supporting native-language literacy—rather than suppressing or eradicating it—results in higher achievement in both English and Spanish. Besides, most recommendations for addressing the academic failure of Latino students have neglected to acknowledge that Latino students who do not speak Spanish *also* have a high level of academic failure. In a word, most solutions offered for the problems of Latino students in U.S. schools have failed to acknowledge that the major problem is *not* that they speak Spanish (many do not), but that their identities as Latinos are dismissed as resources in the development of their literacy. That is, at the core of our society's widespread negative attitudes and beliefs concerning Latino children's intellectual abilities is their status as children of working-class and poor families who speak a devalued language and share a largely disrespected culture.

Until now, few books have focused on the richness of the cultural, linguistic, and experiential resources that Latino students bring to school, and on what teachers need to know and do to tap into these resources. *The Best for Our Children* does just this, and it also challenges generally accepted ideas about language and literacy for Latino children. This exceptional book disputes similarly the efficacy of blueprint-type strategies, from phonics to whole language, as the sole or best answer for improving the academic achievement of Latinos.

The Best for Our Children is unique not only because of *what* it says about Latino students, but also because of *who* is saying it. Here are the voices of

Latino educators themselves—classroom teachers, researchers, teacher educators—who know firsthand what it means to be a Latino student in our nation's schools. Their knowledge and wisdom are based not only on their autobiographies, but also on the hard-learned lessons acquired in classrooms and schools throughout the United States. These educators have themselves, as the editors suggest in their introduction, "cracked the code" of literacy and used it in the service of Latino students. All teachers can learn much from this book.

The Latino educators represented in this volume cover it all. They consider all facets of literacy and provide powerful examples of Latino students also learning to crack the code of literacy. In spite of sometimes overwhelming odds in their lives (a compelling example is Frankie, described in Chapter 12 by Bobbi Ciriza Houtchens), these are young people who yearn to read books *and* life, shattering the stereotype of Latinos as inevitably illiterate. The authors describe Latino students in starkly different ways from how they are described in most mainstream accounts: Unlike the language of despair and failure, they put forth what Luis Moll, in referring to a cultural-historical perspective, calls a "theory of possibilities." Other theories of possibilities developed in these chapters include teaching as sociocultural mediation (Chapter 2, Díaz and Flores), spontaneous biliteracy (Chapter 6, Reyes), literacy as hybridity (Chapter 7, Gutíerrez, Baquedano-López, and Alvarez), and strategic reading (Chapter 9, Jiménez). The metaphors the authors employ are also quite different from the traditional ones: Carmen Mercado, in describing how literacy practices act as gatekeepers to bar Latino students from an equal education in Chapter 10, proposes ways to use literacy to open the gate; rather than see Latino students' language use as fallow ground for literacy, María Berzins and Alice López in Chapter 5 describe how they plant the seeds for biliteracy in their classrooms; and instead of perceiving Latino students as unlikely intellectuals, María Fránquiz discusses in Chapter 13 how Chicano high school students uncover positive academic identities.

But the authors in this volume do not speak with one voice, nor do they suggest that a single strategy works for all. While some propose whole language approaches, others focus on culturally relevant pedagogy, and still others on acquainting Latino students with the dominant cultural capital of our society. Eloise Laliberty, for instance, writes in Chapter 8 about linking literacy to students' lived experiences, while Roberta Maldonado describes in Chapter 11 the stealthful strategies she uses to encourage her adolescent students to become readers, and Alma Flor Ada and Rosa Zubizarreta share their successful strategies for involving Latino parents in the education of their children's literacy in Chapter 14. John Halcón examines in Chapter 4 the impact of a pervasive anti-Latino social and political context in which Latino students are schooled. He, and the others in this book, discuss the need to integrate teachers' attitudes *and* behaviors, their beliefs *and* strategies, and their classroom products *and* processes. In so doing, they reject the dichotomies so prevalent in educational discourse.

The powerful educators who María de la Luz Reyes and John Halcón have gathered in this book have amassed considerable knowledge through their research and practice. While discussing specific strategies, they also advise against relying on any one technique because, in the words of Lilia Bartolomé and María Balderrama in Chapter 3, whether or not teachers are effective with Latino students is above all a question of their "political and ideological clarity." The authors in this volume lay bare the underlying truth about what works best with Latino students: Regardless of strategy or approach, it is about developing a caring, respectful stance concerning the students themselves. They make it clear that it is up to all educators—Latino and non-Latino—to believe in the potential of Latino students and to propose an alternative: that Latino students can learn to read and write, that they can become critically literate, and that they are capable of excellence.

Sonia Nieto
University of Massachusetts, Amherst

Preface

The idea for this book began in 1997 when María de la Luz Reyes conceived of a plan for bringing together a small group of leading Latina and Latino scholars, well known in the area of literacy, to discuss "The Condition of Literacy for Latino Students" within the backdrop of current political, social, and theoretical contexts. Fortuitously, the 1998 annual conference of the American Educational Research Association (AERA), held in San Diego, became the natural public forum to begin this discussion.

Panelists and members of the audience exhibited a great deal of enthusiasm for this topic. Many felt it was a critical issue for the Latino community and agreed that we had a sufficient number of in-house scholars and educators across the country to address this issue ourselves. There was a consensus that this research as praxis was the most appropriate and relevant avenue for seeking solutions and helping our community to improve education for our children.

This book, then, is the result of the efforts of our extended community of scholars and educators who have shared their experiences, research findings, and reflections on the conditions and instructional strategies that foster the development of critical literacy for Latino students. Without their dedication, and commitment to *la causa*, this book would not have been possible. The majority of these contributors are actively involved in writing, teaching, researching, and engaging in activities and projects that will improve the level and quality of literacy in the Latino community. *De todo corazón*, we thank them for their contributions to this book.

There were many others who helped along the way in reviewing, correcting, typing, and supporting this project. In particular, we wish to thank Christina DeNicolo, Alice Laliberty, Roberta Maldonado, and Cinthia Salinas. A special thanks goes to Lisa Costanzo, who spent many extra hours helping with the editorial changes and assisting us in meeting last-minute deadlines. And last but not least, we wish to thank the students and their parents who participate in our research projects and grace our classrooms with their eagerness to unleash their potential.

Introduction

MARÍA DE LA LUZ REYES AND JOHN J. HALCÓN

In putting this literacy book together, it was inevitable that we would reflect on our own route to literacy. How did we become literate? As young children being raised in bicultural homes, what experiences do we have in common with today's Latino students?

María: I think back many years ago when I was in elementary school and recall that, although all my classmates and I were born in the United States, few of us were fluent in English. In spite of this, we thought there was nothing exceptional about us learning to read in English and conducting most of our daily lives in Spanish. The majority of us were from poor, working-class families. In fact, most of us lived "across the tracks"—what many educators today still consider the "cradle of at-risk children." To be more accurate, my family did not live *across* the tracks, we actually lived *in front of* the tracks, in two cold concrete rooms at the end of a barracks-like housing unit owned by the Santa Fe Railroad for whom my father labored. There was no running water, no gas, and, of course, no separate rooms for us to study in, read, or even sleep. We owned no books. The only books that ever graced our home were the hand-me-down textbooks we occasionally were allowed to bring home from Our Lady of Guadalupe School. In spite of these conditions, I learned to read and write English well enough to graduate as eighth-grade valedictorian of my class.

John: I started public school with a strong knowledge of English and Spanish. Unlike María and her classmates at Guadalupe School, where the nuns never punished them for speaking Spanish, I spent many hours standing against a chain-link fence in the hot desert sun of the Imperial Valley (in California) for speaking Spanish in school. As students, we also were subjected to having our mouths washed out with soap, or "taxed" a penny for every Spanish word we spoke. In spite of the punishment, I continued to speak Spanish while developing my literacy skills in English. As a matter of fact, I did quite well in school. In retrospect, I think speaking Spanish in school was a way of rebelling against the imposition of those unjust language policies and my way of affirming my own language and culture.

Triumph of Resilience

We are by no means romanticizing the conditions under which we became literate or implying that if "we did it, so can others." On the contrary, we think back and wonder how much more we (and our classmates) could have accomplished had Spanish been an integral part of our curricula, had we been afforded opportunities for some enrichment activities, and had we been encouraged to graduate from high school and attend college. (Many of our friends did neither.) Actually, we marvel at our resilience to survive, and think of today's Latino students who manage to succeed in an educational climate where, although they are not punished (at least not overtly) for speaking Spanish, the indifference to their cultural and linguistic needs, their hopes, and their talents is even more blatant.

It is not coincidental that today we are professors of education. Both of us have always been interested in the schooling of Spanish-speaking students. We also have been intrigued with the question of why some Spanish speakers become literate in English without knowing the language well, and how some become literate in Spanish with no formal instruction. Although we ourselves were not taught in Spanish, we managed to learn to read and write it without instruction. Did we learn by osmosis? Did we learn because of our exposure to Spanish print at home, in church, in community halls, in barrio stores? Did we learn it because we did not yet feel *disconnected* from it? We are not sure. At one time, we used to consider ourselves and other Latinos who attended minority schools "undereducated." Today we no longer buy into that dominant myth. In fact, we contend that Latinos who grow up bicultural and become biliterate—in spite of an educational system that has little understanding of the linguistic and cultural resources they possess—are "gifted and talented,"—*not* "at-risk," *not* "culturally disadvantaged," *not* "limited English proficient"!

Current Literacy Issues

The question of how children become literate, how they should be taught to read and write, and how they perform in reading and writing evaluations continues to be one of the biggest concerns of school administrators, educators, families, and even legislators. For Latino communities this is also true, but for us there are other concerns: What kind of literate beings do we want our children to be (critical, functional, test-wise)? In which language will our children become literate? How will our children maintain their culture and language and their connection to them in schools that work hard at eradicating all traces of "foreignness" for the price of becoming literate in English? Rosalinda Barrera believes that many adult Latinos are still in need of healing from the "culturalectomies" performed on them when they were children in U.S. schools (see Jiménez, Moll, Rodríguez-Brown, & Barrera, 1999). Indeed, the Richard Rodríguezes and Linda Chavezes of this country may be prominent—the "darlings" of the dominant majority—but we consider them living examples of the hegemonic practices of schools because they gave up their Spanish for the price of becoming literate in English when they could have had both.

Literacy fads and literacy wars have come and gone with no significant positive impact on the literacy development of Latinos. One reason is that these movements rarely consider the needs of Latino students, in spite of demographics indicating that this segment of the student population has doubled in the past 2 decades. Not only are the numbers of Latinos growing at unprecedented rates but also as a group they make up nearly 75% of the speakers of languages other than English (August & Hakuta, 1997). Indeed, as a single bloc, they represent the full spectrum of Spanish- and English-language skills—an enormous challenge to their teachers, who are primarily monolingual English speakers.

In spite of Latino students' growing presence in schools and the formidable task they present to literacy teachers, the majority of educators and researchers ignore their bicultural background and their potential for bilingualism and biliteracy as if these were inconsequential, useless appendages in the process of becoming literate. Tragically, they fail to recognize that Latinos' identity is "intertwined with the meaning and consequences of becoming and being literate" (Ferdman, 1990, p. 182).

The majority of educators prefer, instead, to emphasize the importance of children's early exposure to literature in the home, believing that children who enter school with the language and experience of storybooks (i.e., English) are prime candidates for academic success. On the other hand, they assume that children with little or no experience with books in the home or children from working-class or poor backgrounds are less likely to develop into competent, fluent readers and writers (Anderson, Hiebert, Scott, & Wilkinson, 1985; Teale & Sulzby, 1986). While these views remain viable in many educational circles, they are grounded on narrow definitions of literacy that privilege middle-class speakers of standard English and render useless the rich cultural and linguistic resources of non-mainstream children (Delpit, 1995; Dyson, 1993).

In considering the importance of identity with the consequences of becoming literate, Stuart Hall's (1991) notion of "identity as positionality" is useful in establishing links between different forms of identity and subjectivity. In describing identity as positionality, Hall suggests that we give ourselves or are given identity (or names) by the different ways we are positioned by others or position ourselves within the narratives of the past. Applying Hall's identity as positionality, it is evident that mainstream Euro-American children are "positioned" at the center of the curriculum where their identity is strong and secure, and non-mainstream children are relegated to the outer fringes where cultural and linguistic differences are treated as deviations from the norm.

Identities attributed to Latino students in schools, such as "minorities," "culturally disadvantaged," "second-language learners," "limited English proficient," and "at-risk" students, describe their position vis-à-vis dominant, native English-speaking children who occupy center stage. These labels paint our children as less intellectually capable than they actually are, and ignore their ability to "read" the world (Freire & Macedo, 1987).

As Latino educators we see so much promise in our children. Schools (and society) see so little. One reason is that in schools our children are measured against a monolingual, native English norm that short-circuits their true potential. We continue to read in academic literature, in the popular press, and in the media that Latino students fall short when measured by local and national academic standards. In particular, we read of their dismal performance in standardized reading and writing tests and we recognize the consequences when our children are dismissed, undervalued, or ignored.

We also understand that in schools literacy "plays a vital gatekeeping function in creating or limiting access to postsecondary education" (see Chapter 10) and professional careers. As Latino educators, we feel a sense of urgency to speak on behalf of our children, to write a different narrative that includes our voices, and their voices. Over the past decade or so, the voices of a significant number of Latino scholars from Chicano, Mexican, Puerto Rican, Cuban, and other Latino backgrounds have emerged. In a sense, we have "cracked the code," "crashed the gates of literacy"—we have come of age! We feel compelled to draw another picture of reality—a reality construed by seeing the world not from a single monocular lens that provides no depth (Fishman, 1976), but through the two lenses at our disposal: two linguistic systems and two cultural modes to access and interpret knowledge and information, two lenses that offer broader perception and depth. And so, this volume provides an emic (i.e., insiders') perspective sorely absent in literacy texts written to date. Its purpose is to bring together Latina and Latino educators (both academics and classroom teachers) to address the question of what learning conditions, instructional practices, ideologies, attitudes, and theoretical principles contribute to what is "best for our children" with respect to literacy. Armed with personal and professional experience from which to speak, with knowledge of the culture and language of our community, and cognizant of the institutional structures that marginalize Latinos, we offer a different interpretation of the academic strengths our children bring to school.

Unlike the majority of texts that feature "outsiders looking in," this book focuses on the needs of *our own children*, not "other people's children" (Delpit, 1995). All the contributors to this book are Latinas and Latinos with a strong track-record of working and/or conducting research with Latino students. Many are leading scholars in the field of literacy or outstanding and publicly recognized classroom teachers. This volume brings their voices together under a single cover.

About the Book

We have organized the book into three parts and describe them below, providing a preview of each of the chapters in each part.

In Part I, *Sociocultural, Sociohistorical, and Sociopolitical Contexts of Literacy*, the authors lay out the social, political, and theoretical contexts for understanding literacy for Latinos. In particular, they focus on Vygotsky's (1978) theories because they offer possibilities for understanding issues of cultural diversity.

In Chapter 1, Luis Moll discusses Vygotsky's (1978) cultural-historical theory as a significant tool to address "deculturalization" in educational practice. He contends that, while the writings of Vygotsky and others do not provide immediate, "quick fix" solutions for success, they are "theories of possibilities." As such, they provide conceptual and methodological tools, and principles to address these problems. Moll provides two concrete examples of cultural-historical application in educational settings.

In Chapter 2, Esteban Díaz and Bárbara Flores examine how teachers, as sociocultural and sociohistorical mediators, co-construct with their students teaching and learning experiences that result in either success or failure. They argue that failure is co-constructed by the social interactions that teachers create in classroom lessons and activities. Thus, their "habitudes"—teachers' unexamined attitudes and beliefs about perceived sociocultural and academic "deficiencies" in these children—ultimately result in their failure to provide appropriate, positive, and successful teaching–learning environments.

In Chapter 3, Lilia Bartolomé and María Balderrama challenge conventional explanations for Mexicano/Latino underachievement in schools, such as deficit theories, cultural difference theory, and the myth of meritocracy. They argue the need for educators with "political and ideological clarity" as exemplified in interviews with four exemplary educators who discuss their own ideological beliefs and attitudes about effectively preparing Mexicano/Latino students to succeed academically.

In Chapter 4, John Halcón describes the sociopolitical backdrop in which schools operate and Latino students learn. In particular, he examines anti-Latino, anti-bilingual education sentiment evident in California (and across the country), and discusses how these negative attitudes become part and parcel of the dominant ideology internalized by teachers who teach Latino students.

Part II, *Biliteracy, Hybridity, and Other Literacies*, includes chapters that focus on Latino students' use of hybridity and the emergence of biliteracy. Unlike the old negative view of code-switching (i.e., the alternation of two linguistic codes), which was perceived as the lack of full development of two languages, hybridity is viewed as an advantageous tool for accessing literacy. The development of biliteracy, on the other hand, is discussed as a real possibility when the development of speaking, reading, and writing in two languages is nurtured in the classroom.

In Chapter 5, classroom teachers María Berzins and Alice López lead off this part by discussing how their own advocacy for bilingual education and Latino children helps them construct a supportive teaching and learning environment that fosters close, personal relationships among students. They detail how they "plant the seeds for biliteracy" and how they establish collaborative partnerships with parents to ensure academic success for their students.

In Chapter 6, María de la Luz Reyes describes "spontaneous biliteracy"—the simultaneous development of two distinct linguistic systems without formal instruction. Taking a sociocultural and critical literacy perspective, and challenging the prevailing convention that learning two languages simultaneously might be "too great a challenge for most learners," the author presents a detailed account of the linguistic evolution of four Latina students in kindergarten through second grade as they experiment with biliteracy.

In Chapter 7, Kris Gutiérrez, Patricia Baquedano-López, and Héctor Alvarez present a perspective on "collaborative literacy learning" in the context of Las Redes, an after-school club that nurtures productive learning experiences for children and adults. The authors explain how this program provides an ideal context for collaborative learning where the use of "hybridity"—an unmarked alternation of dominant and alternative discourses—is honored and utilized as a resource for literacy development.

In Chapter 8, Eloise "Alice" Laliberty describes how she was able to influence her monolingual English *and* Spanish speakers to develop a love for writing and literacy that spilled over to literacy development in Spanish and English for her Spanish-speaking students. She discusses the potential power of personal writing based on one's lived experiences.

Part III, *Reading the Word by Reading the World,* consists of chapters that reflect Paulo Freire's (1970) and Friere and Macedo's (1987) idea that we can learn to read the word (i.e., learn to read) by understanding (i.e., reading) the world in which we live and using ideas and events that are important to us as material for developing literacy. Reading the world also requires that we take a critical view of our position in relation to others in the larger social context. Understanding that position helps us become consciously aware of what we must do to improve our condition. The authors in this part provide examples of students in middle school and high school who engage and become literate through nontraditional means.

In Chapter 9, Robert Jiménez reports on his study of Sarah, a 13-year-old, Mexican-origin student assigned to a special education classroom for bilingual Latino students with learning disabilities. Jiménez's curiosity about her was piqued during several observations when he noticed that she was seldom if ever encouraged or provided with opportunities to read, write, or speak in either of her two languages. In this chapter, Jiménez explores Sarah's literacy development and her responses to culturally relevant cognitive strategies that are linguistically sensitive.

In Chapter 10, Carmen Mercado discusses the vitality of Spanish in Latino communities and describes how its use had an impact on the development of English language literacies among Latino youth in a middle school setting in New York City. The author explains how Latino youth continue to harness their bilingualism to gain access to knowledge and information, and to create positive social relationships with esteemed adults, even when Spanish is not the official language of instruction.

In Chapter 11, Roberta Maldonado presents a poignant, yet powerful, case for "living literacy" as she clashes with the established educational system intent on imposing a standardized version of literacy for all, including culturally different, non-mainstream, often poor, non-English-speaking children. She argues that linguistically different and minority children often are wrongly assumed to lack the necessary cultural capital to succeed in deciphering difficult text, when in fact the opposite is often true. Her goal for her students is the achievement of critical literacy so that they might understand "their historical place in the balance of power."

Much like Maldonado, in Chapter 12 Bobbi Ciriza Houtchens discusses the irrelevancy that schools have had for many Mexicano/Latino children, especially high school students. While some may learn to decode well, many fail to develop critical literacy or academic consciousness and often are lost to the streets, succumbing to the pressures around them. Using her own classroom, she demonstrates through her Latino students—typically regarded as unproductive, unmotivated, and resistant to succeeding in school—that they are capable of becoming active, engaged readers.

Examining another group of high school students in an alternative program, María Fránquiz describes in Chapter 13 how culturally relevant projects undertaken by members of a Mexicano/Latino after-school group helped them re-envision the purpose of literacy in their lives. Under the auspices of this group, the students undertake the production of a video and the construction of a large mural depicting their views of themselves and their world. By accepting the challenge of presenting their projects and their meaning at professional conferences, the students demonstrate examples of living literacies.

Finally, in Chapter 14, Alma Flor Ada and Rosa Zubizarreta discuss how parents view their own role in their children's education. In addition, they discuss schools' influence on and responsibility toward families and communities. Specifically, they offer two models of literacy development that invite family and community into the curriculum. They argue that by encouraging dialogue and communication at home and in the community, *in the home language*, teachers support rather than destroy the existing "social capital" of the family.

References

Anderson, R., Hiebert, E., Scott, J., & Wilkinson, I. (1985). *Becoming a nation of readers* (Report of the Commission on Reading). Washington, DC: National Institute of Education.

August, D., & Hakuta, K. (Eds.). (1997). *Improving schooling for language minority children: A research agenda.* Washington, DC: National Academy Press.

Delpit, L. (1995). *Other's people children.* New York: New Press.

Dyson, A. H. (1993). *Social worlds of children learning to write.* New York: Teachers College Press.

Ferdman, B. M. (1990). Literacy and cultural identity. *Harvard Educational Review, 60*(2), 181–204.

Fishman, J. (1976). *An international sociolinguistic view of bilingual education.* Keynote address at the annual meeting of the National Association for Bilingual Education, San Antonio, TX.

Freire, P. (1970). *Pedagogy of the oppressed.* New York: Continuum.

Freire, P., & Macedo, D. (1987). *Literacy: Reading the word and the world.* South Hadley, MA: Bergin & Garvey.

Hall, S. (1991). Old and new identities, old and new ethnicities. In A. D. King (Ed.),
    Culture, globalization and the world-system (pp. 41–68). London: Macmillan.
Jiménez, R., Moll, L., Rodríguez-Brown, F., & Barrera, R. (1999). Conversations:
    Latina and Latino researchers interact on issues related to literacy learning.
    Reading Research Quarterly, 34(2), 217–230.
Teale, W., & Sulzby, E. (Eds.). (1986). *Emergent literacy: Writing and reading.* Norwood,
    NJ: Ablex.
Vygotsky, L. S. (1978). *Mind in society: The development of higher psychological process*
    (M. Cole, v. John-Steiner, S. Scribner, & E. Souberman, Trans. & Eds.). Cam-
    bridge, MA: Harvard University Press.

PART I

Sociocultural, Sociohistorical, and Sociopolitical Context of Literacy

CHAPTER 1

The Diversity of Schooling

A Cultural-Historical Approach

LUIS C. MOLL

The most common response to diversity in schools within the United States, and undoubtedly elsewhere as well, has been to eradicate it, to erase it, to practice what educational historian Joel Spring (1997) has called "deculturalization." This practice, which from this country's beginnings formed part of its "official nationalism," and which forms part of a broader "pedagogy of control," is still very much prevalent today, especially in locations faced with rapid demographic changes. Witness the attempted eradication of bilingual education programs in California, for example, and the designation of Spanish, and the Latino students who speak it, as "pariahs" within the schools (Moll, 1999).

This dual strategy of exclusion and condemnation of one's language and culture, fostering disdain for what one knows and who one is, has another critical consequence in terms of schooling—it influences children's attitudes toward their knowledge and personal competence. That is, it creates a social distance between themselves and the world of school knowledge. It creates the impression that someone else, not they, possesses knowledge and expertise, so that they, including their families, must be unskilled and incompetent; in other words, it creates the impression that their language and knowledge are inadequate, unspecialized, because they are condemned instead of privileged by the schools (see, e.g., Moll, 1999; Olson, 1987). The superiority of the other, and one's own inferiority, is "naturalized," becoming part of an ideology that is easily internalized.

The above points notwithstanding, schools have not been completely unresponsive to the needs of these children. In sharp contrast to the attempts at control and coercion, there are the efforts by some educators who seek to turn the diversity of students into assets for their schooling. For example, one of the most significant educational initiatives of the past 30 years has been the development of bilingual education, but this innovation must be understood within its broader social context. The U.S. version of these programs serve almost exclusively working-class and poor children, precisely the children most neglected and stigmatized by the education system. The primary goal of most bilingual programs has been to teach the children English in order to accommodate them as soon as possible within the broader monolingual system, the very system whose faults motivated the development of bilingual alternatives in the first place. As such, most programs last only 3 years or less, which research has shown repeatedly is an insufficient amount of time to accrue the benefits of bilingualism or to learn well a second language for academic purposes. And, like *all* programs addressing the education of poor children, they have produced mixed results. Nevertheless, it is clear that when bilingual programs are adequately staffed, implemented, and supported, they produce very positive academic and language learning outcomes (Brisk, 1998).

However, even an instructional innovation as limited and as conservative as bilingual education in the United States represents a threat to the status quo, especially in the present demographic context, and xenophobic preoccupations with immigration. In addition, the instrumental view of English as the sole source of social access is a powerful form of language ideology, a point not lost on the enemies of bilingual education. Any analysis of cultural diversity in schools, therefore, must contend not only with pedagogical issues, namely, how to turn such diversity into an asset for instruction, but also with issues of ideology. Prominent among them are language ideologies that not only control how and what children may learn in schools, but mediate how children may come to regulate or limit themselves, a point to which I shall return.

A Cultural-Historical Perspective

In what follows I propose that cultural-historical theory, associated with the writings of L. S. Vygotsky,[1] among others, represents a major tool in addressing issues of diversity in education, because it is at heart a theory of possibilities. The general theoretical premise is that higher psychological functions originate in human sociocultural activities (Vygotsky, 1978). A defining aspect of these sociocultural activities is their "mediation" through artificial means, how humans come to interact with the use of cultural artifacts, tools, and symbol systems, especially language. The use of these artifacts has both social consequences—they mediate how humans communicate with one another—and intellectual consequences—they mediate how humans think, how humans constitute and develop their intellectual capacities (Cole, 1996; Olson, 1986; Scribner, 1990b). Pontecorvo (1993) summarizes well this Vygotskian idea of instrumental mediation.

> Mediation tools include the semiotic systems pertaining to different languages and to various scientific fields; these are procedures, thought methodologies, and cultural objects that have to be appropriated, practices of discourse and reasoning that have to be developed, and play or study practices that have to be exercised. (p. 191)

Thus, the concept of mediation implies a constant reciprocal relationship between the social and the individual, between the cultural and the intellectual. What is central here is not only the presence of cultural artifacts, but how these artifacts are used, that is, how they come to be employed within specific social circumstances of development. How (and why) these artifacts are used, in turn, mediates how humans come to think with these artifacts and, especially important, how they come to regulate their psychological activities through the appropriation and use of these artifacts. Moreover, as Wertsch (e.g., Wertsch & Sohmer, 1995) has emphasized, from a Vygotskian perspective, such mediational means "reflect specific cultural, institutional and historical settings, and their mastery therefore inherently locates individuals in sociocultural history" (p. 334).

Vygotsky assigned central prominence to formal schooling in the development of new psychological processes, perhaps more than any other psychologist (see Baquero, 1996; Moll, 1990b). We could say he conceptualized schools as "cultural settings," with special routines and forms of discourse, where adults help children acquire important mediational means (e.g., literacy and mathematics) of a culture, systems for communicating and representing knowledge, extending and restructuring the children's communicative and cognitive abilities. Therefore, schools (ideally) serve not only retrospective functions, facilitating the acquisition of already existing technologies by a new generation, but prospective functions, facilitating students' potential for learning, and creating a basis for their future development (Kozulin, 1998). Vygotsky's (1978) concept of the "zone of proximal development" captures well this emphasis on creating new possibilities. The concept refers not only to "assisted performance," how "more capable" others assist "less capable" ones in learning, as is usually emphasized, but more broadly to the relationship between development and the cultural resources provided to produce that development (Moll, 1990a; Valsiner, 1988). That is, the zone of proximal development can be understood, as Scribner (1990a) has suggested, in terms of how expert others "use social processes and cultural resources of all kinds" (p. 92) in helping children construct their futures. This orientation, therefore, is very much in line with considering diversity not as an impediment but as a valuable cultural resource that provides important and varied experiences and knowledge for the development of children and their futures (Cole, 1998).

Mediating Agency

A major trend in Vygotskian-inspired research on teaching has been to create "activity settings" that deliberately combine cultural practices and resources in fundamentally new ways (Cole, 1998; Moll, in press). In what follows I will review two such efforts, both concentrating on capitalizing fully on the resources provided by the diversity of the participants. I start with a summary of research we have conducted on what we refer to as "funds of knowledge," those bodies of knowledge generated by the history and productive activities of households (see, e.g., González, Moll, & Amanti, in press; Moll & González, 1997). A goal of this work has been to develop an approach that documents the cultural resources of local communities, namely, the funds of knowledge found in working-class households, and that helps teachers develop pedagogies that build, in a variety of ways, on these resources. We have been particularly successful in helping teachers, as well as others, approach, understand, and define their school's community in terms of these funds of knowledge. For present purposes, I will discuss the development of study-group settings, "mediating structures," in the Vygotskian sense, places where we discuss theory and practice with teachers and that have become a key aspect of the work (Moll, 1997). (For more general discussions of these studies, see, e.g., González, Moll, & Amanti, in press; González et al., 1995; Moll, Amanti, Neff, & Gonzalez 1992; Moll & González, 1997.)

I will then turn to research conducted by Olga Vásquez (1993, 1994) and colleagues on creating community-based settings intended to take full advantage of the cultural resources found in local and distant environments (see also Gallego, Rueda, & Moll, in press; Gutiérrez, Baquedano-López, & Alvarez, in press and Chapter 7). Here I will emphasize the multiple mediations of the research/teaching site and how they incorporate selected cultural practices.

Funds of Knowledge

At the heart of our approach is the work of teachers conducting research in their students' households. This summary is based on Moll & González (1997) and Moll (1999). In contrast to other approaches that emphasize home visits, however, the teachers in our studies visit their students' households and communities, not necessarily as "teachers" attempting to convey educational information, although certainly that may occur, but as "learners" with a perspective that seeks to understand the ways of the households. By focusing theoretically and methodologically on understanding the particulars, the practices of life, we gain a deep appreciation for how people use resources of all kinds, most prominently their funds of knowledge, to engage life.

The orientation of our fieldwork, then, is toward documenting the productive (and other) activities of households and what they reveal about families' knowledge. Entering the household with questions rather than answers provides the context for these inquiry-based visits. The questions typically address such diverse areas as familial histories, family networks, labor history, educational history, language use, and childrearing ideologies. In learning about funds of knowledge, it is particularly important to document how households function as part of a wider economy, both in the formal and informal sectors of the economy, and how family members obtain and distribute their material and intellectual resources through strategic social ties or networks, or through other adaptive arrangements.

From this documentation we have learned that the knowledge and skills that such households and their networks possess are extensive. For example, many of the families know about repairs, carpentry, and masonry, knowledge related to jobs in the working-class segment of the labor market. Some families also have knowledge about matters such as the cultivation of plants, folk remedies, herbal cures, or midwifery, usually learned from older relatives in rural settings. In addition, family members with several years of formal schooling have knowledge about or have worked in professions such as archaeology, biology, and education. In brief, it becomes obvious that these households most definitely contain valuable knowledge and experiences that can serve as important resources for children's schooling.

Our strategy, then, has been to get close to the phenomenon of household life by making repeated visits in our role as learners. These visits, however, must be supplemented by the theoretical work done in the aforementioned study-group settings and by the development of case studies of specific households. Here is where the concept of funds of knowledge plays a major role as a "theoretical tool," in the Vygotskian sense, by helping mediate the teachers' comprehension of social life within the households they study. The concept is intended to make obvious the wealth of resources available within any single household and its social networks, resources that may not necessarily be obvious to teachers or even to the families themselves. However, "documenting funds of knowledge" or "making obvious cultural resources" is also a theoretical activity. The empirical information that teachers collect from households is the starting point; expanding and sharing insights from these visits is part of the theoretical work done at the study-group setting. In other words, through the visits, and through the deliberate elaboration of the concept of funds of knowledge, we appropriate theoretically the families' lived experiences. Accordingly, as with any theoretical enterprise, our conclusions are always tentative, temporary, and subject to revision by further study or scrutiny.

The artifacts that we produce through the inquiry also provide a context for our interpretations and our actions. For example, the field notes and interviews are central in helping us develop a "theoretical vocabulary" to refer to the household dynamics and knowledge. It is through discussions in the study group that we come to share a common language about the households, such as specifying "funds of knowledge" or depicting "zones of proximal development." This common language is also derived through the analysis of "reciprocal relations" and "social networks"; or the identification of "mechanisms of exchange" and of "core households," and so on (see González, Moll, & Amanti, in press). We introduce this vocabulary by examining research articles related to the study, including those which we have authored, and by examining jointly the data collected during the household visits.

Our bilingualism, I should mention, is also a central element in our process of interpretation and in creating these textual representations. Most of the families with whom we have done our work are bilingual, to varying extents, in Spanish and English. This bilingualism is also a general characteristic of the communities. Most of the interviews, therefore, are conducted in a combination of both languages, so much so that we could not imagine conducting the research monolingually; that would be a severe limitation on our ability to understand the families' experiences. We may, for example, conduct the interview in Spanish, summarize the field notes in English, and discuss the findings in both languages, or any other variation of that process. This combination of bilingualism and biliteracy, then, also has become a central cultural tool of the work in all its phases.

As we learn from the families in the study, we all come to know the households not only intellectually but personally and emotionally. Although we have tended to emphasize the documentation of funds of knowledge in our writings, and with good reason, the nature of the social relations created with the families are a key aspect of the studies. For example, it is common for teachers to be invited to dinner, or attend important family functions, such as weddings and *quinceañera* [debutante] celebrations, a prominent cultural activity for many families. These invitations are clear indicators of changes in the relationships between families and teachers. Parent visits to schools or phone calls, if just to say hello, became common as well, as teachers became part of the households' social networks, signaling that a relationship of mutual trust, of *confianza*, had developed. Thus, social relations are an object of study in documenting funds of knowledge and, in a sense, the context for such funds, but they are also method and result of the study. We cannot obtain the sorts of qualitative data we seek in visiting households without taking the time to establish the social relations with the families that allow for the easy and safe exchange of information. Additionally, an important outcome of the studies has been the creation of these relationships, which the teachers credit as an important consequence of doing the household research (see González, Moll, & Amanti, in press).

Many of the teachers also have included within their curricular activities information gathered from households, thus creating strategic connections with classroom instruction. We have, for the most part, avoided curricular prescriptions, but do have a preference for teachers who are willing to experiment with instruction and who consider the making of meaning as the central purpose in their teaching of literacy. These teachers, we have learned, make immediate sense of our excursions into community life and of how funds of knowledge may become assets for developing meaningful instruction for the students. For example, one teacher built a curriculum unit based on the information that many of her students' households had extensive knowledge of the medicinal value of plants and herbs. She was able to draw on this ethno-botanical knowledge in formulating a theme unit that reflected local knowledge of the curative properties of plants. Other teachers have created similar units with a variety of content. In some instances, individuals met during the household visits became participants, visiting the classrooms to contribute, in either English or Spanish, their knowledge or experiences (see González, Moll, & Amanti, in press; Moll & Greenberg, 1990).

We also have proposed how the development of literate competencies in two languages may enable children to take deliberate advantage of the valued resources of their cultures (see Moll & Dworin, 1996; Moll & González, 1994; see also Chapter 6). Let me mention at least two ways, among others, that one can establish mediated relationships between texts and social world in achieving biliteracy. As I have emphasized, one is to connect to local households through the analysis of funds of knowledge. For example, it might be a specific classroom activity (e.g., a science lesson about plants) that motivates the search for resources (e.g., an expert or an example) from the community. Certainly, not all classroom activities need make an immediate connection to household knowledge, but the point is that both teachers and students learn how to appreciate that the funds of knowledge are there and to establish their relevance for classroom learning and for developing various modes of engagement with literacy in either language (Moll & González, 1994).

A second connection between text and social world is through the study of literature. Here biliteracy also can serve an important "mediating" function: It allows teachers and students access to literate resources in not one but two languages. These literate sources allow students to gain knowledge and experiences that may not be found in their immediate community. But this connection also can be mediated in important ways. For example, students can learn how to relate experiences from their communities to issues or problems found in the literature, or to use the knowledge from the literature to rethink issues in the community, thus providing options for thinking that otherwise may not exist (Moll & Whitmore, 1993).

The primary advantage of biliteracy, then, is the intellectual breadth it can facilitate, the expanded possibilities found in developing new social and literate relationships to mediate children's academic learning. The educational emphasis would be on the students' novel use of cultural resources, including people, funds of knowledge, and literature, to facilitate and direct their intellectual work. To this end, we recently have initiated a new study analyzing longitudinally the development of biliteracy in children and the language ideologies that mediate the nature of this biliteracy (Moll, 1999).

La Clase Mágica

The second example is from the work of Vásquez and colleagues, and the activity setting they refer to as "La Clase Mágica" (Vásquez, 1993, 1994). This setting originated as part of a group of related projects called the Fifth Dimension, all community-based, after-school programs (see, e.g., Cole, 1995, 1996, 1998; Nicolopoulou & Cole, 1993; see also Chapter 7). This summary is based on Moll (in press). In brief, all of these projects share a particular social structure, combining play with educational activities, and containing a special set of rules, activities, artifacts, and relationships among participants, including work and electronic connections with local universities. The programs are all conducted after school, usually 3 days a week for 2 hours, at a community site such as a youth club, library, or other community setting. All of the participants are volunteers, including the schoolchildren. The adults typically represent an intergenerational mix of undergraduate students enrolled in child development or education courses at local universities, who act as on-site tutors and research assistants. There are also graduate students majoring in the social sciences, family members of the children in the program, local community members, and university faculty who supervise the implementation of activities and conduct research at each site.

The most noticeable characteristic of each site, however, is the presence of various computers, used by the children to play games or fulfill other educational or communicative activities. The children's use of the computers is partially regulated (mediated) by the activities specified in "task cards" found within a 20-room maze, which is used to represent symbolically the movement of children through several project activities, and recorded in "journey logs" that assess their progress. The newcomers usually start with the first room in the maze, although the selection of room or activity may vary, depending on the age and expertise of the students. As they master the computer games or activities found in that room, they move progressively to the other rooms represented in the maze, as well as assume the expert role, assisting novice members. Throughout, the adults encourage the children to solve problems, formulate goals, and make decisions that will move them toward self-regulation, in the Vygotskian sense.

A key point for present purposes is that there are multiple forms of mediation within each site, including personalized support and assistance with the daily tasks. But perhaps the most novel form of mediation is that provided by an imaginary artifact, the "Wizard," who can be contacted only through electronic mail, and who helps monitor the functioning of the site, providing answers, making suggestions, and even settling disputes. The true identity and gender of the Wizard at each site is a closely guarded secret, but the students usually suspect that the site coordinator or one of the university students is playing the role of the invisible, all-knowing Wizard behind the scenes. This imaginary relationship, as well as those social relations formed by the other project participants, notably those between undergraduates and the younger students, creates multiple social situations for learning unlike those found in a typical classroom setting.

La Clase Mágica, although patterned after the Fifth Dimension, represents a distinct innovation. A most important change is that the site is bilingual in English and Spanish, so that children, or any other person, can participate in all activities in either language or in both. Another is that the Wizard's identity has been adjusted accordingly, becoming El Maga (a neologism combining male and female morphemes), a bilingual and multicultural entity. Vásquez (1993) explains it as follows:

> Transforming the Fifth Dimension was not a simple act of translation from English to Spanish but a fundamental change in the approach to the organization of the pedagogical activity. Although informed throughout by traditional

Mexican cultural knowledge, the Fifth Dimension's evolution into La Clase Mágica was not based solely on the children's home culture. Rather it tapped the multiple knowledge sources available in the children's everyday life. Whenever possible, content knowledge and skills from such learning domains as the family, church, sports, and dance groups were written into tasks accompanying the games. The goal was to build upon the background knowledge of the children at the same time that a new set of experiences and a second language were introduced. (p. 208)

La Clase Mágica represents, therefore, a fundamentally new cultural setting, one that borrows strategically but differs significantly from the children's home culture and from the institutional culture of the Fifth Dimension. Just as clearly, however, this setting is not meant to replace or to replicate classrooms, especially the classroom structure. La Clase Mágica is a deliberate attempt to create an alternative and heterogeneous social situation for learning that mediates the children's access to learning tasks in dynamic ways. The children's experiences and background knowledge form part of the foundation of the site, something that is recognizable by all participants and validated daily through the routines and practices that constitute the setting.

In this sense, perhaps the most notable characteristic of this site is the internal distribution of languages. An important consequence of the particular cultural arrangement of La Clase Mágica is that, to a remarkable extent, language designations, especially in relation to English fluency, which are so powerful in sorting children in schools, become irrelevant within the site's sociolinguistic context. The specific language characteristics of the child, considered temporary, never become a barrier to full participation within the site; they do not control or limit involvement because both languages are found everywhere, fostered, and used routinely in the performance of all tasks.

Another characteristic has to do with the ties fostered with the local community. La Clase Mágica is an open cultural system where the participation of local residents is encouraged and vital to the success of the site. The local residents, especially the children's families, not only represent an additional resource for teaching, contributing their knowledge and experiences, but help establish on a daily basis the cultural identity of the site, that is, how La Clase Mágica defines itself culturally through the nature and content of its routines. Furthermore, local community participants are also key allies in helping sustain the site; their presence helps define it as a worthwhile educational experience for children. The long-term existence of such a nonschool setting depends crucially on the network of support it can generate and how it can mediate existing constraints, especially given fluctuations in funding. The involvement of parents becomes an essential strategy to help perpetuate the site within its host setting, whether a local club, library, or church.

Finally, the site also functions as a broader "mediating structure," helping participants establish contacts and linkages with other important educational settings, especially local colleges and universities. In particular, the students get to know personally the university students and faculty as they interact about social and academic matters for a prolonged time (Vásquez, 1996).

Mediating Ideology

From a cultural-historical perspective, one cannot treat teaching and learning as if they occur outside history, especially in the education of language-minority children and those who live in poverty. These children, in particular, face special institutional practices, such as the devaluing of their home language and culture, or outright hostility and denigration by society, which must be addressed in order to create favorable educational circumstances. The two projects that I have presented, therefore, also address indirectly, in a mediated fashion and primarily through their practices, these broader social concerns and ideologies.

For example, an explicit goal of the funds of knowledge research was to debunk the prevalent idea of working-class households as devoid of intellect or of worthwhile resources. One strategy for addressing this issue was for teachers to conduct research in the households of their students. As mentioned above, documenting concretely the social history of the households, the knowledge generated by this history, and the formation of social relationships inherent in qualitative methods all have contributed to the definition of these households as possessing ample funds of knowledge. As important as the real social relationships established through the visits, however, are the "imagined" relations that can be formed with other families in the school or community. That is, one of the implications of teachers documenting and analyzing funds of knowledge is that the broader school community starts to be defined or imagined on the basis of the findings and the social relationships established with the case study families. We have learned that it is easy to imagine that other families also possess ample funds of knowledge, and by implication the broader community as well. These *imagined communities*, a term I borrow from Benedict Anderson (1991), now based on funds of knowledge, have become important cultural artifacts as well, for they are used to mediate in important ways our actions and our thinking about other children, their families, their lives, and their prospects within schools, even if we have not met them personally (Mercado & Moll, 1997; Moll, 2000).

Along similar lines, La Clase Mágica mediates negative characterizations of children by creating *additive* conditions for teaching and learning. I am using the term *additive* beyond the linguistic sense of creating positive conditions to help children add a second language to their repertoire while developing their first language, a challenging task especially in regard to the minority or socially marked language, even under favorable conditions (see Vásquez, 1993). I am using the term in a broader emotional sense of creating caring or nurturing conditions for the full acceptance of the children and their identities, in terms not only of perceiving their own language and culture as resources for learning, but of having an "unmarked identity" while in the program, without any of the school designations and labels that serve to mark the children as "minority," "different," or "deficient."

My point here is that these projects, by virtue of defining diversity as an asset in theory and practice, are "counterhegemonic" in nature. Although neither project necessarily features explicit discussions of ideologies and power per se, they do provide alternative ways of defining cultural resources, of mediating pedagogical activities through these resources, and of forming new social relations for promoting change. They also provide, through their agency, strategies for developing new "subjectivities" with the participants, either collectively in terms of how groups of people may be defined or in terms of individual children and their potentials for learning.

Conclusion

As several authors have pointed out, the cultural-historical or Vygotskian perspective that I have discussed does not provide straightforward prescriptions to be directly applied in practice for addressing issues of diversity in education (Cole, 1998; Scribner, 1990a). Instead, Vygotskian theory offers a general approach, including what Engeström (1993) has referred to as "conceptual tools and methodological principles, which have to be concretized according to the specific nature of the object under scrutiny" (p. 97). I have provided two examples of such "concretizations"; there are certainly many others (Moll, in press). The cultural-historical theoretical emphasis on understanding human development in social context, how people engage life with the cultural resources at their disposal, and how we come to think through the use of these resources, I have argued, can orient us to positive actions in turning diversity into assets for schooling. It is also important to keep in mind, however, as Eagleton (1989) has argued, that no theory has built into it a self-evident political orientation. This is not to say that theories are politically neutral, but rather that they are politically "polyvalent," capable of generating a multiplicity of sometimes quite contradictory social effects. This is especially true in the field of education, where theories often are incorporated and transformed in unanticipated ways.

Cultural institutions such as schools are not only pedagogical but political sites, with well-known ideological and structural constraints and biases, especially in relation to the social class and ethnic configuration of students. I have suggested that we must examine not only pedagogies but how these ideologies come to mediate what counts as resources in education. As Woolard and Schieffelin (1994) have written, "The term ideology reminds us that the cultural conceptions we study are partial, contestable and contested, and interest-laden" (p. 58). They continue:

> A naturalizing move that drains the conceptual of its historical content, making it seem universally and/or timelessly true, is often seen as key to ideological processes. The emphasis of ideological analysis on the social and experiential origins of systems of signification counters this naturalization of the cultural. (p. 58)

The work presented here complements that suggestion by presenting, in a sense, a social analysis of the ideological. The development of alternative "systems of signification," in one case through research with families and in another with children, provides evidence that the realities of schooling could always be otherwise. It fosters the possibility that we can develop pedagogies that privilege what children and families possess and that treat their knowledge with respect and care, regardless of languages or social origins.

Note

1. A comprehensive review of this perspective is obviously beyond the scope of this chapter. An extended corpus of Vygotsky's writings is now available in several languages; see Elhammoumi (1997), Moll (in press), and Van der Veer and Valsiner (1991, 1994). In addition, several books devoted to addressing the educational implications of Vygotsky's ideas are now available: Alvarez (1997), Baquero (1996), Berk and Winsler (1995), Bodrova and Leong (1996), Daniels (1993), Dixon-Krauss (1996), Forman, Minick, and Stone (1993), Hicks (1996), Kozulin (1998), Moll (1990b), Terré and Bell (1995), and Tharp and Gallimore (1988).

References

Alvarez, A. (Ed.). (1997). *Hacia un currículum cultural: La vigencia de Vygotski en la educación* [Toward a cultural curriculum: The relevance of Vygotsky]. Madrid: Fundación Infancia y Aprendizaje.

Anderson, B. (1991). *Imagined communities* (rev. ed.). London: Verso.

Baquero, R. (1996). *Vigotsky y el aprendizaje escolar* [Vygotsky and school learning]. Buenos Aires: Aique.

Berk, L., & Winsler, A. (1995). *Scaffolding children's learning: Vygotsky and early childhood education*. Washington, DC: National Association for the Education of Young Children.

Bodrova, E., & Leong, D. (1996). *Tools of the mind: The Vygotskian approach to early childhood education*. Englewood Cliffs, NJ: Prentice-Hall.

Brisk, M. E. (1998). *Bilingual education: From compensatory to quality schooling*. Mahwah, NJ: Erlbaum.

Cole, M. (1995). Cultural-historical psychology: A meso-genetic approach. In L. M. W. Martin, K. Nelson, & E. Tobach (Eds.), *Sociocultural psychology: Theory and practice of doing and knowing* (pp. 168–204). Cambridge: Cambridge University Press.

Cole, M. (1996). *Cultural psychology: A once and future discipline*. Cambridge, MA: Belknap Press of Harvard University Press.

Cole, M. (1998). Can cultural psychology help us think about diversity? *Mind, Culture, and Activity, 5*(4), 291–304.

Daniels, H. (Ed.). (1993). *Charting the agenda: Educational activity after Vygotsky*. London: Routledge.

Dixon-Krauss, L. (Ed.). (1996). *Vygotsky in the classroom*. White Plains, NY: Longman.

Eagleton, T. (1989). *The significance of theory*. London: Basil Blackwell.

Elhammoumi, M. (1997). *Socio-historicocultural psychology: Lev Semenovich Vygotsky (1896–1934): Bibliographical notes*. Lanham, MD: University Press of America.

Engeström, Y. (1993). Developmental studies of work as a test bench of activity theory: The case of primary care medical practice. In S. Chaiklin & J. Lave (Eds.), *Understanding practice: Perspectives on activity and context* (pp. 64–103). Cambridge: Cambridge University Press.

Forman, E. A., Minick, N., & Stone, C. A. (Eds.). (1993). *Contexts for learning: Sociocultural dynamics in children's development*. Oxford: Oxford University Press.

Gallego, M., Rueda, R., & Moll, L. C. (in press). Understanding dual language and (bi)literacy in an after-school setting: A cultural-historical activity approach. In J. Tinajero & R. DeVillar (Eds.), *The power of two languages: Effective dual language use across the curriculum for academic success*. New York: McGraw-Hill.

González, N., Moll, L. C., & Amanti, C. (Eds.). (in press). *Theorizing practices: Funds of knowledge in households and classrooms*. Cresskill, NJ: Hampton.

González, N., Moll, L. C., Floyd-Tenery, M., Rivera, A., Rendón, P., Gonzales, R., & Amanti, C. (1995). Funds of knowledge for teaching in Latino households. *Urban Education, 29*(4), 443–470.

Gutiérrez, K., Baquedano-López, P., & Alvarez, H. (in press). A cultural-historical approach to collaboration: Building a culture of collaboration through hybrid language practices. *Theory into Practice.*

Hicks, D. (Ed.). (1996). *Discourse, learning, and schooling*. New York: Cambridge University Press.

Kozulin, A. (1998). *Psychological tools: A sociocultural approach to education*. Cambridge, MA: Harvard University Press.

Mercado, C., & Moll, L. C. (1997). The study of funds of knowledge: Collaborative research in Latino homes. *Centro, 9*(9), 26–42.

Moll, L. C. (in press). Through the mediation of others: Vygotskian research on teaching. In V. Richardson (Ed.), *Handbook of research on teaching*. Washington, DC: American Educational Research Association.

Moll, L. C. (1990a). Introduction. In L. C. Moll (Ed.), *Vygotsky and education* (pp. 1–27). Cambridge: Cambridge University Press.

Moll, L. C. (1990b). (Ed.). *Vygotsky and education*. Cambridge: Cambridge University Press.

Moll, L. C. (1997). The creation of mediating settings. *Mind, Culture, and Activity, 4*(3), 192–199.

Moll, L. C. (1999). *Captives of words: Challenging the pedagogy of control*. Invited address, AERA Distinguished Lecture, Montreal.

Moll, L. C. (2000). Inspired by Vygotsky: Ethnographic experiments in education. In C. D. Lee & P. Smagorinsky (Eds.), *Vygotskian perspectives on literacy research*. Cambridge: Cambridge University Press.

Moll, L. C., Amanti, C., Neff, D., & González, N. (1992). Funds of knowledge for teaching: Using a qualitative approach to connect homes and classrooms. *Theory into Practice, 31*(2), 132–141.

Moll, L. C., & Dworin, J. (1996). Biliteracy development in classrooms: Social dynamics and cultural possibilities. In D. Hicks (Ed.), *Discourse, learning, and schooling* (pp. 221–246). New York: Cambridge University Press.

Moll, L. C., & González, N. (1994). Lessons from research with language minority students. *Journal of Reading Behavior, 26*(4), 439–461.

Moll, L. C., & González, N. (1997). Teachers as social scientists: Learning about culture from household research. In P. M. Hall (Ed.), *Race, ethnicity and multiculturalism* (pp. 89–114). New York: Garland.

Moll, L. C., & Greenberg, J. (1990). Creating zones of possibilities: Combining social contexts for instruction. In L. C. Moll (Ed.), *Vygotsky and education* (pp. 319–348). Cambridge: Cambridge University Press.

Moll, L. C., & Whitmore, K. (1993). Vygotsky in educational practice. In E. A. Forman, N. Minick, & C. A. Stone (Eds.), *Contexts for learning: Sociocultural dynamics in children's development* (pp. 19–42). New York: Oxford University Press.

Nicolopoulou, A., & Cole, M. (1993). Generation and transmission of shared knowledge in the culture of collaborative learning: The fifth dimension, its playworld, and its institutional contexts. In E. A. Forman, N. Minick, & C. A. Stone (Eds.), *Contexts for learning: Sociocultural dynamics in children's development* (pp. 283–314). New York: Oxford University Press.

Olson, D. (1986). Intelligence and literacy: The relationship between intelligence and the technologies of representation and communication. In R. Sternberg & R. Wagner (Eds.), *Practical intelligence: Nature and origins of competence in the everyday world* (pp. 338–360). Cambridge: Cambridge University Press.

Olson, D. (1987). Schooling and the transformation of common sense. In F. van Holtoon & D. Olson (Eds.), *Common sense: The foundations for social science* (pp. 319–344). Lanham, MD: University Press of America.

Pontecorvo, C. (1993). Forms of discourse and shared thinking. *Cognition and Instruction, 11*(3 & 4), 189–196.

Scribner, S. (1990a). Reflections on a model. *The Quarterly Newsletter of the Laboratory of Comparative Human Cognition, 12*(3), 90–94.

Scribner, S. (1990b). A sociocultural approach to the study of mind. In C. Greenberg & E. Tobach (Eds.), *Theories of the evolution of knowing* (pp. 107–120). Hillsdale, NJ: Erlbaum.

Spring, J. (1997). *Deculturalization and the struggle for equality* (2nd ed.). New York: McGraw-Hill.

Terré, O., & Bell, R. (1995). *La psicología cognitiva contemporanea y sus implicancias en el aprendizaje* [Contemporary cognitive psychology and its implications for learning]. Lima, Peru: Ediciones Libro Amigo.

Tharp, R., & Gallimore, R. (1988). *Rousing minds to life.* Cambridge: Cambridge University Press.

Valsiner, J. (1988). L. S. Vygotsky and contemporary developmental psychology. *Developmental psychology in the Soviet Union* (pp. 117–165). Sussex, England: Harvester Press.

Van der Veer, R., & Valsiner, J. (1991). *Understanding Vygotsky.* London: Blackwell.

Van der Veer, R., & Valsiner, J. (1994). *The Vygotsky reader.* London: Blackwell.

Vásquez, O. (1993). A look at language as a resource: Lessons from La Clase Mágica. In M. B. Arias & U. Casanova (Eds.), *Bilingual education: Politics, practice, and research* (pp. 199–224). Ninety-second Yearbook of the National Society for the Study of Education, Part 2. Chicago: University of Chicago Press.

Vásquez, O. (1994). The magic of La Clase Mágica: Enhancing the learning potential of bilingual children. *Australian Journal of Language and Literacy, 17*(2), 120–128.

Vásquez, O. (1996). A model system of institutional linkages: Transforming the educational pipeline. In A. Hurtado, R. Figueroa, & E. García (Eds.), *Strategic interventions in education: Expanding the Latina/Latino perspective* (pp. 137–166). Regents of the University of California, Santa Cruz.

Vygotsky, L. S. (1978). *Mind in society: The development of higher psychological process* (M. Cole, V. John-Steiner, S. Scribner, & E Souberman, Trans. & Eds.). Cambridge, MA: Harvard University Press.

Wertsch, J., & Sohmer, R. (1995). Vygotsky on learning and development. *Human Development, 38*, 332–337.

Woolard, K., & Schieffelin, B. (1994). Language ideology. *Annual Review of Anthropology, 23*, 55–83.

CHAPTER 2

Teacher as Sociocultural, Sociohistorical Mediator

Teaching to the Potential

ESTEBAN DÍAZ AND BÁRBARA FLORES

This chapter focuses on how teachers as sociocultural, sociohistorical mediators co-construct teaching–learning experiences with their students that result in either success or failure. We call these teaching–learning experiences socioeducational contexts because they are social in nature and occur exclusively in schooling. Our efforts to create appropriate academic experiences and organize successful schooling practices for children from lower-socioeconomic (SES) working classes, and different language and cultural backgrounds, are guided principally by Vygotsky's (1978) sociocultural, sociohistorical theoretical framework.

On the whole, school has not been a very successful place for these students despite extensive "remedial" efforts by educators. In our view (Flores, Cousin, & Díaz, 1991), the failure of these efforts is due to the deficit perspective inherent in them. We argue that failure is co-constructed by means of the social interactions that teachers help create in classroom "lessons and activities" (Díaz, Moll, & Mehan, 1986; McDermott, 1976). Failure or success in "lessons" is seen as a function of teachers' pedagogical knowledge, expectations, beliefs, and attitudes about language, culture, teaching–learning, and, most recently, "mandated" ways of teaching statewide curricula. We hold that the basis for failure is due to defective organization of lessons and activities based on teachers' unexamined attitudes and beliefs about the perceived "deficiencies" of minority and poor students and their families. We call these habitual unexamined attitudes and beliefs, "habitudes" (Flores, 1982).

In this chapter we will examine how academic success rather than failure can be organized for minority students. We do this by (1) presenting and discussing Vygotsky's sociocultural, sociohistorical framework; (2) discussing the teacher as sociocultural, sociohistorical mediator in the teaching–learning process and how the social interaction between teacher and student(s) is deliberate and guided by pedagogical understandings; (3) explaining how teachers need to organize teaching–learning aimed at the potential and not at the developmental level of the children in one socioeducational context that supports and promotes literacy and biliteracy; and (4) making visible the pedagogical implications of this knowledge for the academic achievement of children who are poor and working class and come from different language and cultural backgrounds.

Sociocultural, Sociohistorical Perspective

Within this chapter we want to continue the development of a framework that fully captures the power of the social interactions that comprise classroom "lessons." As stated earlier, it is our contention that the failure of minority students in the United States has been the function of the deficit habitudes and low academic expectations that predominate American classrooms and the subsequent social interactions that create failure (see also Chapter 4). Thus, the question that we raise and have used to guide our query is: How can the sociocultural, sociohistorical perspective give us another perspective on the nature of teaching–learning? Wertsch (1993) has proposed that the goal of sociohistorical theory is to "develop an explanation of mental processes which recognizes the essential relation between these processes and their cultural, historical and institutional setting" (p. 6). This quote captures an essential tenet of Vygotsky's theory, which basically argues that who we are and how we think is a function of the social interactions in which we participate. Further, the interactions are significantly determined by cultural, historical, and institutional settings. Therefore, it follows that we, as teachers, critically examine, reflect, interrogate, and transform our social interactions across these multiple settings. It is critical that teachers understand that we are key links in the continuing personal development of a child.

Vygotsky's view that development of mind is a social construction helps us to understand that social relationships are key to the mental and personal development of individuals. He notes, "The very mechanism underlying higher mental functions is a copy from social interactions: All higher mental functions are internalized social relationships, their whole nature is social" (Vygotsky, 1978, p. 128).

Therefore, if our social interactions do, in fact, become internalized as mental functions, then it follows that we, as teachers, have the power to organize for failure or success. This premise not only has great implications for the teaching–learning that occurs within socioeducational contexts, but also challenges the common belief that we must teach to the developmental level of the student(s). Our challenge, then, becomes to organize the teaching–learning process to the potential and not the perceived developmental level of our children.

Vygotsky's (1978) law of cultural development also supports the notion that social interactions underlie higher mental functions. For example, he says:

> Every function in children's cultural development appears twice, on two levels. First, on the social, and later on the psychological level, first, between people as an interpsychological category, and then inside the child, as an intrapsychological category. (p.128)

Thus, this law of cultural development underscores for us the importance of social interactions organized for children as they develop. There is little doubt that in most cultures children are raised with the goal of optimal development. Their parents and caregivers go to great lengths to ensure that they grow into healthy adults. Unfortunately, this great effort and concern does not always continue when the child enters school. Often the cultural, socioeconomic, and linguistic differences of students are seen as handicaps that are likely to hinder their academic progress unless "compensated for" in some way through appropriate educational treatment. A strong indicator of this view can be seen by the title "Compensatory Education" given to federal policies and programs aimed at improving the education of children who are poor and from different cultural and linguistic backgrounds. Educators often appropriate the views of policy makers and ascribe the poor academic performance of such students to their cultural, socioeconomic, and linguistic differences. This perspective, we argue, leads teachers to organize instruction for poor and minority students at the "lower" end of their abilities rather than at a level that maximizes their full potential. This cycle of failure begins with low expectations, which beget low levels of instruction and result in poor academic achievement. In the following sections we will examine how this cycle can be broken. We will see that teachers can become sociocultural, sociohistorical mediators in the schooling of diverse students.

Vygotsky considered schooling to be critical to the continuing cognitive, emotional, and personal development of a child. Parents take the lead in this developmental process by creating social interactions for sharing important cultural knowledge with the child. According to Vygotsky (1978), the learning that takes place in these social interactions create zones of proximal development and this "learning awakens a variety of internal developmental processes that are able to operate only when the child is interacting with people in his environment and in cooperation with his peers" (p. 90). The zone of proximal development (ZOPD) is defined by Vygotsky as the "distance between the actual developmental level of the learner as determined by independent problem solving and the level of potential development as determined through problem solving under adult guidance or in collaboration with more capable peers" (p. 86).

It is easy to picture that in caring familial and cultural settings, children develop and grow cognitively, personally, and emotionally. It is more difficult to see how ZOPDs such as these can be constructed in schools when teachers base the organization of instruction on a "deficit" perspective. In our view, this means that teachers actually organize "negative zones of development." The "proximal" or positive potential is removed or critically diluted by lessons that focus on dead-end skills and waste precious hours of school time that could be used for the appropriate development of all students.

In this chapter, we propose a reconceptualization of the schooling practices that views them as part of an ecological model that captures the multiple layers of contexts within which individuals develop. In a sociocultural, sociohistorical perspective, individuals are ontological constructs of the social interactions within their culture. Therefore, we must view districts and schools, like families and communities, as existing in social and political contexts that strongly influence children's development. For example, some schools attract solid, experienced teachers, while others see only newly credentialed candidates who leave as quickly as possible. Likewise, quantity and quality of resources vary as do the characteristics of students. All of these factors, singly and collectively, constrain the development of individuals who go to school there.

Teacher as Sociocultural, Sociohistorical Mediator

As noted above, it is important to recognize that schooling plays a significant role in the cognitive, social, and personal development of children. Part of who children become is a function of the experiences that they have in school. Thus, socioeducational contexts continue the process of development in critical and powerful ways. And the teacher becomes the link between the child's sociocultural experiences at home and school. That is, the teacher becomes the sociocultural, sociohistorical mediator of important formal and informal knowledge about the culture and society in which children develop.

Likewise, it is difficult to overemphasize how important the teacher is in the continuing cognitive, affective, and personal developmental processes of the child. While the child has been participating in ZOPDs since birth, successful negotiation of ZOPDs becomes critical in school because of their links to success or failure in society. The teacher, as a professional educator, is responsible for creating social systems that organize optimal ZOPDs for all students. Teaching–learning occurs as a function of the social interactions within the ZOPDs that the teacher co-constructs with students.

For example, students enter the classroom at an actual level of development that has been a function of their everyday familial, cultural, and communal experiences. If the teacher does not respect and properly take into account these previous experiences as indicative of the students' actual level of development, then the child is put "at-risk" within the socioeducational contexts and cannot participate appropriately within the ZOPDs. This is where children from different cultural and language backgrounds are likely to fail. The failure, however, is not of their making; it is the direct result of the social interactions set up by the teacher. If the students' language and cultural experiences are not included in socioeducational contexts, then they will have great difficulty reaching their level of potential development. We also argue that the teacher's pedagogical knowledge of language (oral and written, first and second) development and learning plays a significant role as well. That is, the teacher's theoretical understanding of and experiences with language development and learning guides him or her in organizing teaching–learning, mediating, and assessing the children's progress, too. And, since literacy is one of the educational yardsticks used to measure academic achievement, it becomes paramount that the teacher's pedagogical knowledge, habitudes, beliefs about teaching–learning, development, culture, and expectations determine the sociocultural link between failure and success in schooling.

The teacher as the sociocultural link or sociocultural mediator must deliberately mediate. For Vygotsky all human activity is mediated. In fact, he considered mediation by means of tools to be the defining characteristic of humans. Language is such a tool, as are mathematical formulae, written language, art, music, drama, dance, and so forth. These tools form vital links between the learner and the object that an individual seeks to possess, influence, or change in the sociocultural context. Thus, in the context of educational practice, the teacher also becomes a tool, a mediating "device" that deliberately teaches students to achieve important objectives/goals. In order to continue positive development of an individual, the teacher must be a sociocultural mediator—a "tool"—who mediates teaching-learning experiences so that students achieve their fullest potential. In helping students become literate, teachers must deliberately seek to connect students across many levels of understanding. This is particularly true for so-called, at-risk students. As sociocultural mediators, teachers must understand that literacy development and its teaching-learning process is a sociocultural, sociohistorical act, especially for children from low-SES groups or who speak a language other than English. Freire (1970) would add that literacy development is also a sociopolitical act. In other words, teachers must deeply understand and appreciate the relationships between literacy processes and the cultural, historical, institutional, and political factors at play in the classroom (see Chapter 3). In order for teachers to create positive ZOPDs for literacy development, they must mediate across multiple types of knowledge. That is, they must be deeply aware of the children's cultural experiences, respect their cultural knowledge, appreciate their differences, and accept their developmental capacity to learn. Also, teachers must view the learner as capable of generating knowledge, as a knowing subject and worthy of the best education possible.

A Socioeducational Context: Interactive Dialogue Journal

One of the most important roles of the teacher is to help create appropriate socioeducational contexts. These are contexts that are co-constructed within school lessons or activities as part of the teaching-learning process. They are ZOPDs, social in nature, that are designed to create positive, potential development within students (Díaz & Flores, 1990). In whole language classrooms teachers work to organize multiple socioeducational contexts for the development of reading and writing. One such context is created by interactive dialogue journals. Interactive dialogue journals (Flores, 1990; Goodman, Goodman, & Flores, 1979) are used by teachers to assist students in the appropriation of reading and writing. This is accomplished by having students select a topic, draw a picture, and then write something in their own way about the picture. The child then reads his or her entry to the teacher. The teacher accepts the child's "reading" of the text, noting the child's writing behavior and naming the developmental level to herself or himself. Next, the teacher, on a one-on-one basis, authentically responds to the child's message both orally and in written language, that is, as she or he writes, the teacher says the words in a syllabic cadence so that the written text matches the oral text. The best way to demonstrate this type of mediation is to discuss one student's developmental progress.

Before presenting the case study, we would like to provide a brief description of the larger social context in which the student lives. His name is

Daniel. He is of Chinese descent, immigrated from Mexico, and is at this time mostly bilingual in Spanish and Chinese, but also understands some English. He is 5 years old and lives in a town along the California–Mexico border. Ninety-eight percent of the students are Latino and a large majority of them are Spanish dominant and/or bilingual. The economy of the town is based on commerce and agricultural labor from the Mexican city across the border, which is the state capital. There is an average unemployment rate of 20%–30%. Stated succinctly, this town is a poor, working-class Latino community.

Daniel is a kindergartner in the classroom of a highly competent teacher, who at the time of this data collection had just begun to implement a holistic approach in his classroom. In an interview, he stated that prior to implementing this approach his expectations for his students at the end of the year were that they be able to count to 20, know their ABCs in Spanish, write their name, know all their shapes, and write their numbers. He considered himself an excellent teacher because he regularly met this goal, despite "the incredible deficiencies of his students." The expectations were low because these students were predominantly from very low-income families. However, as the teachers at this school began to learn how to reorganize the teaching–learning of literacy and biliteracy, their expectations shifted dramatically. This, in part, was due to their growing pedagogical knowledge from psychogenesis research (Ferreiro & Teberosky, 1984; Goodman, 1991), the sociopsycholinguistic nature of the reading process (Goodman, 1986, 1994, 1996), the sociocultural tradition (Díaz, Moll, & Mehan, 1986; Moll, 1990; Vygotsky, 1978; Wertsch, 1984), and the sociopolitical nature of teaching–learning (Freire, 1970; Freire & Macedo, 1987).

Daniel's Monthly Interactive Journal Samples: A Socioeducational Context

The journal begins in September with Daniel, a kindergartner, drawing and writing about an event at home. As one can tell, he drew a picture of a mouse and a house then wrote in capital letters, DANHEE (see Figure 2.1). Upon first glance it looks like he wrote his name. But, when he read it, he said, "Tenemos un raton en mi casa." [We have a rat in my house.] He also wrote the alphabet so that his teacher would know that he knew his "letters." Daniel's actual level of development is demonstrated by his use of a string of letters to represent a meaningful event. According to Ferreiro and Teberosky's (1984) psychogenesis theory, he is at a presyllabic conceptual interpretation level of literacy. In other words, this is his way of

FIGURE 2.1: Daniel's September Journal Entry

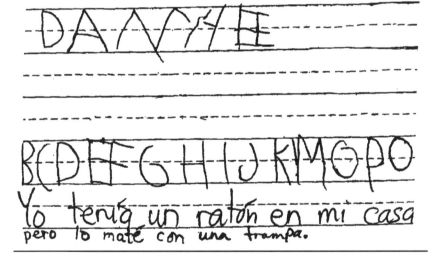

writing and representing meaning. He is not yet at the adult's alphabetic conceptual interpretation, which is the use of a one-to-one letter/sound correspondence.

His teacher cannot read his writing nor can Daniel read his teacher's writing. They are in the same situation; thus they are on equal footing. Since the teacher cannot read Daniel's current appropriation of writing and vice versa, both must resort to the use of a common mediational system to which both are privy—oral communication in Spanish. Vygotsky would describe this social interaction as a zone of proximal development, that is, Daniel's actual development is manifested in the writing of his "name" when asked to write independently. The teacher's response, in turn, is at the potential: the level he wants Daniel to reach. As the teacher responds to Daniel, Daniel watches, and the teacher writes the words in a syllabic cadence as he says them. (The teacher's writing is at the bottom of the page in Figure 2.1.) This deliberate mediation of matching the oral with the written in a slower syllabic cadence makes visible the correspondence between oral and written language in a meaningful and genuine way. Thus, the use of oral language mediates across the gulf that exists between the two different written representations.

In October Daniel shows some progress in the use of more letters to represent his message. He definitely is not afraid to write his way. He is still at a presyllabic conceptual interpretation level, which we simply consider to be where he is writing at this time. He will continue to make progress. We do not consider this level to be "low." His teacher continues to respond in the same manner described above—to the potential, where we want him to grow. It is important to note that the teacher does not organize the teaching only at the child's developmental level. Rather he creates a ZOPD that aims at the potential with each interaction and response. Although it may seem that the child is learning through osmosis, this is not the case. The teacher is deliberately mediating, encouraging the child to write his way but to pay attention to the teacher's response as it is produced, and teaching to the potential. The teacher is, in fact, acting as a sociocultural mediator.

By December Daniel is appropriating words in his own idiosyncratic way, such as the use of quotation marks to indicate borrowed words or phrases. According to his teacher, Daniel explained that his use of quotation marks was based on a comment the teacher made while reading a story. "When you use someone else's words from another language, you use quotation marks to show it."

Using Ferreiro and Teberosky's (1984) psychogenesis model, in January we begin to see advanced syllabic, and alphabetic writing. For example, "Loa" means los go-bots ("The go-bots"[name of a toy]), that is, *L* for "los," *o* for "go," and *a* for "bots." In the advanced syllabic conceptual interpretation, children use one letter per syllable, which matches one of the sound/letter correspondences within the syllable. The use of one-to-one alphabetic hypothesis, that is, one letter per sound, is represented by the words "Yo," "Bi," and "MaLo" in Figure 2.2. Daniel is no longer just writing a string of random letters. He is now moving toward an adult's representation of the alphabetic writing system. In February, Daniel writes, "MIMAMIIBA

FIGURE 2.2: Daniel's January Journal Entry

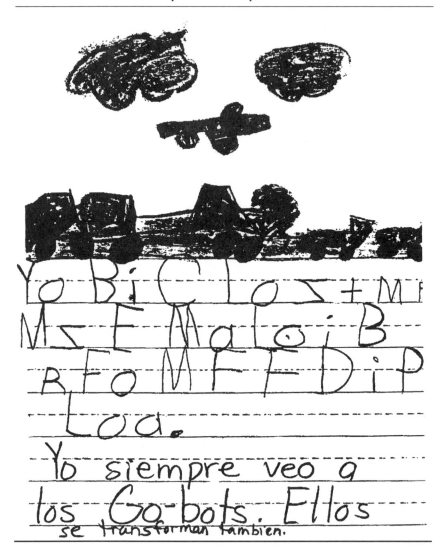

ACOMARUAPUEA" (Mi mami iba a comprar una puerta [My mommy was going to buy a door]. See Figure 2.3).

Daniel definitely is using at advanced syllabic, syllabic/alphabetic, and alphabetic writing systems (conceptual interpretations). Even though Daniel does not segment his words conventionally (the use of standard spaces between words), he is writing at a more advanced level after only 6 months in

FIGURE 2.3: Daniel's February Journal Entry

kindergarten. This is phenomenal given his teacher's previous expectations. His teacher continues to respond at the potential, still mediating the oral with the written.

Three months later, Daniel writes, "mi MAMA me compro unos Tenis" [my MOM bought me some tennis shoes] (see Figure 2.4). Notably, he no longer has to mediate his written language because now he is approximating the adult cultural representation. His segmentation is conventional as is his orthography. His teacher continues to mediate his written response until Daniel can read it without the teacher's oral mediation. When this occurs, Daniel has reached the potential, that is, he can read and write at the alphabetic level.

FIGURE 2.4: Daniel's April Journal Entry

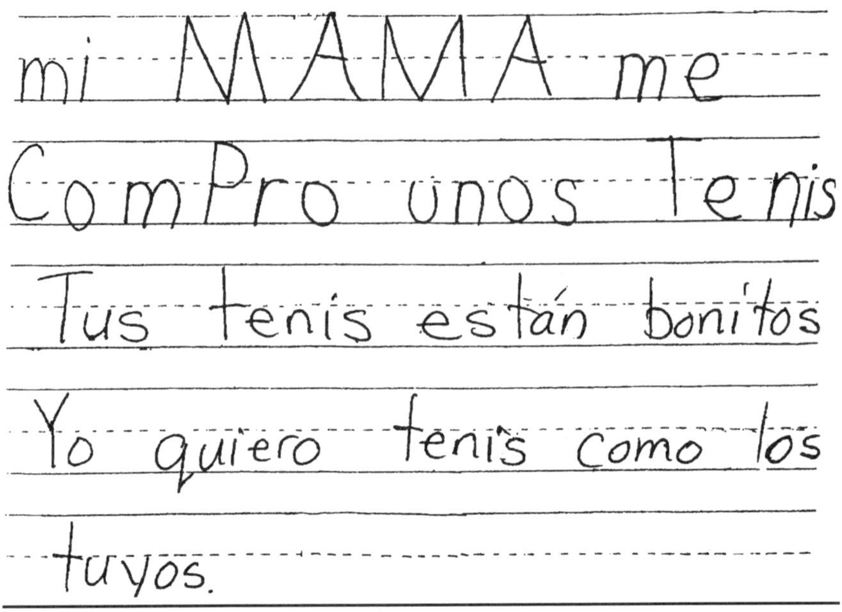

mi MAMA me
ComPro unos Tenis
Tus tenis están bonitos
Yo quiero tenis como los
tuyos.

In June, Daniel writes, "Yo Fui afuera a pasearme en mi bisicleta" [I went outside to ride my bicycle] (see Figure 2.5). Daniel can read the teacher's written response without mediation, and the teacher also can read Daniel's entry without his mediation. How did this occur? As we stated from the beginning, the teacher organized for the potential, accepted the child's developmental level, socially organized the interaction, expected the child to write his way, deliberately mediated, and abandoned his deficit beliefs, habitudes, and myths about language, learning, and culture.

In addition, the teacher's pedagogical knowledge from psychogenesis allowed him to name Daniel's developmental levels each time they interacted in the dialogue journal and to abandon his previous assessment of the child's ability to use random letters as "low." Likewise, his sociocultural knowledge of teaching–learning permitted him to set up the zone of proximal development, engage in meaningful social interactions, mediate deliberately, and teach to the potential. The teacher used conventions of written language: the orthographic system (standard spelling, punctuation, capitalization), the semantic system (representing meaning), and the syntactic system (word order). The response reflected the adult level of literacy that

FIGURE 2.5: Daniel's June Journal Entry

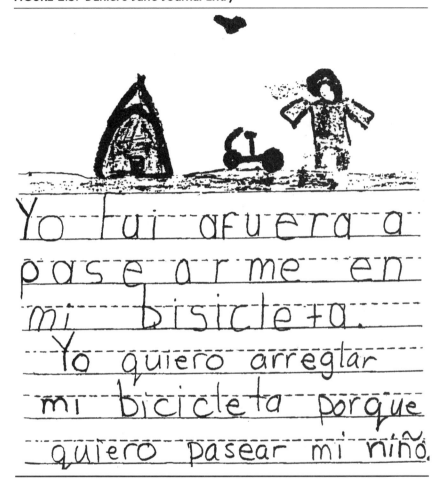

Daniel was expected to reach—his potential. With every interactive journal writing, the teacher made visible all the cueing systems in a meaningful context so that the child could learn them even though he was developmentally at another level. We contend that if we teach merely to the developmental level of our children, they do not achieve their full potential in literacy. Daniel's developmental story is representative of those of hundreds of children whose writing samples we have collected over 15 years of research in dozens of schools. We hope that this chapter will extend the success achieved by Daniel to thousands of other Latino and minority children.

Daniel's Literacy Success: A Sociocultural Explanation

In this section we analyze Daniel's progress from a sociocultural perspective by examining his journal via the mechanisms of the ZOPD identified by Wertsch (1984). He identifies three ZOPD mechanisms; (1) situation definition; (2) intersubjectivity; and (3) semiotic mediation. By situation definition Wertsch refers to the way in which a setting or context is represented. Even though the adult and child are in the same spatiotemporal context, they often understand this context in such different ways that they are not really doing the same task. As we noted above, in his first journal entry, Daniel responded to the teacher's request to "draw and write something." His rendering, in terms of his ability to communicate clearly by using letters from the alphabet, is quite distant from that of his teacher. But, by means of Spanish oral communication, the interactive dialogue journal, and shared cultural understanding, they are able to co-construct an understanding of what is going on during journal writing. That is, they are able to construct a situation definition. Across time this understanding grows as the teacher continues mediating within and across socioeducational contexts. In so doing, a critical qualitative change has taken place in the basic understanding of what reading and writing is and the process by which a novice comes to know it. Wertsch (1984) states that "we must recognize that a previously existing situation definition has been replaced in favor of a qualitatively new one" (p. 11).

Intersubjectivity for Wertsch (1984) exists "between two interlocutors in a task setting [i.e., a lesson] when they share the same situation definition and know that they share the same definition" (p. 12). Intersubjectivity takes time. Our previous classroom investigations (Díaz & Flores, 1990; Flores, Cousin, & Díaz, 1991) indicate that at times students have very little idea of what the teacher wants or means when he or she asks them to "write in your journals." This is accomplished slowly, by the daily interactions between the teacher and student (see Chapter 12). At one extreme, it can consist of no more than agreement on the location of concrete objects in a communication setting. At the other extreme, nearly complete intersubjectivity exists when two interlocutors represent objects and events in identical ways (Wertsch, 1984).

In the case of Daniel, the latter is seen in his June entry when he clearly has appropriated the adult's use of the alphabetic system for communication. In the course of reinventing the writing system of our adult culture at this point, there occurred many communications between the teacher and Daniel in order to co-construct this intersubjectivity. Comments such as, "No puedo escribir, maestro" [I don't know how to write, teacher], on the part of Daniel and the teacher's response, "Escribe de tu manera; está bien que escribas de tu manera porque algun día vas a aprender a escribir como escriben los adultos" [Write your way; it's okay to write your way because by watching me respond, you'll learn to write like adults some day], is but a single example among many of the dynamics that take place in the creation of intersubjectivity within the ZOPD offered by this socioeducational context.

The third mechanism that Wertsch (1984) proposes is that of semiotic mediation. For Vygotsky, mediation by linguistic signs plays a fundamental role in the creation of intersubjectivity and the construction of meaning (semiotic mediation). For Daniel, "coming to know" how to use the alphabetic writing system to communicate involved extensive negotiations across different levels of understanding. This was accomplished by the use of oral language for communication. It might have occurred, for example, on an occasion when the teacher noticed that Daniel was beginning to establish sound/letter correspondence. He then would deliberately mediate by saying, "Now write all the letters that you hear; say the words slowly so that you can capture the letters with the sounds that you hear" [Ahora escribe todas las letras que oígas; dí las palabras despasito para captar las letras que van con los sonidos que oyes]. The teacher knows that Daniel knows the letter/sound correspondences, but in this context he still continues to write only random letters and occasionally some letter/sound correspondences. So, the teacher notices this and strategically makes visible to the child that he can now use this knowledge in this social context, too.

This verbal exchange or negotiation is called deliberate mediation on the part of the teacher to bridge the child's current actual developmental level of understanding of literacy. At this moment the teacher is acting as a sociocultural mediator. In other words, alone the child uses the presyllabic and the beginnings of the syllabic system, but with deliberate mediation the child uses the advanced syllabic and syllabic/alphabetic writing systems (Díaz & Flores, 1990; Flores, 1990; Flores, Cousin, & Diaz, 1991). Since knowledge is socially constructed, this social interaction shows the child not only the next level of development, but also how to write it now. Showing the child and telling him that the teacher knows that he knows the letter/sound correspondences raises the expectation and sets a new goal. The child is now expected to write the letters that he hears in this context. Daniel knew letter/sound correspondences in another context, but the teacher had to make visible to him that he already knew this and could use it in the social context, too. We have seen this behavior over and over, that is, children knowing something in one context and not being able to apply it or appropriate it to another, similar context. Thus, it is the teacher's responsibility to act as the sociocultural mediator across socioeducational contexts. This leads us to posit the notion that perhaps teaching–learning is context specific until teachers help children to create links to other contexts.

The child also can make bids for negotiation by asking how to spell a specific word. The teacher, using professional judgment about the appropriateness of his or her response, might ask the student first to write the letters that he hears, or to ask a more knowledgeable peer, or simply to write the word his own way. These mediational responses bridge the child across his developmental level to the potential. Teachers must make professional judgments based on their knowledge of a child's level of development, the nature of the curricular task or material, and the goal of the given lesson or activity within a socioeducational context. Wertsch (1984) refers to this as semiotic flexibility, wherein adults adjust their directives (responses) based on the difficulty of the specific task at the moment and the child's ability level.

In summary, we have shown how the teacher has co-constructed a ZOPD for the development, teaching, and learning of reading and writing in the socioeducational context of an interactive dialogue journal. Originally the teacher was more than satisfied with having his students achieve the modest curricular goals noted above: the ABCs, counting and writing the numbers from 1 to 20, writing their name, knowing shapes, and so on. By implementing this holistic approach the teacher also has had to change his views of children's capacities to generate knowledge through sociocultural mediation, for learning, and for successful development of a child's intellectual potential. Teaching to the potential is a powerful concept, as demonstrated by Daniel's literacy journey.

Summary and Conclusions

The central purposes of this chapter were fourfold: (1) demonstrate how sociocultural knowledge can advance the academic area of literacy development within one socioeducational context, the interactive dialogue journal; (2) examine the role of the teacher as a sociocultural, sociohistorical mediator; (3) explain how development is mediated within the ZOPD; and (4) make visible the benefits of teaching to the potential.

Vygotskian theory offers us great insight into both why this is so important and how it can be accomplished. First, it emphasizes the importance and value of cultural and social experiences in the process of individual human development. These experiences, in fact, constitute the child's identity; they are who he or she is. Therefore, to deny those experiences in the schooling process is to negate the process of an individual's cognitive, emotional, and personal development. We are, in a sense, developing the child's academic identity in schooling practices. Therefore, our teaching–learning needs to be organized for success and the potential.

The zone of proximal development is the second Vygotskian contribution that helps educators continue the positive process of development begun within the family. Teachers must take the lead in organizing appropriate socioeducational contexts for supporting the continued development of all students. These contexts should be organized not from a deficit perspective, but rather from a perspective that capitalizes on students' previous experiences and incorporates the highest expectations possible (see Chapter 11). Stated more directly, teachers must not organize "negative" ZOPDs that lead to academic dead ends for students. Instead, teachers should structure ZOPDs that organize for the optimal potential of each student. As for the teacher, the challenge is to figure out how to respond, deliberately mediate, and strategically structure teaching–learning to the potential in each socioeducational context.

The acceptance of this theoretical framework represents a very important shift in the view of the value of experiences that children bring to school and how children learn. This is particularly important for students whose experiences prior to school do not give them easy entry to school. In schools there is often the view that these students are deficient because they come from poor or working-class backgrounds or have a different language and culture (see Chapter 4). Viewed from this perspective it is easy to see why school does not enrich them. Rather, it creates an artificial academic "deficiency" that is a function of the attitudes and practices embedded in the social interactions of classroom lessons. We could call them zones of negative development. It is where institutional failure is created.

Cummins's (1986) model supports this perspective. He argues that the views and attitudes inherent in the structure imposed by the dominant majority have an impact on the education of minority students in the classroom. For example, he would consider the intent of the English-only movement to privilege those from the dominant society who speak English. Privileging English in classroom interactions privileges the experiences of English-dominant persons and those who come from predominantly English environments. Those who are not such are by implication considered deficient. If schools are not able to alter this dominant structure, Cummins fears, bilingual and bicultural students are doomed to fail. However, privileging mediational means in the classroom is within the purview of the teacher. Either teachers can choose to organize social interactions that recapitulate the status quo—massive academic failure of minority children—or they can choose to restructure their teaching–learning across socioeducational contexts in order to counter the negative societal influences and, in turn, organize academic success. In conclusion, then, the goal of education should not be to recapitulate the inequities that exist in society, but rather to offer students opportunities to defeat the limitations placed on them by social status, home language, and cultural background. In the United States there is much pride taken in the belief of equal educational opportunity for everyone. However, we must recognize that equal opportunity does not mean equal access. Equal opportunity is merely a policy. Equal educational access is socially constructed in the classroom. It is organized by teachers who choose to provide it for all students and by the administrators who support them. Vygotsky's sociocultural framework not only offers all teachers a means for valuing the cultural and community experiences of their students. It also provides them with a mechanism—the ZOPD—by which they can help everyone reach their fullest potential.

References

Cummins, J. (1986). *Empowering language minority students*. Sacramento: California Association of Bilingual Education.

Díaz, E., & Flores, B. (1990, April). *Teacher as sociocultural mediator in literacy development*. Paper presented at the fifty-seventh annual Claremont Reading Conference, Claremont, CA.

Díaz, E., Moll, L., & Mehan, H. (1986). Sociocultural resources in instruction: A context-specific approach. In California Department of Education (Ed.), *Beyond language: Social and cultural factors in schooling language minority students* (pp. 186–230). Sacramento: California Department of Education.

Ferreiro, E., & Teberosky, A. (1984). *Literacy before schooling*. Portsmouth, NH: Heinemann.

Flores, B. (1982). *Toward a Hispanic theory of bilingualism: Language influence or interference*. Unpublished doctoral dissertation, University of Arizona, Tucson.

Flores, B. (1990). The sociopsychogenesis of literacy and biliteracy. *Proceedings of the First Research Symposium of the Office of Bilingual Education and Minority Language Affairs* (pp. 281–320). Washington, DC: U.S. Department of Education.

Flores, B., Cousin, P., & Díaz, E. (1991). Transforming deficit myths about language, literacy, and culture. *Language Arts, 68*(5), 369–379.

Freire, P. (1970). *Pedagogy of the oppressed*. New York: Continuum.

Freire, P., & Macedo, D. (1987). *Literacy: Reading the word and the world*. South Hadley, MA: Bergin & Garvey.

Goodman, K. S. (1986). *What's whole in whole language*. Portsmouth, NH: Heinemann.

Goodman, K. S. (1994). *Phonics phacts*. Portsmouth, NH: Heinemann.

Goodman, K. S. (1996). *On reading*. Portsmouth, NH: Heinemann.

Goodman, K., Goodman, Y., & Flores, B. (1979). *Reading in a bilingual classroom: Literacy and biliteracy*. Rosslyn, VA: Clearinghouse for Bilingual Education.

Goodman, Y. M. (Ed.). (1991). *How children construct literacy*. Newark, DE: International Reading Association.

McDermott, R. (1976). *Kids make sense: An ethnographic account of interactional management of success and failure in one first grade classroom*. Unpublished doctoral dissertation, Stanford University, Stanford.

Moll, L. C. (Ed.). (1990). *Vygotsky and education*. Cambridge: Cambridge University Press.

Vygotsky, L. S. (1978). *Mind in society: The development of higher psychological process* (M. Cole, V. John-Steiner, S. Scribner, & E. Souberman, Trans. & Eds.). Cambridge, MA: Harvard University Press.

Vygotsky, L. (1981). The genesis of higher mental functions. In J. Wertsch (Ed.), *The concept of activity in Soviet psychology* (pp. 144–188). Armonk, NY: M. E. Sharpe.

Wertsch, J. (1984). The zone of proximal development: Some conceptual issues. In B. Rogoff & J. Wertsch (Eds.), *Children's learning in the zone of proximal development: New directions for child development* (pp. 7–18). San Francisco: Jossey-Bass.

Wertsch, J. (1993). *Voices of the mind*. Cambridge, MA: Harvard University Press.

CHAPTER 3

The Need for Educators with Political and Ideological Clarity

Providing Our Children with "The Best"

LILIA I. BARTOLOMÉ AND MARÍA V. BALDERRAMA

Much of the current discussion on improving Latino students' academic and literacy performance centers on best strategies and methods. Our focus, however, is on teachers' political and ideological clarity and its significance in preparing Mexicano/Latino students academically. By "political clarity" we mean the process by which individuals achieve a deepening awareness of the sociopolitical and economic realities that shape their lives and their capacity to transform their lives. It also refers to the process by which individuals come to understand better the possible linkages between macro-level political, economic, and social variables, and subordinated groups' academic performance at the micro-level classroom. Thus, it invariably requires that educators struggle to link sociocultural structures and schooling (for a more detailed discussion of the influence of sociocultural structures, see Chapter 1 and 2). A related concept, ideology, refers to the framework of thought used by members of a society to justify or rationalize an existing social [dis]order (see Chapter 4). Thus, "ideological clarity" refers to the process by which individuals struggle to identify both the dominant society's explanations for the existing societal socioeconomic and political hierarchy as well as their own explanation of the social order and any resulting inequalities. Ideological clarity requires that teachers' individual explanations be compared and contrasted with those propagated by the dominant society.

Our perspective, as working-class Chicana educators, educated in public and Ivy League institutions, affords us a variety of lenses with which to view the phenomenon of Mexicano/Latino academic underachievement as well as potential long-term solutions to this education crisis. We tap into various epistemological sources of knowledge to examine the historical, pervasive, and disproportionate academic underachievement of Mexicano/Latino and other subordinated populations. These sources include: (1) lived experiences in rural and urban settings, (2) personal and professional experience in public schools working with predominantly bilingual, Mexicano/Latino students, (3) research experience in both qualitative and quantitative methods, and (4) active involvement in teacher education programs.

As critical researchers we share an interest in identifying the often-unspoken and negated ideological dimensions of education that we believe inform minority education efforts and practices. As Chicanas, we learned early of the often-unrecognized but very real negative perceptions toward Mexicano/Latinos and other low-status ethnic/socioeconomic groups held by society in general and educators in particular. We have experienced and observed firsthand discrimination, as well as occasional preferential treatment because of our relatively "lighter" skin color, our gender, and our mastery of standard English. These experiences have led us to question conventional explanations for Latino underachievement, such as the seemingly apolitical deficit and cultural explanations, including those grounded in meritocratic myths. Meritocratic ideology reflects the belief that in schools, "the talented are chosen and moved ahead on the basis of their achievement alone" (Darder, 1991). She continues:

> "The talented for the most part, are members of the dominant culture whose values comprise the very foundations that inform the knowledge and skills a student must possess or achieve to be designated as an individual who merits reward. . . . Public schools persistently legitimize this myth of meritocracy to guarantee that successful participation in the educational system becomes the visible process by which individuals are allocated or rewarded with higher social status. Through a system of merit, the process of unequal privilege and entitlement is successfully smoke screened under the guise of democratic schools." (pp. 11–12)

Thus, we are interested in engaging in a dialogue beyond strategies and methods, since focus solely on technical issues often distracts educators from examining ideological and political dimensions of minority education.

In this chapter, we specifically discuss how four educators, identified as exemplary by administrators and peers, describe their ideological beliefs and attitudes about effectively preparing Mexicano/Latino high school students for literacy. Our discussion utilizes the broader definition of literacy suggesting that literacy is more than teaching students to read and write the "word." The educators in this study were adamant in their belief that preparing Mexicano/Latino students for academic success required not only that students encode and decode "words" but that they also develop the ability to read a variety of "worlds." Examples of these "worlds" include their school's academic and social cultures, their immediate community, and the English-speaking, White mainstream culture. Following this orientation, we discuss Latino student literacy as encompassing both the reading of the word and the reading of the world (Freire & Macedo, 1987).

The chapter is organized in the following fashion. First, we provide some key definitions of terms as we use them in this chapter. Second, we discuss the historical negation of the politics and ideology of teaching. Third, we describe the four exemplary educators' ideological beliefs about Mexicano/ Latino education and their attempts to operationalize their belief systems. Finally, we interpret these findings, offering general recommendations for providing "the best" for our Latino children.

Definitions

To assist readers in understanding how we use certain terms, we provide the following brief definitions:

Latino, as used throughout this chapter, is a term used in the United States to identify persons of Spanish-speaking origin or descent who designate themselves as being Mexican American, Chicano, Puerto Rican, Cuban, or of other Hispanic origin (Carrasquillo, 1991). We use the term *Mexicano/Latino* to describe the student population at Riverview High School. Historically and currently, the Latino population has been of Mexican ancestry, but we nevertheless want to acknowledge those Latino students who may not be of Mexican ancestry. The term *Mexicano* is utilized instead of the more common Mexican American or Chicano because a significant number of the Latino students are first-generation or immigrant Mexicanos.

Subordinated refers to cultural groups that are politically, socially, and economically subordinate in the greater society. These groups often are described as culturally diverse, minority students, at-risk, and disadvantaged. The use of subordinate implies the centrality of lower-status accordance due to membership in non-White, non-middle-class, and non-standard-English-speaking groups.

The term *technical* refers to the positivist tradition in education that presents teaching as a precise and scientific undertaking and teachers as technicians responsible for carrying out (preselected) instructional programs and strategies.

Historical Negation of Ideology in Teacher Education: The Need to Name Its Existence

As mentioned earlier, the issue of teacher ideology and the role that it plays in teachers' thinking and classroom practice remains unnamed and often negated, particularly in reference to Latino education. The dominant tradition equates teacher preparation with an industry, emphasizing training and imparting of technical skills in instruction, management, and curriculum (Bartolomé, 1994, 1998; Freire, 1987; Giroux & McLaren, 1986). Given this tradition, the role and effects of teacher political and ideological orientation have not been sufficiently acknowledged as relevant to the task of teacher preparation.

For example, when reviewing the 1998 American Educational Research Association (AERA) conference program, we were struck by the variety of conference presentations dedicated to discussing teacher "beliefs," "predispositions," "unconscious perceptions," and "assumptions," and their "thoughts" about "culturally diverse student populations" (a euphemism for non-White and non-middle-class students). Virtually none of the educators "named" their ideology or discussed it in explicit terms. Given our nation's history of negating the political nature of education, it is not surprising to witness that, even though ideology is at the core of many current minority education debates, there is no overt acceptance of this reality by those engaged in the debate. Although there have been, and continue to be, efforts to examine teacher beliefs and attitudes, there have been few systematic attempts to examine the *political and ideological dimensions* of educators' "beliefs," "assumptions," and "unconscious perceptions," and how these worldviews are part of a particular ideological orientation.

Indeed, educators' beliefs and attitudes have been treated as apolitical, overly psychologized constructs. One perception is that these merely reflect personality types, individual values and predispositions that have little to do with the existing larger political, social, and economic order. Educators' conscious and unconscious beliefs and attitudes regarding the legitimacy of the greater social order and of the resulting unequal power relations among various cultural groups in schools historically have not been acknowledged as significant to improving the educational process and outcome of linguistic-minority education.

However, even without utilizing the term *ideology*, the literature suggests that prospective teachers tend to uncritically and, often, unconsciously hold beliefs and attitudes about the existing social order that reflect the dominant ideology (Gomez, 1994; Gonzalez, 1996; Haberman, 1991; Sleeter, 1992; see also Chapter 4). Unfortunately, this reproduction of thinking often translates into teachers' uncritical acceptance of assimilationist and deficit-based

views of Latino students (see Chapter 2). We believe that these deficit ideologies held by most White and many non-White educators continue to have
detrimental consequences for the education of Latino students. In fact, we
argue that the combination of an assimilationist belief system and a deficit
ideology proves to be an especially deadly one. It is so because it justifies
disrespecting Latino students' native language and culture, misteaching
them dominant culture and English, and then blaming their academic difficulties on their "pathological deficiencies."

More recently, the examination of teachers' beliefs about teaching
linguistic-minority students has become a topic of research interest (Bloom,
1991; García, 1991; Howard, 1997; Jiménez, Gersten, & Rivera, 1996; Rueda
& García, 1996). This work, however, does not explicitly discuss teachers'
racist and classist beliefs about working with historically subordinated student populations (see Chapter 11). Eugene García's (1991) work on effective bilingual teachers' thinking and practice moves closer to examining elements of teachers' political and ideological clarity. Although he
discusses these teachers' "attributes" as apolitical constructs, we believe that
these attributes clearly contain elements of teacher political and ideological clarity. For example, the teachers in one of the studies are described
as knowledgeable and skilled practitioners who go beyond the content
knowledge and technical aspects of their job when they explain that

> [P]art of their job . . . is to provide the kind of cultural and linguistic *valida-
> tion* that is missing in Field Town [the local community], a community known
> for *deprecating* the Latino [Mexican American] culture and the Spanish lan-
> guage. (García, 1991, p. 139, emphasis added)

The teachers appear to recognize the subordinate status accorded to
Latinos in the greater society and in the immediate community and take
steps to validate them in school, firmly rejecting feeling sorry for or treat-
ing the students in a condescending manner. Instead, they describe creative
ways for circumventing obstacles preventing their students from receiving
an academically rigorous education. All the teachers reported a conscious
rejection of the "pobrecito" (poor little one) syndrome and the belief that
schools can do little to teach children from low-socioeconomic backgrounds
(see also comments on this syndrome in Chapter 5). They have an unwa-
vering support of their students and their idealistic, yet realistic, belief that
they can create "safe" learning spaces for their students to protect them from
negative experiences. While García does not distinguish between teachers
who are well-prepared, caring and loving individuals and those who are well-
prepared, caring and loving human beings *driven by a political and ideological
quest for greater social justice,* Tamara Beaubouef (1997) clearly and explicitly
explains this important distinction.

In her research, Beaubouef (1997) interviews six effective African American teachers regarding their beliefs, attitudes, and actual instructional practices. Her African American teachers resemble the Mexican American teachers García describes in his research. Beaubouef similarly describes her teachers as well-prepared, caring, and committed to incorporating their students' life experiences and cultures into the curriculum—yet *consciously dedicated* to preventing unequal power relations from being reproduced in their classrooms and schools. Beauboeuf reports that the teachers she studied have come to see education for social justice through maternal, *political*, and moral lenses. She describes their teaching as "politicized mothering" and explains her renaming of "culturally relevant teaching" to "political relevant teaching" precisely because of the significant role the teachers' political and ideological clarity plays in their attempts to transform their classrooms and schools into more just and democratic institutions for *all* students. Beauboeuf's work begins to name the existence and significance of teacher political and ideological clarity in the work of effective teachers. The classroom teachers featured in this volume (Berzins & López; Ciriza Houtchens; Laliberty, and Maldonado) are examples of the kinds of teachers Beaubouef describes.

The Study

Riverview High School (pseudonym) is located in a coastal southern California community close to the Mexican border. It recently celebrated its one hundredth birthday and currently enjoys impressive success with its students, recognition as a "California Distinguished School, 1996," and *Redbook Magazine*'s "Best High School in 1994." In addition, it boasts many notable people on its list of distinguished alumni. Riverview High School is considered successful because it sends approximately 80% of its graduating classes to community and 4-year colleges, and secures millions of dollars in student scholarships.

Riverview High School is surprisingly effective in schooling its 1,955 students. The school has a majority "minority" student enrollment of which 70% is Mexicano/Latino, 8% is Filipino American, with Whites, African Americans, and Pacific Islanders constituting the remainder. In addition, home languages are diverse, with Spanish and Tagalog the most common. Sixty-two percent of all Riverview students come from homes where a language other than English is spoken. According to school records, non-English-speaking students and those learning English constitute 23% of the current enrollment, "with the number of students who are English language learners continuing to increase while those who are fluent in English or

English speaking only continues to decrease. Furthermore, because the number of students coming from low-income and AFDC families comprise the majority of students, all students receive free nutrition and lunch services" ([*Riverview*] *High School Profile Information*, 1996, pp. 1–2).

The Findings: Four Educators Working Toward Political and Ideological Clarity

Four exemplary high school educators were invited to discuss their beliefs about how to work effectively with and prepare Mexicano/Latino students. The interview consisted of open-ended questions intended to elicit teacher-centered explanations and views about their own beliefs regarding Latino students (and other linguistic-minority students) and factors related to educating them. The educators ranged in experience (8 to 25 years) and consisted of (1) one White female principal, Dr. Peabody; (2) one Chicano history teacher, Mr. Tijerina; (3) one White female English teacher, Mrs. Cortland; and (4) one White male math teacher, Mr. Broadbent (all names are pseudonyms).

Our findings support Lawrence Sternhouse's (1985) assertion that it is the teachers who, in the end, will change the world of the school by understanding it. Our findings highlight the significance of teacher ideology in deconstructing what one counselor called a previous, "plantation" school model where Latino students were treated like second-class citizens. Instead, teacher ideology has transformed it into a school where working-class Latino students are welcomed and where serious and strategic efforts are made to ensure their academic and social success.

These educators attributed their students' success to the school personnel's ability to create and sustain a caring, just, and equal playing field for students who historically have not been treated well in schools or in the greater society. Common ideological beliefs shared by the four educators included rejection of (1) meritocratic explanations of the existing social order; (2) assimilationist orientation and deficit views of Mexicano/Latino students; and (3) romanticized and White supremacist views of White middle-class culture. In addition, the four participants reported having engaged in cultural border crossing, where they personally experienced or witnessed someone else's subordination. *Cultural border crossers* refers to individuals who demonstrate the ability to understand and participate in various social and cultural realities or "discourses" (Gee, 1990). Discourse refers to "a socially accepted association among ways of using language, of thinking, feeling, believing, valuing, and of acting that can be used to identify oneself as a member of a *socially meaningful group,* 'social network,' or culture" (p. 143, emphasis added). In other words, a discourse is like an "identity kit" that participants adopt or are expected to assume. The identity kits vary in terms of status and power (e.g., the discourse of White, male doctors versus the discourse of Mexican, male farm workers). The individuals in this study engaged in border-crossing experiences where they became clearly cognizant of issues of subordination and unequal power relations across cultures. These shared educator ideological beliefs and their experiences as cultural border crossers are elaborated on next.

"There is no equal playing field": Interrogating Meritocratic Explanations of the Social Order

Despite educators' differing explanations for the existing social order, they all question the validity of a "meritocratic" explanation of it. As a result of their questioning, these high school educators work hard to protect and shelter their students from the hardships present in their personal lives and from possible discrimination and ill treatment encountered inside and outside school.

For example, one teacher, Mr. Broadbent, reasons that Mexicano/Latino academic failure can be partly countered if teachers somehow get their working-class students to get a "taste of the better life" or to see "how the other half lives." Mr. Broadbent reported that had his father not been moved up from enlisted man to officer, he, too, might not "have been pushed by someone who had seen it." He explained that, by a fluke of good luck, his father had been promoted to officer (despite the fact that he was not a college graduate). Mr. Broadbent believes that his father's employment and promotion provided his father with a taste of a better life.

> He wasn't a college graduate, but he got a taste of the better life when he was in the army after the war . . . he got raised up from an enlisted man to an officer . . . and so he saw how the other half lived.

Given this experience, Mr. Broadbent's father aggressively pushed his two sons to go to college. This teacher points out that because of working-class limitations, life is not fair and often those most capable are not exposed to the outside world. As a result, they do not feel confident enough to "grab for it." Mr. Broadbent emphasized repeatedly that there is no equal playing field and that students, through no fault of their own, often are put into a disadvantaged position unless concerted efforts are made to "equalize the playing field." Another teacher, Mrs. Cortland, also questioned the meritocratic notion of success and achievement of the most able, as commonly subscribed by schools. She cited an incident during which the drama club was eliminated from county and state competitions because "they [couldn't] afford to compete." She discussed, at great length, how "competition requires more than merit and much economic support."

Similarly, the principal, Dr. Peabody, questioned the uncritical belief in a merit system where racism is a reality in the lives of her students of color. She reports reminding White teachers and peers that

> Even if you were oppressed as an Anglo, being poor or whatever . . . what I know is that the worst day or the worst part of all of that is never as challenging as [that encountered by] a Black person or Brown person. That whole color issue brings in a whole different thing.

She admits that a big part of her job is trying continuously to change the racist lenses of some of her teachers. Dr. Peabody explains that there aren't many teachers she would consider racist and that she avoids using the term *racist* in the school context because "it isn't that they're deliberately that way." She added that racism is a fact of life that has to be dealt with in an aggressive manner and she shared examples of her interventions. For instance, the California Scholarship Federation (CSF) advisor did not encourage her students to participate in a district-wide CSF scholarship competition because the advisor did not believe that her minority students were qualified to compete against White students from more affluent schools. Dr. Peabody spoke of this incident with great indignation: "I mean every flag in my head just went off . . . I just went through the ceiling . . . that's a deficit model, that is, 'How could these kids compete with anybody else?'" She went on to describe how she confronted the teacher and used CSF alumni college graduation information to prove to this teacher just how qualified and outstanding her minority CSF students truly were.

The educators in this sample articulate their awareness that other factors, such as racism and classism, often assume greater importance than pure merit and ability in the lives of working-class and non-White students. They relate this reality in a matter of fact tone, yet they do not fall into negative or deterministic views of their students' life chances. Instead, in taking this more political and comprehensive understanding of the social order and its potential manifestations at the school level, they can strategically create a more equal playing field for their students at the classroom and school levels.

"You have to . . . love Brown [people]!":
Rejecting Assimilationist and Deficit Views of Mexicanos/Latinos

A second belief system shared by these educators is their rejection of deficit views of Mexicano/Latino students and their refusal to assume assimilationist views in educating these students. In fact, these educators promote native-language instruction so that students, in the words of Mr. Tijerina, "can learn academic subject matter appropriate to their grade level and to maintain positive self-esteem and cultural pride."

In rejecting assimilationist views, the majority of these teachers voiced their belief that cultures in contact (such as Mexican Americans and Whites in the southwest) should inform and transform each other. This can be done with each cultural group taking the "best" from the other culture and discarding the "worst" from their respective cultures. Mr. Tijerina also emphasized his belief that effective teachers of Mexicano/Latino students and other minorities have to be conscious of cultural and ethnic differences and of their own racist tendencies and beliefs. He explained that to be effective teachers of Mexicanos/Latinos, "you have to like people of color—you have to authentically like dark colors, you have to love Brown [people]!" He elaborated:

> I think we have the feeling here [at Riverview] that minorities aren't inferior. I think there's a difference between patronizing in some schools where they really think a person is inferior to some degree, but, "Hey, you can make it if you try harder." The White people here—I don't think they feel that here. I think that they feel that our kids are equal—they have the same brains as kids in [more affluent predominantly White schools such as] Playa Dorada or Buena Vista or anyplace else. They *do* have the same brains—only the background is definitively disadvantaged—for lots of reasons.

As a part of his efforts to work against the students' acceptance of deficit views of Mexican culture, Mr. Tijerina works to transform his students into what he terms "Mexican Jews." He believes that students from "formerly colonized groups" should emulate Jewish practice of studying one's history, feeling pride in one's heritage, and working to uplift the collective. However, he argues against attempting to politicize high school students ("They're much too young."). He believes that an emphasis on the positive aspects of Mexican culture ("just like middle-class White kids always get regarding their culture") encourages students to feel good about themselves as individuals and as members of a larger collective. This type of education prepares Mexicanos/Latinos well for the racism they may confront once they leave Riverview High School. Mr. Tijerina proves his success in producing "Mexican Jews" by pointing out the significant number of students who have gone on to assume leadership positions at the college level (e.g., Movímiento Estudiantil Chicanos de Aztlán [MECha] officials, Associated Student Body [ASB] officials, etc.).

Throughout our conversations with Riverview educators, we discovered their common belief that the disproportionate academic problems among Mexicano/Latino students are not a result of their culture, language, or some innate racial pathological disorder. In fact, the participants distinguish between the very poor restrictive life circumstances in which their students live, and their students' innate potential. These educators understand that their students "*do* have the same brains" but that, through no fault of their own, have experienced difficult life conditions as a result of living in poverty. They see their students' chief problem as that—as not having money. However, they do not restrict their students' academic potential because of the students' low-socioeconomic standing. They believe, as Paulo Freire (1993) eloquently states, that students' lack of familiarity with the dominant culture "does not mean . . . that the lack of these experiences develop in these [students] a different 'nature' that determines their absolute incompetence" (p. 17). Instead, these educators consciously reject deficit explanations, utilizing, building, and infusing into the school culture the numerous cultural strengths that they perceive their Mexicano/Latino students bring to school.

"They play this game, 'all these [White and middle-class] students are smart and wonderful'": Questioning Romanticized Views of Dominant Culture

In addition to rejecting deficit views of minority students and assimilationist approaches to dealing with cultural diversity, the educators in our sample questioned the superordinate status typically conferred on "mainstream," middle-class, White culture. Mr. Tijerina, for example, emphasized the highly desirable values and ways of behaving that Mexicanos/Latinos possess. He described these students as generally respectful toward adults and desirous of improving their lot in life as well as their family's, but unsure as to how to go about it and in need of teachers' guidance. He explained that he actually preferred working with Mexicano/Latino students instead of the more affluent White students in other schools. He shared with us:

> I would not teach in [more affluent White schools such as] Playa Dorada or Buena Vista. See, I like these kids and I don't think I would like being in a White school because the students are, by my standards, they're disrespectful. I think they're "muy igualados."

"Muy igualados" is a good way to describe them. They are "muy igualados," like you owe them and "you're here to teach me," you know, "teach me, we pay your salary," kind of an attitude. The kids here are just very, very respectful and they're very accepting and tolerant of each other.

Igualado, in Mexican colloquial language, refers to someone who is in a subordinate position but acts as if equal to a superior. Mr. Tijerina's example refers specifically to students who assume equal status with their teachers and in behaving as equals come across as improper, disrespectful, and impolite. Mr. Tijerina emphasized the importance of maintaining traditional Mexicano/Latino cultural values and belief systems and incorporating them into the mainstream high school culture. For example, he mentioned that Mexicano/Latino students, by custom, demonstrate their respect for teachers and peers by cordially greeting others when they encounter them in hallways and other school sites. He compared their behavior with his perceptions that White middle-class students are rude, distant, and accustomed to ignoring people. He argued that mainstream middle-class, White culture would benefit tremendously if aspects of Mexicano/Latino culture were incorporated into it. Mr. Tijerina shared his belief that many aspects of middle-class, White culture serve to dehumanize people of color and promote the erroneous and arrogant belief that Whites are superior. He believed that if the mainstream could adopt traditional Mexican values of respect, humility, and acceptance of difference, our society might become more humane and the feelings of disconnection and alienation that so many of its own members feel might be reduced.

Beliefs about the superiority of White, middle- and upper-middle-class culture were debunked also by Mrs. Cortland when she spoke of the hypocrisy, dishonesty, arrogance, and disrespectful behavior exhibited by many of the affluent White students she had worked with in the past. She pointed out that White students, their parents, and their teachers delude themselves about just how superior the students are in comparison to poorer students and those of color. She found many of the White students seriously lacking in numerous human qualities such as respect and empathy for others. She shared her views, acquired when she began to substitute teach at Buena Vista High School: "I never had one kid ever, as I was walking across the campus, come up to me and say, 'Are you new here? Can I help you? Do you need help in finding the room?'" Furthermore, she observed that

They [the students and their teachers] played this "game"—"All these students are smart and wonderful." And the kids would come and go, "We'll pretend we are smart and wonderful." And I mean, the lady I took over for . . . I think she had a nervous breakdown. They never told me but I walked in and the first class was, what they called, 122 English and it was all . . . Anglo kids. [When the assistant principal left me in the classroom], they [the students] all stood on their desks and sang, "Ding-Dong the Witch Is Dead," and thought it was funny.

Mrs. Cortland discussed how her father advised her not to work at Riverview High School because of the roughness of that part of town and of the disrespectful minority students. She explained, however, that she had yet to encounter at Riverview, the disrespectful and somewhat boorish behavior exhibited by the Buena Vista High School White students that she had taught.

The educators in this study consciously challenged and rejected romanticized perceptions of White, mainstream culture. Their attitude seemed to be that they "knew better" than to believe unrealistic and uncritical views of White, middle-class culture. Too often, the norm in schools and in society is to compare poor, non-White students with that invisible, yet highly romanticized, White, middle-class standard. These educators are not impressed by and do not subscribe to myths of White supremacy or, conversely, to myths about Mexican or working-class inferiority. On the contrary, they very realistically name the invisible "center," middle-class, White culture—and point out numerous undesirable aspects of it. They work to maintain their Mexicano/Latino students' culture and to prevent the students from uncritically assimilating negative Anglo cultural elements.

"These experiences have shown me that if you are a person of color, it is more difficult for you to achieve": Becoming Cultural Border Crossers

In describing their experiences as cultural border crossers, these educators reported having lived or witnessed the arbitrariness and unfairness of being relegated to low status at some point in their lives. For instance, Mr. Tijerina spoke of his life experiences as a working-class Chicano who grew up in Rancho Nación and attended Riverview High School approximately 35 years earlier. Obviously, as a member of the working-class minority, he was forced to cross social and cultural borders in order to survive a middle-class, White school culture.

He reported that in his generation at Riverview High School (from 1960–1964), Mexican Americans constituted approximately 30% of the student population. Despite their numbers, they remained invisible in the mainstream high school culture. He remembered vividly the second-class citizenship to which the majority of Mexican American students were relegated. He related the condescending attitude (at best) directed at Mexicans as well as the outright disrespectful treatment (at worst) that he and his peers experienced. The maximum insult was to be called a "dirty Mexican" or "beaner" and told to "go back to Mexico." He explained that these derogatory comments lay just under the surface of Mexican and White interactions and frequently were utilized by White students at the slightest, real or perceived, provocation.

Mr. Tijerina explained that throughout his youth, he was always conscious of the low status ascribed to his working-class, Mexican background. He attributed his resilience to the strong pride he felt in being Mexicano (a value his father inculcated) and to his increasing conscious understanding of racism and its manifestations. His later experiences with the Chicano movement in the 1970s provided him with opportunities to formally study White supremacist ideology and colonialization models.

The high school principal, Dr. Peabody, attributed her early cultural border-crossing experiences to growing up as one of a few Whites in inner-city, predominantly African American Pittsburgh. She explained that as a working-class White girl growing up in an African American community, she learned early on about the advantages of cultural pluralism. She, too, like Mr. Tijerina, experienced firsthand what it means to be relegated to low status, given her position as a "minority" White person in an African American community. However, she recognized the lifelong privilege and preferential treatment she received by virtue of being White. She told of her exposure to racism and discrimination chiefly as a result of her close work with people of color.

> In Corpus Christi, Texas, is where I met man's inhumanity to man in terms of Hispanics. I remember clearly the kids being forced to speak English—kids who could not speak English. How do you force somebody to do something they can't do? . . . I remember that was the year that Texas turned back a lot of free lunch program money so those kids didn't eat . . . there was a barrio situation in Corpus Christi so I spent some time there. . . . These experiences have shown me that if you are a person of color, usually it is more difficult for you to achieve. You know, being poor, disadvantaged and if you're going to add on top of that, Black or Brown or Red or something else, it becomes a greater challenge.

She also shared her belief in allowing people of color to "use" her position as a White person (and therefore perceived by other Whites as a more legitimate spokesperson) to carry their messages. Dr. Peabody shared her conscious decision to utilize her privileged position as a White woman to become a change agent in school settings.

The educators in this sample experienced at some point in their lives, opportunities to cross cultural and social class borders. These border-crossing experiences, however, did not resemble the experiences that White, upper- and middle-class individuals have when they travel abroad or when they "visit" lower-class, predominantly minority urban areas. During these more typical types of cross-cultural experiences, members of the dominant majority often become unconscious "voyeurs" who view their new situations through never-acknowledged assimilationist and deficit ideological lenses. In addition, they usually do not consciously recognize their positions of dominance and higher status vis-à-vis the poor and non-White people they encounter. As a result, they emerge from these experiences ever more bound to their unquestioned classist and White supremacist ideologies.

The border-crossing experiences of the educators in this sample varied from typical "White border crossings" in that the educators either lived or witnessed others' subordination. For a variety of reasons, the reality of asymmetrical power relations among cultural groups became evident to them. For example, Dr. Peabody, whose experience as a child living in a predominantly African American community and later working with Mexican Americans, clearly understood that, by virtue of her Whiteness, she was considered higher status and given greater legitimacy in comparison to her non-White peers. Mr. Tijerina painfully experienced consistent efforts to subordinate him, given his working-class, Chicano status. Given their "baptism of fire" during their border-crossing experiences, these educators better understand asymmetrical power relations among cultural groups and consciously work toward reducing/preventing their reproduction at Riverview High School.

Educator Political and Ideological Clarity: Providing Our Children with "The Best"

The purpose of this chapter was to contribute to the book's discussion of better literacy instruction for Latino students. Although we do not offer specific reading and writing instructional recommendations, we believe that our findings, related to broader definitions of literacy, can powerfully inform the discussion of how best to educate Latino children. We contend that in discussing successful academic instruction for students from subordinated populations, a fundamental issue that needs to be addressed is that of educator (teacher, administrator, counselor, etc.) political and ideological clarity. We believe that when discussing subordinated Latino populations such as Mexican Americans, Chicanas/os, and Puerto Ricans, we need to acknowledge candidly and courageously issues of unequal power relations and how they may get played out in school settings. There are scholars who argue that, short of a revolution, the equalization of asymmetrical power relations at the school and societal level cannot occur. Our findings, however, suggest the powerful agency that teachers and other educators, as change agents, possess in their work in creating more just and democratic schools.

Despite the significance of educator political and ideological clarity for Latino academic achievement, few studies address educators' beliefs and attitudes as ideological and political constructs. As mentioned earlier, the tendency has been to treat educator beliefs and attitudes as overly psychologized, individual predispositions reflective of the educator's personality.

Given our life experiences as working-class Chicanas who have crossed (and continue to cross) numerous cultural and ideological borders, we believe our findings confirm the perspective that educating subordinated students is not solely a pedagogical issue, but a political and ideological one as well. The educators in our sample understand that teaching is not an apolitical undertaking. Although the educators vary in terms of political and ideological clarity, they nevertheless understand that Mexicano/Latino students often, through no fault of their own, are viewed and treated as low status, in the greater society and in schools. These educators question narrow meritocratic explanations of the existing social [dis]order that suggest that Mexicano/Latino students occupy the lower end of the hierarchy because they lack merit and ability. They list numerous factors, such as racism and monetary limitations, that often eclipse merit and ability.

In addition, these educators reject deficit and assimilationist ideologies imposed on their students. They recognize aspects of working-class and Mexicano/Latino cultures as extremely positive and desire that their students maintain their cultural values. Similarly, while they recognize the need for their students to critically appropriate aspects of mainstream culture, they reject romanticizing middle-class, White culture and do not expect Mexicano/Latino students to assimilate uncritically and blindly into it.

Given their life experiences as cultural border crossers, they recognize how low status often is unfairly assigned to members of lower-class and non-White groups. These educators' political clarity, solidarity with students, and sense of ethics make them true advocates and cultural brokers for their students so that they can "equalize the unequal playing field" and provide students with "the best" educational experience.

References

Bartolomé, L. (1994). Beyond the methods fetish: Toward a humanizing pedagogy. *Harvard Educational Review, 64*(2), 173–194.

Bartolomé, L. (1998). *The misteaching of academic discourses: The politics of language in the classroom.* Boulder, CO: Westview Press.

Beaubouef, T. (1997). Politicized mothering among African American women teachers: A qualitative inquiry. Unpublished doctoral dissertation, Harvard Graduate School of Education, Cambridge, MA.

Bloom, G. M. (1991). The effects of speech style and skin color on bilingual teaching candidates' and bilingual teachers' attitudes toward Mexican American pupils. Unpublished doctoral dissertation, Stanford University, Stanford.

Carrasquillo, A. L. (1991). *Hispanic children and youth in the United States.* New York: Garland.

Darder, A. (1991). *Culture and power in the classroom: A critical foundation for bicultural education.* New York: Bergin & Garvey.

Freire, P. (1987). Letter to North American teachers. In I. Shor (Ed.), *Freire for the classroom* (pp. 211–214). Portsmouth, NH: Boynton Cook/Heinemann.

Freire, P. (1993). *A pedagogy of the city.* New York: Continuum.

Freire, P., & Macedo, D. (1987). *Literacy: Reading the word and the world.* South Hadley, MA: Bergin & Garvey.

García, E. (1991). Effective instruction for language minority students: The teacher. *Boston University Journal of Education, 173*(2), 130–141.

Gee, J. P. (1990). *Sociolinguistics and literacies: Ideology in discourses.* London: Falmer.

Giroux, H., & McLaren, P. (1986). Politics of teacher education. *Harvard Educational Review, 56*(3), 213–238.

Gomez, M. L. (1994). Teacher education reform and prospective teachers' perspectives on teaching "other people's children." *Teaching and Teacher Education, 10*(3), 319–334.

Gonzalez, R. (1996). *Resistance in the multicultural education classroom.* Unpublished manuscript, Harvard Graduate School of Education, Cambridge, MA.

Haberman, M. (1991). Can culture awareness be taught in teacher education programs? *Teacher Education, 4*(1), 25–31.

Howard, E. (1997). Teachers' beliefs about effective educational practices for language-minority students: A case study. Qualifying paper, Harvard Graduate School of Education, Cambridge, MA.

Jiménez, R. T., Gersten, R., & Rivera, A. (1996). Conversations with a Chicana teacher: Supporting students' transition from native to English language instruction. *The Elementary School Journal, 96*(3), 333–341.

Rueda, R., & García, H. (1996). Teachers' perspectives on literacy, assessment and instruction with language minority students: A comparative study. *The Elementary School Journal, 96*(3), 311–332.

Sleeter, C. (1992, March–April). Restructuring schools for multicultural education. *Journal of Teacher Education, 43*(2), 141–148.

Sternhouse, L. (1985). *Research as a basis for teaching: Readings from the work of Lawrence Sternhouse.* Portsmouth, NH: Heinemann.

CHAPTER 4

Mainstream Ideology and Literacy Instruction for Spanish-Speaking Children

JOHN J. HALCÓN

Latino educators who promote primary-language instruction have long been at odds with educators and policy makers who espouse mainstream educational policy about how best to educate Spanish-speaking children, especially with respect to literacy instruction (San Miguel & Valencia, 1998). In control of the direction of public education since the passage of compulsory school attendance laws, majority educators and policy makers have promoted and imposed English as the sole medium of instruction for U.S. schools, and for all subjects. Even after the passage of Title VII ESEA, the Bilingual Education Act of 1968, the development of programs designed to promote primary-language instruction for Spanish-speaking children has been consistently blocked and weakened. Throughout the years, non-English languages and cultural differences have been treated as if they were irrelevant to the learning process. As a result, over the decades, Latinos who have had virtually no voice in their children's education have railed against the imposition of deliberate language policies and practices that have subordinated them to second-class-citizen status (San Miguel & Valencia, 1998).

In the 1920s and 1930s, for example, there was widespread use of IQ testing of Spanish-speaking students, *in English*. This practice served as a means of placing a disproportionate number of Mexican children in remedial education programs. The rationale was that IQ tests provided the necessary "scientific evidence" that gave those in charge of schools the license to prescribe what was best for Mexican children. These tests purportedly showed that Spanish speakers failed to achieve academically because they were: (1) non-English speakers, (2) culturally deprived, (3) mentally retarded, (4) bilingual, (5) poor, or (6) not interested in learning (Valencia, 1997b). As early as 1934, George I. Sánchez, a Chicano psychologist, challenged the use of these IQ tests to place Mexican children into segregated classrooms and separate schools. Not unlike the experience of today's Latino educators, his voice was dismissed as irrelevant and radical.

Mainstream Ideology

What I refer to as "mainstream ideology" is a set of beliefs about what constitutes America. At the heart of this ideology is a strong sense of nationalism: a pride and love of all that is believed to be American, to the exclusion or subordination of other beliefs. According to this ideology, it is the responsibility of those who reside in, or immigrate to, the United States to embrace the ideals of the "model American" embodied in and synonymous with White, Anglo-Saxon, *English-speaking* Protestant. This model is the measure by which "the other" (i.e., those perceived as non-Americans, those who deviate from the norm) is evaluated.

Mainstream ideology has reigned supreme since the late nineteenth century when nationalistic policies and the "melting pot" theory were popular rallying cries for a young nation (Crawford, 1997). Latino educators, however, have viewed the melting pot theory and "Americanization" policies as hegemonic practices. The purpose of Americanization, according to Carlson (1975), was to rid immigrants of the foreignness of their culture. This ideology is based on misperceptions and misdirected notions that the "other" would somehow "melt" their cultural and linguistic differences and thus become "real" Americans. While some groups of immigrants chose to "melt," the majority of Latinos did not or could not. For this reason, Latinos continue to be viewed as falling short of the ideal American virtues: assimilation into the mainstream and English fluency. Mainstream ideology permeates all facets of Latinos' lives and continues to dominate current educational policies and practices affecting their children.

In this chapter I attempt to show that what lies at the heart of today's debate over what is "best for our (Latino) children," is really a continuation of a long struggle between dominant majority policy makers and educators, and Latinos over who has the right to define whom. In spite of research conducted by Latinos that challenges present practices, Latinos continue to be defined as "deviations from the norm" (Valencia, 1991), thereby justifying educational policies that result in placing our children at the margins of a mainstream school curriculum (see Chapters 11 and 12). Having learned to "read the world," we recognize not only the asymmetrical power relations that exist between us, but our responsibility and right, as Latinos, to define ourselves and thus determine what is best for our children. In discussing our ability to read the world and the imposition of mainstream policy making with respect to literacy instruction, I examine briefly the historical treatment of Mexicanos/Latinos in schools, recent legislative initiatives in California that have had an impact on the education of Latinos, and the manifestation of this mainstream ideology in teacher practices and attitudes that, ultimately, negatively affect the education of Latino children.

Historical Treatment of Mexican American Children

Historically, the majority of Mexican children (many of whom were American born) not only looked different from mainstream children, but spoke a language different from that used in schools. Further, their parents adamantly persisted in maintaining their culture and language in spite of serious attempts by the schools to assimilate and Americanize the children. As a consequence, Mexicans were viewed as irresponsible, dependent on others, dirty, stupid, lawless, and spreaders of disease, and thus unsuited to attend schools with Anglo children (Donato, 1997). Others viewed them as "illiterate, perversely immoral, superstitious, 'densely ignorant,' and lacking in civilized customs" (San Miguel & Valencia, 1998).

The popular and common solution to the "Mexican problem" was to segregate the children into "Mexican" classrooms and schools that provided a strict diet of English-language instruction, a rigid mainstream curriculum, and corporal punishment for speaking Spanish (Carter, 1970; Carter & Segura, 1979). The goal was to impose English at all costs, even if it meant forcing the children to lose their language and culture (San Miguel & Valencia, 1998). Again, Sánchez (1951) challenged policies that advocated the segregation of Spanish-speaking children and the loss of their primary language in exchange for learning English. He also opposed the tacit, de jure policies that ignored their language differences and resulted in the labeling of hundreds of thousands of Mexican children as educable mentally retarded (Carter & Segura, 1979).

By the 1930s, 85% of Mexican children in the southwest were forced to attend segregated public schools (Donato, 1997). Chicano educators such as Sánchez (1934) argued that the "scientific evidence" that governed the education of Mexicans was biased, prejudiced, and motivated by xenophobia. In spite of their objections, segregation, mislabeling of Mexican children, and an English-only curriculum prevailed (Carter, 1970; Carter & Segura, 1979). These policies prevented a great majority of Mexicano/Latino students from achieving more than a minimal education. Donato (1997) attributes the high Mexicano enrollments in elementary schools and the disproportionately low enrollments in high schools during this same era to the negative impact of these policies.

There is evidence to suggest that the goal of schooling for Spanish-speaking children was not intended to promote their academic capabilities but to restrict their access to mainstream society. According to Donato (1997), "Schooling of Mexican Americans during the first half of the twentieth century in the Southwest functioned as a means of social control, an attempt to socialize them into loyal and disciplined workers, and the instrument by which social relations between Mexican and white communities were reproduced" (p. 12). Judging by educational policies for Spanish-speaking children during this time, it is clear that a solution to the "Mexican problem" was more about the imposition of mainstream ideology (i.e., hegemony) than about sound educational pedagogy.

Fortunately, the "scientific evidence" that defined the academic problems of Mexicans in those early years has largely been discredited, or, as Foley (1997) states, "All of these studies have left the culture of poverty concept of culture and deficit thinking in the dust bin of intellectual history" (p. 124). Over the past 50 years, Latino educators and other scholars have developed important language theories, promising bilingual programs, and sound pedagogy. Their research has debunked most of these early theories. For example, educators now acknowledge that the concept of "educable mentally retarded" is a subjective social construct with little useful meaning and, thus, inappropriate for describing Spanish-speaking children in the process of learning English. Educators today understand that non-mainstream children are simply different and not "culturally deprived," and they recognize that poor children are equally capable of academic success, although their struggles might be exacerbated by biases against them. There is ample research that shows that speaking two languages does not confuse children. Most important, educators know that bilingual, biliterate children are *not* retarded but enhanced intellectually by their ability to access two distinct linguistic codes (Hakuta, 1986; McLaughlin, 1985; also see Chapters 1 and 6).

What we have learned from the most recent studies on teaching literacy is that all teachers need to understand the importance of sociocultural factors in the construction of knowledge (Freire, 1985; Freire & Macedo, 1987; Moll, 1990; Vygotsky, 1978). This means not only that they need to understand the social nature of learning between expert and novice (teacher and student, or student and student), but that building on the cultural and linguistic background of students is the best foundation for learning. When one understands this process of learning, and the importance of developing not just literacy, but *critical* literacy (Freire, 1985), it is easier to accept the fact that a child's native language (and culture) is critical in the process of becoming literate in the native language.

Literacy Instruction for Latinos

The current literacy debates over what method and what language should be used for teaching literacy to the growing number of Latino students suggest that, despite new research findings about bilingual learners, the nineteenth-century deficit model of "the other" still prevails (Valencia, 1997b). Educational policy concerning Spanish-speaking children continues virtually unchanged, albeit masked in different terms. Spanish-speaking children are still segregated in mainstream classrooms because of their language (Valencia, 1991). They are still considered by mainstream educators to be "at-risk" if they enter schools without speaking English (Carter & Segura, 1979). The practice of testing them in English still continues even when teachers know these children don't understand the language of the test. Equally insidious is the fact that mainstream educators ignore or dismiss Latino scholars when their research findings and recommendations call for literacy instruction in the native language, consideration of sociocultural factors, and utilization of children's funds of knowledge as a basis for literacy development (see Chapter 1).

Many Latino scholars with expertise in literacy attended U.S. schools and experienced the same kinds of problems that today's Mexicano/Latino children experience. One might expect that given their "emic" (insider's) perspective on these issues, their professional expertise might carry some weight and be considered seriously enough to influence current literacy policies and practices. Instead, their expert knowledge, research, and new theories fall on deaf ears, especially when they challenge the status quo. The consequence is that those in charge of schools continue to tweak the traditional curriculum (designed for English speakers) in hopes that some benefits might trickle down magically to culturally and linguistically diverse children. In doing so, they fail to understand the role of Spanish, and other languages, in the development of English fluency, English literacy, and biliteracy (Reyes, 1992). They continue to believe that English is the only language children need, and the only language that should be taught in public schools. It should not be surprising, then, that we currently are witnessing the gradual erosion of bilingual education (Crawford, 1997) and the dismissal of the kind of literacy instruction designed to improve the literacy skills of Spanish-speakers—all because these views do not conform to mainstream ideology (see Chapter 11).

A brief review of the historical treatment of Latinos in U.S. schools reveals that the dominant (but hidden) curriculum has been about measuring and defining "the other" against a mythical model American that does not now exist, and never has existed. I borrow from Shannon (1995) to suggest that literacy instruction for Spanish-speaking children, historically, has been nothing less than educational hegemony. In fact, educational policy today continues to be about maintaining the dominance of the Euro-American mainstream. It has never been about what is best educationally for Latino children. This is evident today on two fronts: the general public's antipathy toward the education of Mexicano/Latino children as manifested in the initiative process in California, and the resistance of classroom teachers to accepting literacy instruction in languages other than English.

The California Initiatives

As educated Latinos, not only have we learned to "read the word"—to access knowledge through reading and writing—but, for our own survival, we have learned to "read the world" (Freire & Macedo, 1987). In reading the world, we recognize the asymmetrical power relations between Latinos and others in society. Further, we understand that programs and policies potentially beneficial for our communities are under attack by those who mean to keep Latinos in check. A review of recent California legislation introduced through the initiative process, specifically Proposition 63, Proposition 187, Proposition 209, and Proposition 227, clearly supports this assertion. I discuss each one below.

Proposition 63

Proposition 63 proposed making English the official language of California (Crawford, 1989). With strong support from U.S. English, an anti-bilingual education group, it passed by a 3–to–1 margin in 1986. This initiative required all official documents to be printed *only in English* and all government proceedings to be conducted *only in English*. While technically not eliminating bilingual education, the passage of an official English amendment created enough anti-bilingual sentiment to pave the way for the elimination of state funding for bilingual education programs in California. In 1987, then Assembly Speaker Willie Brown introduced Assembly Bill 2813, which would have extended the bilingual education law (and state funding for bilingual education) in California. In spite of the support of "virtually every school board and educator's organization in California" and the state legislature, Governor George Deukmejian, heavily influenced by the strong support for Proposition 63, vetoed the measure (Crawford, 1989).

The passage of this initiative in California sparked anti-bilingual education policies in other states, empowered English-only advocates, and opened the flood doors to similar initiatives around the country. According to Crawford (1989), "Proposition 63 [was] a boon to English-Only advocates in giving legislative form to a backlash against bilingualism" (p. 53). In 1987 and 1988, similar proposals were considered by voters and lawmakers in 39 states, passing in 8 and bringing the total "official-English" states to 16. With support from U.S. English and English-only advocates, by 1999, 30 states had passed "official-English" legislation. While no such legislation has passed at the federal level, conservative members of Congress have introduced "official-English" legislation regularly over the past several years.

Members of the U.S. English movement have pushed to impose English as the "official" language of the nation, declaring it the only legitimate language for public policy, education, and social interaction. Despite this seemingly benign intent, Latinos recognize it for what it is: a way to curtail the use of languages other than English and to diminish the growing influence of Spanish.

Proposition 187

In November 1994, Proposition 187—a ballot initiative aimed at curtailing immigrants—passed successfully in California. Proposition 187, the anti-immigration bill, as it was known, proposed to ban undocumented immigrants (especially from Mexico) from public education, as well as from other social services provided by the state. It is estimated that over 300,000 children in California were targeted by this proposition, which passed by a large margin (3–to–2). Although unstated, the aim of Proposition 187 was to identify and limit public school attendance of Latino children if they, or their parents, lacked proper identification, proof of U.S. citizenship, or resident alien status (Mailman, 1995). Latinos and their supporters filed for a court injunction against this initiative. In 1997, Proposition 187 was declared unconstitutional by a federal judge in Los Angeles (Los Angeles Times, 1997).

Proposition 209

In November 1996, California voters placed yet another initiative on the ballot. This was Proposition 209, the California Civil Rights Initiative (better known as the "anti-Affirmative Action" legislation). The intent of this initiative was to amend the California Constitution to ban preferences based on race or gender in public education, employment, and contracting. Proposition 209 was supported and embraced by conservative voters, and passed without a problem. Although it was initially enjoined, the Ninth Circuit Court of Appeals declared it constitutional. This proposition went into effect on August 28, 1997.

In November of the same year, the Supreme Court declined to review the Ninth Circuit decision, effectively supporting the prohibition on gender- and race-based preferences (Egelko, 1997). Its passage resulted in denying Latinos, other minorities, and women equal access to California's public colleges and universities. What this initiative has done is to reverse the civil rights gains made by Latinos since the 1960s. To many Latinos, Proposition 209 is another example of a blatant attempt by California's dominant mainstream voters to control them and other minorities.

Proposition 227

The latest, most direct attack against Latinos' growing influence in California was the 1998 passage of Proposition 227, better known as the "Unz initiative." Attacks on Latinos' demands for bilingual education are not new; they have been going on since the inception of the demands over 3 decades ago. Under the guise of improving the academic achievement of non-English learners, and claiming to provide "what is best for them," mainstream policy makers, conservative educators, and opponents of bilingual education steadfastly have undermined every effort to improve and expand bilingual programs. This has occurred in spite of research that shows improved academic performance and steady acquisition of English among students enrolled in bilingual education programs when programs are implemented correctly (Ramírez, Yuen, & Ramey 1991; Thomas & Collier, 1995).

In recent years, the goal of English-only proponents to eradicate bilingual education has become more focused and virulent. When Proposition 227 passed in June 1998, it outlawed bilingual education programs in California public schools. This initiative passed by a margin of 62% to 38%. While Unz and his supporters claim it as a "victory for Spanish-speaking children," in truth, the Unz initiative was designed to undermine and, ultimately, eliminate bilingual programs (Crawford, 1997). In truth, this is a good example of how members of the dominant majority presume to know what is best for other people's children, in this case *our* children.

While these legislative initiatives in California may seem far removed from the classroom and irrelevant to the teaching of literacy, they have had a far-reaching influence in shaping negative public attitudes toward Latinos and toward the use of Spanish in the classrooms. The truth is, we live in a society that currently boasts of its intolerance for non-English speakers through passage of English-only amendments, anti-immigrant, anti-bilingual education, and passage of anti-affirmative action amendments to keep "foreigners," especially Mexicans, in check. This negative rhetoric does not remain in the public domain, but filters down from the mass media and the larger sociopolitical context to Mexicano/Latino homes, to parents and their children who embrace it, subconsciously and uncritically, without understanding it. The result is, at best, ambivalence toward one's language and, culture, and, at worst, a self-hate that hinders learning (see Chapter 1).

To illustrate the impact of this insidious anti-Mexicano/Latino sentiment, María de la Luz Reyes (personal communication, 1999) tells of an incident involving two first graders, 6-year-old Iliana from Mexico and 6-year-old Greg, a U.S.-born Chicano.

> On hearing Greg taunt others with the word "caca, caca," Iliana reprimanded him saying: "It's not nice to say that word!" Without a moment's hesitation and pointing his index finger in an angry gesture Greg glared at her and retorted, "I don't *have* to listen to *you*. YOU WEREN'T EVEN BORN HERE!"
>
> The following morning when the first-grade bilingual teacher called the Spanish-dominant group for reading, Iliana complained, "Why can't we read English? *I don't like Spanish anymore.*" This was unusual coming from Iliana, but it was obvious that the incident with Greg had deeply hurt her and left her feeling insecure about her culture and language.
>
> Fortunately for Iliana, her bilingual teacher nipped the problem in the bud. She asked five students from the non-bilingual class (some Anglos and Chicanos) to come and discuss with her class how they felt about learning Spanish (something they were doing in a team-teaching exchange). These students talked about how much fun it was to learn Spanish and how they wished they could speak two languages like the bilingual kids. After this session Iliana continued with literacy instruction in Spanish without complaint.

The sad part about this incident is that it illustrates that despite the close cultural connection between Chicanos and Mexicanos, Chicano students also assimilate the negative anti-Mexicano/Latino sentiment without realizing that they are part of what the dominant majority views as the "Mexican" problem.

Teach Me to Teach "Them"

As a university professor, I teach undergraduate students preparing to become classroom teachers, and graduate students who return for a master's degree, generally with an ESL or bilingual endorsement. The majority of these students are Euro-American females who are teaching Spanish-speaking students or will one day do so. Although most aspire to be good teachers, few succeed with Spanish-speaking students because they have tacitly accepted mainstream ideology and its deficit views of the "them" they have to teach (see Chapter 3).

They rarely, if ever, consider that the problems they encounter in teaching second-language learners are due to their own lack of preparation, lack of ideological clarity (see Chapter 3), or unexamined attitudes about "them" (see Chapter 2). Consistent with the mainstream ideology, they have learned to view Spanish-speaking children as "deficient" because they do not speak English. Although most are unaware of it, their instruction is based on a deficit model and, as such, requires "remediation." The majority of these teachers find it difficult to consider bilingualism an asset, and as a consequence view biliteracy as an impossibility.

They enroll in my classes eager to learn how to teach "them"—desperately searching for the quick fix, tricks, answers, and/or easy solutions to solve literacy problems in their classrooms. Initially, they are not interested in theory. They want answers and a "one-size-fits-all" approach to literacy (Reyes, 1992) for all their students. They desperately seek the magic bullet to solve all their problems, fundamentally failing to recognize that these children are individuals whose literacy needs may not be similar to those of their mainstream students. The inadequacies of their initial teacher preparation become evident, preventing them from even considering learning a second language as a tool for teaching Spanish-speaking monolingual children.

From district-wide inservices they learn how to prepare lessons for "them," how to manage "them" in their respective classrooms, and how to create learning activities that might benefit "them." Few reflect on their own lack of preparation for teaching diverse populations. Few question the inadequacies of the dominant pedagogy, and even fewer examine the biases in their own attitudes, beliefs, or behaviors. As noted in Chapter 3, they lack ideological clarity. Teachers' lack of success with Latinos is discussed in greater detail in Chapter 2.

Most of these teachers do not recognize that mainstream curricula are dominated by negative views of Spanish-speaking children (Valencia, 1991). As a result, they view non-English speakers as "at-risk" not because they are not intelligent or capable of learning, but because they do not speak English (Arias, 1986). So, the teachers focus on teaching the children the English language, but in the process fail to help them become literate. Reyes (1992) discusses the need to separate the concept of learning the English language from the concept of literacy. These are not mutually inclusive terms; one can exist without the other, yet, mistakenly, they often are used synonymously. In other words, one can be literate in languages other than English, in English, and in both (referred to as biliteracy). Unfortunately, most mainstream teachers' "habitudes" (see Chapter 2) toward Spanish-speaking children translate into a primary goal of teaching them *in English*.

Language learning and literacy instruction for Spanish-speaking children in American public schools reflect hegemonic practices (Macedo, 1994). Under the guise of doing what is "best" for Latino students, the history of mainstream instructional practices for Mexicano/Latino students is replete with examples of the failure of these strategies (San Miguel, 1987). Irrespective of Latino educators' best efforts, these practices continue in spite of the accumulating evidence to the contrary (Valencia, 1997a).

Conclusion

In this chapter, I have tried to show that mainstream political ideology has long governed educational policy toward Spanish-speaking children. Although complex, the heart of the debate between policy makers and Latino educators over several decades has been about how best to educate Spanish-speaking children. Those who control schools still treat Spanish as a deficit to be eliminated if Latinos are to succeed in schools. In contrast, Latinos argue that affirming the primary language is a necessary component of academic success. Acknowledging the sociocultural nature of learning (Vygotsky, 1978) is, in fact, a vehicle for higher-order skills (i.e., critical literacy).

Since policy makers at the turn of the twentieth century insisted that Spanish speakers were to be educated only minimally (Donato, 1997), few serious attempts were made to improve the quality of their education. In spite of educational innovation and widespread reform in mainstream pedagogy since then, including those aimed at Spanish-speaking children, the conundrum of the "Mexican" problem still remains. In essence, mainstream educational policy continuously and irrevocably has frustrated the educational development of generations of Spanish-speaking children.

To reverse the trend, to ensure better than a minimal education for these children, mainstream policy toward Spanish speakers must change. And it must do so quickly before the schools are completely inundated by the sheer weight of the increasing numbers (Valencia, 1997b) of Latino children, a trend that will continue into the foreseeable future with no signs of abating. Educational policy must shift away from old, unworkable and hegemonic ideologies that held Spanish-speaking children to be deficient because they didn't speak English, to new theory and practice that accept their home language as an asset. Teachers trained to work with Spanish-speaking children must examine their preconceived ideas about Spanish-speaking children and develop an acceptance of cultural and linguistic differences as strengths to be developed rather than as weaknesses to be overcome. They must develop a keener sense of "ideological clarity" in understanding the impact of the norms of mainstream society on them and the curriculum they teach as they address the needs of these children. Further, they must learn that sociocultural factors such as children's language, culture, family, and community have an equal impact on the potential for their educational successes. These are not extraneous to the function of schooling, but, in fact, are an integral part of it (see Chapter 11). Finally, teachers and policy makers must learn to "trust" the expertise of Latino educators.

References

Arias, M. B. (1986). The context of education for Hispanic students: An overview. *American Journal of Education, 95*(1), 26–57.

Carlson, R. A. (1975). *The quest for conformity: Americanization through education.* New York: Wiley.

Carter, T. P. (1970). *Mexican Americans in school: A history of educational neglect.* New York: College Entrance Examination Board.

Carter, T. P., & Segura, R. D. (1979). *Mexican Americans in school: A decade of change.* New York: College Entrance Examination Board.

Crawford, J. (1989). *Bilingual education: History, politics, theory and practice.* Trenton, NJ: Crane.

Crawford, J. (1997). The campaign against Proposition 227: A post mortem. *Bilingual Research Journal, 21*(1), 1–29.

Donato, R. (1997). *The other struggle for equal schools: Mexican Americans during the civil rights era.* Albany: State University of New York Press.

Egelko, B. (1997, April). Appeals court upholds California ban of affirmative action [on-line]. Available: www.detnews.com/1997/nation/9704/09/04090079.htm

Foley, D. (1997). Deficit thinking models based on culture: The anthropological protest. In R. R. Valencia (Ed.), *The evolution of deficit thinking: Educational thought and practice* (pp. 113–131). Stanford Series on Education and Public Policy. Washington, DC: Falmer Press.

Freire, P. (1985). *The politics of education: Culture, power, and liberation.* South Hadley, MA: Bergin & Garvey.

Freire, P., & Macedo, D. (1987). *Literacy: Reading the word and the world.* South Hadley, MA: Bergin & Garvey.

Hakuta, K. (1986). *Mirror of language: The debate on bilingualism.* New York: Basic Books.

Los Angeles Times. (1997, November 15). Proposition 187 found unconstitutional by federal judge [on-line]. Available: www.humnet.ucla.edu/people/macswan/LAT23.htm

Macedo, D. (1994). *Literacies of power: What Americans are not allowed to know.* Boulder, CO: Westview Press.

Mailman, S. (1995). California's Proposition 187 and its lessons. *New York Law Journal* p. 3, col. 1.

McLaughlin, B. (1985). *Second-language acquisition in childhood: Vol. 2. School-age children* (2nd ed.). Hillsdale, NJ: Lawrence Erlbaum.

Moll, L. C. (Ed.). (1990). *Vygotsky and education.* Cambridge: Cambridge University Press.

Ramírez, J. D., Yuen, S. D., & Ramey, D. R. (1991). *Final report: Longitudinal study of structured immersion strategy, early-exit, and late-exit transitional bilingual education programs for language-minority children* (Executive Summary). San Mateo, CA: Aguirre International.

Reyes, M. de la Luz (1992). Challenging venerable assumptions: Literacy instruction for linguistically different students. *Harvard Educational Review, 62*(4), 427–446.

Sánchez, G. I. (1934). *The education of bilinguals in a state university system.* Unpublished doctoral dissertation, University of California, Berkeley.

Sánchez, G. I. (1951). *Concerning segregation of Spanish-speaking children in the public schools* (Inter-American Education Occasional Papers IX). Austin: University of Texas.

San Miguel, G., Jr. (1987). *"Let all of them take heed": Mexican-Americans and the campaign for educational equity in Texas, 1910–1981.* Austin: University of Texas Press.

San Miguel, G., Jr., & Valencia, R. R. (1998). From the Treaty of Guadalupe Hidalgo to Hopwood: The educational plight and struggle of Mexican Americans in the southwest. *Harvard Educational Review, 68*(3), 353–412.

Shannon, S. M. (1995). Hegemony of English: A case study of one bilingual classroom as a site of resistance. *Linguistics and Education, 7*(3), 175–200.

Thomas, W., & Collier, V. (1995). *Language minority student achievement and program effectiveness.* Washington, DC: National Clearinghouse for Bilingual Education.

Valencia, R. R. (1991). *Chicano school failure and success: Research and policy agendas for the 1990's.* New York: Falmer.

Valencia, R. R. (Ed.). (1997a). *The evolution of deficit thinking: Educational thought and practice.* Stanford Series on Education and Public Policy. Washington, DC: Falmer.

Valencia, R. R. (1997b). Genetic pathology model of deficit thinking. In R. R. Valencia (Ed.), *The evolution of deficit thinking: Educational thought and practice* (pp. 242–255). Stanford Series on Education and Public Policy. Washington, DC: Falmer.

Vygotsky, L. S. (1978). *Mind in society: The development of higher psychological process* (M. Cole, V. John-Steiner, S. Scribner, & E. Souberman, Trans. & Eds.). Cambridge, MA: Harvard University Press.

PART II

Biliteracy, Hybridity, and Other Literacies

Chapter 5

Starting Off Right

Planting the Seeds for Biliteracy

MARÍA ECHIBURU BERZINS
AND ALICE E. LÓPEZ

As public education crosses the threshold of a new millennium, meeting the needs of the growing number of Latino students continues to be one of the major challenges for today's teachers, who are primarily White, middle-class, monolingual English speakers. The stakeholders in education consist primarily of two distinct camps with clearly defined, even diametrically opposed approaches and solutions for how to teach reading and writing to Latinos.

The larger, more dominant camp believes that the key to the education of the large number of Spanish-speaking students, who cling so tenaciously to their native language and culture, is to immerse them in English-only instruction. One of the primary goals of this camp, as evidenced by the passage of Proposition 227 in California, is to eradicate bilingual education programs that, according to these stakeholders, prevent children from acquiring English. The second camp is made up largely of advocates of bilingual education. Among them are educators (including those in this volume) who view literacy as a sociocultural process (Vygotsky, 1978) that recognizes the importance of validating and incorporating the wealth of knowledge, experiences, and resources that Latino children bring to school. This group views proficiency in Spanish as an asset rather than an obstacle to learning. Blame (if any) for the academic failure of Latino students is placed squarely on schools and teachers who fail to build on students' background knowledge and natural resources.

Locating Ourselves and Our Assumptions

As a Chicana and a Latina with a combined total of 40 years of experience teaching in elementary schools with high numbers of Mexicano/ Latino students, we locate ourselves in the second camp. We declare openly and firmly that we are advocates for *all* children, but especially for bilingual students whose native language and culture often are demeaned, omitted, or excluded in schools. Throughout our teaching careers, we have been "las espinas" (thorns) in the side of those who cling to the status quo and treat non-English languages and cultures as inconsequential to learning. We acknowledge a vested interest in improving the condition of education for children in our community, in providing essential learning strategies to enable them to transform their own experiences into a new reality where they have better control of their own learning. Paolo Freire (1970) calls this process *conscientização*. Through this process, children can learn to maintain their language, preserve their culture, and take advantage of multiple opportunities for development of dual-language literacy.

Our assumptions are that: (1) teaching is a political act (Freire, 1970; Freire & Macedo, 1987) and therefore teachers must be advocates for the intellectual well-being of the *whole* child, (2) all children can learn, (3) children come to school ready to learn, (4) children learn best when their native language and culture are used as the springboard for learning (Freire, 1970; Vygotsky, 1978) and as a vehicle for the acquisition of English (Cummins, 1981), and (5) parents are indispensable partners in the education of their children (see Chapter 14).

Planting the Seeds of Biliteracy

It has been our experience that the majority of today's teachers are ill prepared to meet the unique academic needs of dual-language learners (see Chapter 4). In this chapter, we provide information that may be helpful for those teachers. Specifically, we describe how we begin planting the seeds for biliteracy in our kindergarten and first-grade classes. This includes how we construct a supportive environment that fosters close relationships among students and is conducive to successful learning, how we organize instruction for academic learning in English and Spanish, how we establish collaborative partnerships with parents, and, finally, how children have responded to these opportunities.

Creating a Supportive Learning Environment

Over the years we have learned that planning for and creating a safe learning environment are critical to the development of bilingualism and essential for planting the seeds for biliteracy. (It is like preparing the soil, making sure it is rich with minerals before planting the seeds.) We recognize that early on, Latino children learn the primacy of English and often enter school with feelings of inadequacy because they speak Spanish (see Chapter 8). In subtle and not-so-subtle ways, they discover that their native language is neither valued nor respected outside their homes. As a result, many students and even their parents develop ambivalence toward their language and culture that often hinders learning.

Because of this reality, what we try to do from the first day of classes is to use both Spanish and English as a way of letting students (and their parents) know that both are valued in our classrooms. During the first week of school we meet with parents for an orientation. One purpose is to find out all we can about the language(s) used at home by the children and other family members. As might be expected, the majority of our students are Spanish-dominant speakers with limited exposure to English. Some students are bilingual, and a few are English-dominant speakers whose parents want them to learn Spanish so they can communicate with grandparents or other relatives. Some parents believe that learning Spanish is an asset for their children's future; others wonder out loud if their children will learn enough English in a bilingual program. Their views and opinions about bilingual education usually run the whole gamut. Knowing this only reminds us that to be successful with our students we must help educate the parents about the value and goals of bilingual education. (We will discuss our collaboration with parents in a later section.)

To determine each child's dominant language, we conduct a short informal interview with the child. We generally ask the children to tell us about their family. In addition, we ask them to identify the language(s) they speak. If a child's self-assessment is different from his or her parents', this gives us an idea of how the child perceives English and Spanish. Later a more formal language assessment is conducted to determine expressive and receptive abilities in the areas of oral language, comprehension, vocabulary, and so on.

We document all this information on the student's registration form for future reference. At the same time we find out about the child's strengths and weaknesses as well as likes and dislikes. This information helps us determine the appropriate language of instruction for each child. Our aim is to build on the child's strengths, provide full development of the first language, foster the second language, and nurture self-esteem (Freeman & Freeman, 1992) so that the seeds of biliteracy can grow.

Bilingual children in our classrooms often withdraw because they fear being ridiculed. Thus, from the start we foster a positive attitude toward bilingualism and biliteracy by letting the children know that if they are bilingual they have the option to respond and/or participate in English or Spanish. We also practice culturally compatible ways of showing respect and concern for others. Lewis, Schapf, and Watson (1996) contend that "when kids care about one another—and are motivated by important, challenging work—they're more apt to care about learning" (p. 16). Consistent with this belief, we communicate and model our learning expectations and classroom procedures for our students. In fact, we practice procedures and behaviors until they become a natural part of students' daily routine. Students quickly learn that others will not laugh if they make mistakes. On the contrary, as a community of learners, we celebrate every child's effort and work hard at creating a close bond with all members of the class.

Budding Bilingualism

Students put great effort into learning a second language. Early in the first semester of kindergarten, we hear such efforts as: "Maestra, Maestra. Mi mamá hoy . . . aaah picks me up . . . a escuela a tarde" [Teacher, Teacher. My mom today . . . aaah she'll pick me up at school this afternoon]. For example, an English-dominant girl announced to a small group of friends that she would read because she was the teacher: "yo . lee . book . Shhh . . . Yo maiestra, okay?" (I . read . a book . Shhh . . . I'm the teacher, okay?] Children in our classroom begin to code switch as soon as they learn some words in the second language. This is their way of demonstrating that they are learning English and Spanish.

We have found that allowing our students to code switch fosters greater participation. It is an opportunity for students to practice their emerging (budding) second language. Our students take the risk in using both languages to construct meaning and to communicate developing knowledge. These students are pleased to be acknowledged and complimented for their efforts. We view code-switching as an important linguistic resource. Chapter 7 discusses "hybridity," which is an unmarked, nonpejorative type of alternation between linguistic codes. Like Martha in the case study described in that chapter, our children also use two linguistic codes to construct meaning and engage in learning activities.

Building a Community of Learners

Our classrooms become a cohesive unit, with students demonstrating concern for one another. Students work in groups or with partners using both languages without any problems. They become adept at taking care of both personal and group needs. One interesting result is that our students learn to use each other as resources, knowing who possesses particular talents. They are not inhibited in soliciting assistance from more capable peers.

Over the years we have visited our former students who move up to second and third grade, and we have observed that these social skills have become a natural part of who they are. Some of our students take nonreader peers under their wing. They see it as their responsibility to help others who might need academic help. For example, as noted in Chapter 6, Brittany (Berzins's former kindergarten student) still plays teacher and helps nonreaders. Without being asked, children who readily acquire English generally tutor less-English-proficient classmates.

Survival Strategies

We know that our students will not always have the luxury of having bilingual teachers, and that they often have limited ways of asking or responding to questions, so we teach them some strategies conducive to successful learning. One of these, introduced in kindergarten, and maintained through first, second, and third grade, is the art of questioning (Cecil, 1995). We help children distinguish between questions that reflect affective and those that reflect cognitive domains, as well as to recognize questions that are representative of all levels of Bloom's (1984) taxonomy. By "affective" we mean questions that reflect feelings or emotion, for example, "Were dinosaurs friendly to people?" In contrast, a question in the cognitive domain reflects desire for specific knowledge or information, for example, "What was the gestation period of dinosaurs?"

We begin by actually gathering the students around us and engaging them in a series of role-playing sessions on asking a variety of questions. For example, we tell the children we are going to ask them some questions that we are fairly confident that they do not know the answers to. The students are then directed to ask numerous questions to help them understand better what the teacher is asking. For example, "Sra. Lopez, I didn't understand what you said. Could you say it again?" or "Sra. Berzins, I'm not sure I understood what you mean. Could you say it again in a different way?" "Sra. Lopez, Could you give me an example or show me what you want me to do?" Asking these types of questions *places the burden on the teacher* to accommodate her instruction to the needs of the learners. She is required to explain more clearly what she is asking, to elaborate on the question, to pose it in a different manner, to provide examples, and to model what she wants from the students. This line of inquiry also helps students demonstrate to teachers that they are interested in learning, but need further elaboration, or mediation. Questioning strategies such as these are meant to elicit this mediation from the teacher who may not be in tune with what English-language learners need in order to be successful. The process also gives bilingual students a better opportunity to respond correctly, more time to process the question (especially if it is in their second language), a way of scaffolding information, and greater access to academic learning. The students quickly internalize the process and learn the value of "questioning." The result is that they become empowered with a useful tool to advance their own learning, even in situations where the teacher may not be bilingual.

Consistency and High Expectations

Consistency in providing directions and explicitly expressing our expectations for children is the key to success. Some teachers find it difficult to demand the best from students who come from poor backgrounds or broken homes, or speak little or no English. They take on a "pobrecito" (poor little one) attitude, which generally results in a watered-down curriculum (see Chapter 3). Our position is that for these students it is even more critical to provide some structure and a solid academic foundation so that they will have a strong education on which to fall back (see Chapter 12).

Organization of Bilingual Instruction

Our bilingual program is based on an alternate-day model; instruction is provided one day in English, one day in Spanish, building upon the previous day's skills and concepts, without repetition or translation. This model validates both languages and puts them on equal footing. It also provides students access to academic learning by allowing them to use their native language while developing skills in the second language. Although we encourage students to use the language of the day, they may choose to use Spanish or English when this is needed for clarification. We believe it is more important that students understand the concept being taught than to penalize them for not using the target language. As their teachers, however, we maintain instruction in the target language of the day for greetings, openings, directions, story time, and any type of conversations with students.

Our students learn academic concepts in their primary language. We encourage them to draw from their own experiences for learning. Students do this in their journals and literature response notebooks. We continually emphasize the importance of retelling these experiences in written form, and students respond well. For example, Sonia, a first grader, did not let the school bell interrupt her enthusiasm for writing about penguins. She continued her writing at home and shared it in class the following morning (see Figure 5.1).

In this writing sample, Sonia writes: "Penguins know what to eat. Some eat krill, others eat fish, and some eat shrimp." Although the writing has been edited for capitalization, this student shows remarkable control of writing. In spite of the fact that the words *pinguinos* [penguins], *algunos* [some], and *camarones* [shrimp] are difficult words, Sonia shows mastery of them as well as the rest of the writing.

Our students also have the opportunity to become actively engaged in culturally relevant and high-interest learning opportunities that are inclusive of all members of the learning community. As a result, the cultural and linguistic resources they bring from home are affirmed.

FIGURE 5.1: Sonia's First-Grade Writing Sample

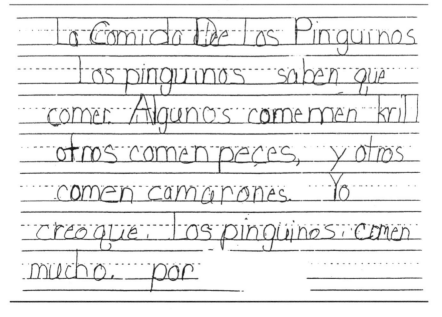

One exception to the use of the target language is literacy instruction that we provide in the student's primary language. Students are grouped accordingly. In kindergarten and first grade we make a conscious effort to supplement our guided reading program with culturally and linguistically diverse literature that incorporates a strong reading and writing connection.

Although there is much controversy as to whether teachers should or should not teach phonics, we believe in a balance between phonics/phonemic awareness and a strong literature component. Thus, we plan activities designed to develop phonemic awareness, as well as vocabulary development within context, through listening, reading, writing, and literature responses to a variety of authentic reading texts. We ensure an enjoyable experience by offering our students opportunities to select reading materials at their independent reading level and sufficient time to read alone or to their peers.

By reading Spanish and English literature and developing emergent literacy in the two languages, students establish social groups and ways of interacting with others. They gain and learn to maintain status and social position by acquiring culturally appropriate ways of thinking, problem solving, valuing, and feeling (McGinley et al., 1997). When students are allowed to read and write about things that are congruent with their home culture, they generally read and write quantitatively and qualitatively better (Reyes, 1992).

One story that usually generates a tremendous amount of involvement and response from the children is *Los Amigos del Otro Lado* (*Friends from the Other Side*) (Anzaldúa, 1993). This is a story about Prietita, a young Mexican American girl, and Joaquin, a Mexican boy who crosses the border daily from Mexico to the United States to sell dried firewood as a means of helping support his family. Prietita's friends find him easy prey for ridicule and humiliation; they call him *mojado* [wetback]. Prietita finds herself caught between loyalty to her old friends and her desire to help Joaquin. As a result of these two children's friendship, emotions such as fear, hurt, anger, and frustration soon give way to *cariño* [caring], *compasión* [compassion], *fé* [faith], and *esperanza* [hope]. After listening to the experiences of the characters, our students are usually eager to share their own experiences relative to the themes raised in this story. For example, Marta, a first grader, wasted no time in telling the class the benefits and wisdom of the *curandera* [healer] who cured her aunt of some unknown ailment for which the medical doctors had no answers. Yesenia recounted a time when some family members were picked up by *La Migra* [immigration officials] for trying to cross over into the United States from Mexico. Milagro felt it necessary to share with her classmates the importance and significance of *El Santo Niñito de*

Atocha (a Catholic statue of baby Jesus with his mother) and *La Virgen de Guadalupe*, pictures that could be seen in the background detail of the illustrations in the book. Each student was eager to share a story of great importance to him or her. Children's oral and written responses to stories such as these are profoundly important because they generate a broad range of emotions and responses that help them find meaning in their own lived experiences. Connecting with texts also legitimizes their funds of knowledge (see Chapter 1).

Computer Lab

In addition to the literacy instruction in class, students go to the computer lab daily for 40 minutes of a Spanish language arts program (Jostens Learning Corporation, 1995). Each literacy unit in the program consists of a story that students listen to while following the text on the screen. This is followed by a read along passage, then comprehension questions. We expect students to answer these questions with 85% accuracy or they have to repeat the activity. Decoding activities using pictures and syllabication also are provided. Our students find a great deal of enjoyment in these activities. Because of the culturally relevant content of this program and the high interest level, our students' decoding skills are reinforced and their vocabularies show dramatic growth. This growth in literacy is evident in their writing by the second semester. Figures 5.2 and 5.3 show two examples of kindergartners' writing completed in March.

In Figure 5.2 a Mexican American native-English speaker, Shelley, writes about one of her favorite holidays, Christmas. For a 5-year-old, her writing shows remarkable command of the conventions of writing. She has written two complete sentences requiring no editing; even Christmas and Santa Claus are spelled correctly and each sentence ends with a period.

Alex, a Spanish-dominant, 5-year-old, writes about his trip to Vail with his friend Luis [On Sunday I went with my friend Luis to ski and swim at Vail] (Figure 5.3). With the exception of capitalizing "el" at the beginning of the sentence and changing "bail" to "Vail," the only editing had to do with formation of letters. In Spanish, the rendering of the letters /b/ and /v/ is almost identical. Slight differences in the pronunciation of these phonemes do not make a difference in meaning. In English, however, these letters not only yield different phonemes but different meanings. This is a contrastive linguistic element that Spanish speakers have to learn in acquiring English. Again, this writing sample is quite impressive for a kindergartner. The word *esquiar* is a difficult word, yet Alex manages to sound it out and provides the correct spelling.

FIGURE 5.2: Shelley's Kindergarten Writing Sample

Name _____

My library book was about the Night Before christmas It's about Santa Claus and the way he brings toys.

FIGURE 5.3: Alex's Kindergarten Writing Sample

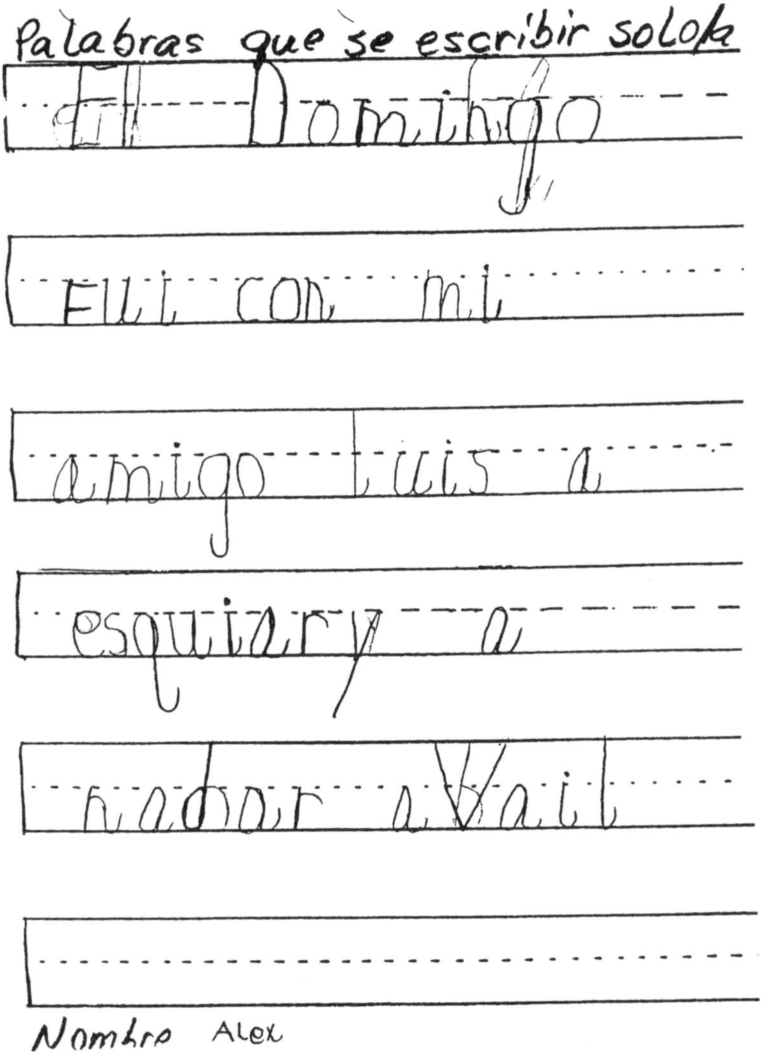

Palabras que se escribir solo

El Domingo

Fui con mi

amigo luis a

esquiar y a

nadar a Vail

Nombre Alex

Collaborative Partnerships with Parents

To nurture the seeds of biliteracy, we recognize the importance of involving parents in their children's education as much as possible. As we mentioned earlier, during orientation day we ask parents to sign up to help with classroom activities. We give them some choices as to when or how to help. Some sign up to help during specific times and/or activities; others sign up to be called as needed. At all times, we also encourage parents to drop in to observe at their convenience. We feel that the more they know about their children's schoolwork, the more their children's learning will improve.

Each year we have five or more parents in the room helping with classroom activities. One mother liked it so much that she continued coming every afternoon to help with groups or individual students. Several parents drop in and stay from half an hour to half a day. Some parents also help with clerical activities at the office and in the library. All parents sign up to contribute snacks for the class.

Knowing that communication with parents is crucial, we send bilingual monthly letters. We make phone calls letting parents know what concepts we are working on, as well as suggesting home activities for the children to work on while at the same time having fun. The extra practice needed to master concepts is done at home under the supervision and guidance of parents. If children are absent, we call to find out the reasons and whether they will be arriving late, or to find out if a student is returning for the next semester.

To facilitate the process of involving parents in helping with homework, Berzins sends kindergarten class homework twice a month. Homework folders include reinforcement activities to be done by the students during a period of 10 days and to be returned in the same folder. Included is a letter in the child's native language letting parents know about the activities and expectations. A book to be colored by the child and to be read to him or her is always one of the assignments. Parents interact with their children by reading the directions, supplying the materials needed, and pacing the work. Homework folders are signed by the parents and returned with all the completed work, often with optional written comments.

In López's first grade, *Pasaportes* [passports] become an integral extension of the students' classroom learning experience. At the beginning of the year, she makes every effort to impress upon parents the value of daily "homework" assignments and uses the analogy of Pasaportes as a way to ensure a more successful academic future for the students. This presents an opportunity to reinforce the importance of parents' role as instructional "tour guides" for their children. In an effort to make this experience aesthetically appealing and educationally beneficial, López takes a picture of each student with a Polaroid camera, glues it on the cover of the Pasaportes, and laminates it. Inside the cover folder, she inserts a blank sheet of paper on which the students receive a "stamp" to acknowledge completed assignments. After the students receive ten "stamps," they are free to choose any item from a classroom "treasure chest." On the back cover of the folder is a comment form to facilitate communication between the parents and the teacher. Parents feel very comfortable asking questions, making comments, or sharing resources relative to the concepts or themes we are studying.

We make accommodations for students with special needs, such as sending home books with audio tapes for students whose parents are nonreaders. If a student fails to return the homework on time, we send a note home and follow up with a phone call. By October the routine is established and continues until the end of the year. It is significant to note that the majority of parents cooperate without complaints and are grateful to participate in their children's academic development. For example, one mother expressed her opinion.

> Señora Berzins, I'm so glad that you take the time to give the children homework. It helps me know what my daughter needs help with and it gives her the chance to show us what she is learning. My husband is really impressed and since your note says *mom and dad*, now my husband feels he has to read to our daughter and help her with the numbers. (translation)

Another way to involve parents in the development of their children's biliteracy is through the implementation of two home-based reading programs, *Home Literacy Bags* and *Book Swap*. Through the Home Literacy Bags program, each student takes a canvas bag home once a week. This contains a book and a journal in the native language, a pencil and crayons, and a book in the second language. Part of the task is to have someone read a book to the child. In addition, children have to respond to a book using one of the activities in their journal. Later children share this experience with their peers in the classroom.

The Swap Book program consists of creating a collection of used books for students to "swap" for books they bring from home. In the event that a child does not have a book of her or his own, we provide the child with an initial swap book, thereby ensuring the participation of all students. Students are then directed to take the book home and have someone read it to them. Frequently, the students enjoy the story so much they ask for time to share it with the class.

To make sure that the necessary resources are available, we take inventory of our school library to determine the various types of books available. Initially, we discovered that the quality and quantity of Spanish books were limited. As a result, we consulted and collaborated with our "distributors," the librarian, and the building principal, and quickly made expanding our collection of Spanish books a priority. Over the past 4 years we have made every effort to stock our library shelves with more current and varied multicultural books.

Conclusion

In recent years we have truly seen the seeds of biliteracy that we plant in kindergarten and first grade flower and bloom. The students' writing samples presented in this chapter are evidence of how naturally the development of biliteracy takes place in an environment that nurtures the *whole* child; that is, his or her culture(s) and language(s), not just the development of English literacy. Because we share membership in the Latino community, we believe it is our advocacy for these children that fuels our determination that they can and will succeed in school without sacrificing their native language or culture. We too have experienced the undervaluing of our expertise because of our cultural background so we work hard at shielding our students from these negative experiences in school. We strongly believe, however, that *any* teacher can be a strong advocate for children. If she values the whole child, she will affirm his or her cultural and linguistic background and understand how these play a significant role in academic development.

Implementing the activities described above, being flexible with language boundaries, incorporating students' language and culture in their learning, promoting biliteracy, and involving parents in their children's academic development have produced impressive results as early as kindergarten and first grade. Students feel good about themselves and are eager to learn; parents are proud of their children. This feeling of success feeds on itself. The result is very low absenteeism. Further, not only are our students on a par with their native-English counterparts, but, we dare say, their use of two linguistic systems for reading and writing puts them far ahead of monolingual students in every regard. We have learned that the earlier we plant the seeds for biliteracy, the better our children will succeed.

References

Anzaldúa, G. (1993). *Friends from the other side.* San Francisco: Children's Book Press.
Bloom, B. S. (Ed.). (1984). *Taxonomy of educational objectives.* White Plains, NY: Longman.

Cecil, N. L. (1995). *The art of inquiry.* Winnipeg, MB: Peguis.

Cummins, J. (1981). The role of primary language development in promoting educational success for language minority students. In California State Department of Education (Ed.), *Schooling and language minority students: A theoretical framework* (pp. 3–49). Los Angeles: California State University, Education, Dissemination, and Assessment Center.

Freeman, Y., & Freeman, D. (1992). *Whole language for second language learners.* Portsmouth, NH: Heinemann.

Freire, P. (1970). *Pedagogía del oprimido.* [Pedagogy of the oppressed]. Mexico, DF: Siglo Veintiuno Editores.

Freire, P., & Macedo, D. (1987). *Literacy: Reading the word and the world.* South Hadley, MA: Bergin & Garvey.

Jostens Learning Corporation. (1995). *Spanish language arts: Cuentos de Coquí* (4th Ed.). San Diego, CA: Author.

Lewis, C., Schapf, E., & Watson, M. F. (1996). The caring classroom: Academic edge. *Educational Leadership, 54*(1), 16–21.

McGinley, W., Kamberelis, G., Mahoney, T., Madigan, D., Rybicki, V. & Oliver, J. (1997). Re-visioning reading and teaching literature through the lens of narrative theory. In T. Rogers & A. O. Soter (Eds.), *Reading across cultures: Teaching literature in a diverse society* (pp. 42–68). New York: Teachers College Press.

Reyes, M. de la Luz. (1992). Challenging venerable assumptions: Literacy instruction for linguistically different students. *Harvard Educational Review, 62*(4), 427–446.

Vygotsky, L. S. (1978). *Mind in society: The development of higher psychological process* (M. Cole, V. John-Steiner, S. Scribner, & E. Souberman, Trans. & Eds.). Cambridge, MA: Harvard University Press.

CHAPTER 6

Unleashing Possibilities

Biliteracy in the Primary Grades

MARÍA DE LA LUZ REYES

It's 9:00 and the second graders in Ms. Espinoza's class are spread out throughout the room, on the floor, on the sofa, at their desks, on the stairs to a small upper room. Two boys are lying under a round table reading—their heads propped up on cushions. Scrunched between them is their captive listener, a large teddy bear.

Ashley, a Spanish-dominant bilingual student, is at her desk writing a response to *Así es Josefina* (Tripp, 1997), a chapter book that she has just finished reading today. She writes the following response: "Se trata de Josefina Vive con sus Ermanas y con su papá vivian en un rancho avia vacas y chivas y vino su tia y Josefina le dio un abrazo." (The child's writing has *not* been edited; it includes her original spelling and grammar.) The edited English translation is: "It's about Josefina. She lives with her sisters and with her father. They live in a ranch. There were cows and goats. And her aunt arrived and Josefina gave her a hug."

Brittany, fluent in both English and Spanish, is reading a *Spanish* book to a girl who has been identified for special education and is not yet reading independently. The girl makes brief comments about the pictures. Brittany smiles at her proudly, enjoying her own role as "teacher."

Iliana, who arrived from Mexico 2 years earlier, is on the sofa reading an *English* book, *Today Was a Terrible Day* (Giff, 1980). She reads aloud to herself:

Today was a terrible day. It started when I dropped my pencil. Miss Tyler asked, "Ronald Morgan, Why are you crawling under the table like a snake?" Now all the children call me Snakey. (p. 1)

She laughs and turns the page, oblivious to those around her who also are reading.

On the floor in the corner, sandwiched between the sofa and a bookshelf, Lucia, by far the most accelerated bilingual student, is reading *Meet Kristen, An American Girl* (Shaw, 1986). She seems to be the only one in the classroom reading silently. Lucia is completely absorbed in her book with a kind of concentration that shields her from all the oral reading and chatter of the other students around her.

A slight variation of this scene is played out each day—a scene where seven or eight 8-year-olds move easily through permeable linguistic boundaries (Reyes, 1998). For the four little girls above, Ashley, Brittany, Iliana, and Lucia,[1] the natural and seamless movement from Spanish to English and English to Spanish belies the complexity of their achievement—the simultaneous development of two distinct linguistic systems (Zentella, 1997). Even more impressive than their oral fluency is their ability to access the two distinct graphophonic systems of English and Spanish for their own reading and writing purposes.

What is it about these four particular students that makes it possible for them to move rather successfully along the path of biliteracy without formal literacy instruction in *both* languages? Is this a mere aberration that defies those who claim that bilingual programs retard the acquisition of English, result in negative cognitive consequences for Mexicano/Latino children, and waste financial resources on expensive language programs (see Crawford, 1997)? How unique are these case studies?

In this chapter I explore these questions as I discuss four case studies, in particular, the development of what I refer to as the "spontaneous biliteracy" of these four little girls (from Mexicano, Chicano, and Central and South American parentage) beginning in kindergarten and extending through second grade. Just as Clark (1976) and Durkin (1966) use "spontaneous reading" to refer to a child's ability to read without receiving instruction, I use "spontaneous biliteracy" to indicate that the child is acquiring literacy in Spanish *and* English *without formal instruction in both* languages. (Each girl was receiving literacy instruction only in her dominant language.)

Although each girl began her literacy journey at a different linguistic and learning juncture, in the short span of 2 years each is achieving remarkable fluency in Spanish and English. Furthermore, each, for her age, is reading and writing at an impressive pace in not one, but *two*, languages.

In the sections that follow, I take a sociocultural and critical approach (Freire & Macedo, 1987; Vygotsky, 1978) to understanding the broader social context of their schooling. This includes the language and literacy instruction that takes place in the classroom as well as how the social, cultural, and linguistic influences from their families play out. In particular, I discuss each girl's idiosyncratic experimentation with biliteracy as she gains mastery over the two writing systems and self-regulates her interactions with language and texts (Vygotsky, 1978). Finally, I discuss the implications for unleashing the potential for biliteracy for other Mexicano/Latino children.

Theoretical Underpinnings

Through a sociocultural approach I view the processes of reading and writing as social, cultural, and linguistic acts situated in a particular sociohistorical context (Vygotsky, 1978). As Freire and Macedo (1987) assert, "Reading does not consist merely of decoding the written word or language; rather it is preceded by and intertwined with knowledge of the world" (p. 29). Further, becoming literate is not simply an individual act; rather, it is "transpersonal (a distributed phenomenon, not simply something residing within a single head)" (Erickson, 1996, p. 29). Reading and writing, like all learning, are rooted in social interaction where an expert other and a learner engage in the "zone of proximal development" using various cultural tools (verbal and nonverbal language, artifacts, signs, or written symbols) to arrive at a more in-depth or clearer understanding of a concept. The construction of meaning takes place in dialogue and interactions with others (Giroux, 1987).

Additionally, taking a sociocultural perspective means rejecting single-cause explanations of perceived outcomes (Cortés, 1986). In explaining a child's academic performance in biliteracy, for example, a sociocultural approach takes into account the multiple encapsulating layers of contexts in which biliteracy is situated. First, one examines the broader social context, which includes the prevailing views on biliteracy held by public institutions such as government, schools, churches, mass media, and so on. Second, one evaluates the influence of the home context, for example: Do the parents speak two languages? What are their attitudes toward maintaining or using these languages? Third, and very important, is an examination of the social organization of the school context. What is the staff's knowledge of biliteracy, their attitudes toward biliteracy and bilingualism? What curriculum is used? Do the materials support the development of two languages? What is the learner's own attitude and motivation toward biliteracy, and toward learning? Each of these layers, like an inverse ripple effect, influences the final student outcome.

The term *biliteracy* as I use it here refers to mastery of the fundamentals of speaking, reading, and writing (knowing sound/symbol connections, conventions of print, accessing and conveying meaning through oral or print mode, etc.) in two linguistic systems. It also includes constructing meaning by making relevant cultural and linguistic connections with print and the learner's own lived experiences (Reyes & Costanzo, 1999), as well as the interaction of the two linguistic systems to make meaning.

What We Know About Biliteracy

Much research has been conducted on emergent literacy for English speakers, but little or none addresses the development of biliteracy by students who speak both Spanish and English. Until recently, even bilingual educators had been largely silent on the subject, possibly due to a narrow interpretation of the research on second-language acquisition conducted by Jim Cummins (1981). He argues that to avoid negative cognitive effects, a second language should not be introduced until a child has mastered the first language (see Legaretta, 1979; Wong-Fillmore & Valadez, 1986). For most teachers this "mastery" generally is defined as grade-level competence in speaking, reading, and writing in the child's first language. Research on immigrant children conducted by Collier and Thomas (1989) and Skutnabb-Kangas (1981) is also consistent with this interpretation. This research indicates that immigrant children who have had 2 to 3 years of school in their native countries perform better academically than those who have had no previous schooling before arriving in the United States. Better performance is attributed to the fact that they can build on their native language and prior experiences. Indeed, August and Hakuta's (1997) report, *Improving Schools for Language Minority Students*, supports this interpretation. It states:

> Clearly one of the major intellectual stimuli to bilingual education programs has been the belief that initial reading instruction in a language not yet mastered orally to some reasonable level is too great a cognitive challenge for most learners. (p. 59)

Fear of challenging Cummins's (1981) universally accepted "minimum threshold hypothesis" is perhaps another reason why bilingual advocates have been hesitant to write about the biliteracy development observed in elementary grades. Neither Cummins nor the literature on bilingual education really defines what this minimum threshold is. Most bilingual teachers assume that this threshold is the end of third grade, when children generally are exited from bilingual programs. Before this time, few attempt to introduce formal instruction in the students' second language.

It should be evident to the reader that there is considerable controversy over the level of second-language proficiency needed to support literacy in that language. Among a large number of bilingual educators, the prevailing view is that the simultaneous introduction of two graphophonic systems might seriously jeopardize the development of literacy because it might be "too great a challenge for most learners."

Some exceptions to this view are the emerging number of studies reporting Chicano/Latino children's experimentation with literacy in two languages. Edelsky's (1986) extensive study of children's writing in Spanish, for example, dispelled the myth that "to begin literacy acquisition in Spanish and then to add English leads to interference with English literacy" (p. 73). On the contrary, she concluded that native-language (Spanish) literacy supported the acquisition of literacy in the second language (English). Children applied what they knew about literacy in their first language to second-language literacy. In another study, Hudleson (1984) found that bilingual children could read and write in a second language at the same time they were developing oral competency in that language.

Reyes and Laliberty (1992) found in their study of fourth-grade bilingual students that "the widely held belief that the negative effects of language mixing on the acquisition of English (Legaretta, 1979) and on the development of literacy skills did not prove true" (p. 274). Specifically, they found that "students seemed to use their native language as a way of demonstrating their academic potential and as a way of participating in the same academic activities as their peers while learning English *in a meaningful context*" (p. 275, emphasis in original).

Moll and Dworin (1996) examined some case studies of elementary students' development of biliteracy. Their findings suggest that there are multiple paths to dual-language literacy. According to them, those paths are formed by the student's history, the social context of learning, and opportunities students receive for engaging in language and literacy events in both languages. They assert that the key to "mediating external social constraints is that teachers create conditions in which both languages are treated, to the extent possible, as unmarked languages (cf. Griego Jones, 1993)" (p. 240). Additionally, Moll and Dworin reach an important conclusion: that terms such as *native language* and *second-language learners* become meaningless in bilingual contexts where the simultaneous development of literacy in two languages is taking place. This, they point out, may result in "misleading assumptions about children's learning" (p. 241) based on a required set or sequences of skills. Their conclusion rings true in the study presented in this chapter.

The School Context

In the section that follows, I describe the school context, including the teachers who taught the focal students, the instructional program in which the students participated, and each of the focal students. In particular, I discuss what language (Spanish or English) was used for literacy instruction for each of the four girls.

School and Staff

Williams Elementary School (pseudonym) is part of a small district just outside a large urban center in Colorado. At the time of the study, the school boasted an enrollment of about 600 students, 45% of whom were Mexican-origin students, with 61% of students on a free or reduced-cost lunch program—an indicator of the low-socioeconomic status of the families in the district. The bilingual program within this K–5 school is transitional, with one designated bilingual classroom per grade, totaling about 125 students. Administrative support of the bilingual program in the first year of the study seemed tenuous, but that support grew stronger as it became increasingly evident that more students benefit from bilingual education.

In general, the school's bilingual program model utilized an alternate-day approach: Spanish one day, English another. At the kindergarten and second-grade levels, the teachers were Latinas. The other teachers in the program were Euro-American women with bilingualism ranging from moderate to fluent. The kindergarten teacher followed this alternation religiously, but the first- and second-grade teachers did not adhere strictly to the target language of the day. The first-grade teacher, a Euro-American woman with moderate command of Spanish, used English nearly 80% of the time on any given day. The second-grade teacher (a Mexican American) often alternated between the two languages on any given day, making it difficult to determine the target language.

Instruction

In kindergarten, first, and second grades, literacy instruction was provided for all students in their primary or dominant language. For the focal students this meant that Ashley and Iliana were taught literacy only in Spanish, while Brittany and Lucia were taught only in English. The content area subjects (science, math, social studies) in first grade were taught in both languages in a team teaching arrangement between a bilingual and a non-bilingual first-grade teacher. The children were divided into two groups; one half stayed with the bilingual teacher who taught the content subject *in Spanish*, and the other half went to the non-bilingual teacher who conducted another lesson with similar content, but *in English*. On the following day, the groups exchanged classrooms for a follow-up lesson in the other language. This plan was used to provide opportunities for students to learn content area concepts in both Spanish and English. In second grade, the homeroom teacher (following the alternate-day language model) taught the content area subjects. For all students in all grades, art, music, and physical education were conducted in English outside the homeroom.

Structured phonics instruction for Spanish and English reading was provided in kindergarten by the teacher and via a computer literacy program in Spanish that consisted of relevant themes, literature, phonemes, and grammatical concepts. In first and second grade, only minimal phonics was taught.

Focal Students

Ashley, Brittany, Iliana, and Lucia entered the same bilingual kindergarten class at Williams Elementary School in the academic year 1996–97. They moved as a cohort to the same bilingual class in first and second grade. All four girls come from working-class families, as do most of the students enrolled in the school's bilingual program.

Ashley: "Me gusta leer en dos idiomas." Initially, Ashley seems shy. When she speaks she bows her head down a bit, but looks up with her big almond eyes and then responds with an air of confidence. It is obvious that she enjoys school—she exudes a sense of pride in doing her schoolwork. Unlike others, she is rarely seen engaging in useless chatter with her peers unless her work is completed.

Ashley's parents are from Mexico. They attended school in Mexico with the mother completing secondary school, and the father elementary school. Ashley was born in the United States. When asked how she learned English, she says: "I learned a little bit of English in preschool." As the only Spanish speaker at the child-care center, she began learning some English. At Williams School, her parents enrolled her in the only bilingual kindergarten class available. Ashley knew a few English phrases, but spoke mostly Spanish. Her parents speak mostly Spanish at home, although Ashley has a teenage brother who speaks English. During her entire kindergarten year, Ashley spoke little English. She rarely used more than single words or short phrases in English: *yes, no, thank you, okay,* and such, but she showed a great deal of interest in learning.

In first grade, she demonstrated the competency of a beginning English speaker, using more conversation, but preferring Spanish for most social interactions with her peers as well as for reading and writing. Her mother helped Ashley with her schoolwork in Spanish, but confessed that she and her husband worried that their daughter might not be learning enough English in a bilingual class. They considered transferring her to a private school at the beginning of second grade. Before making the move, however, they decided to discuss this with the teacher, and after getting an explanation of the goals of the bilingual program, they changed their minds and kept Ashley enrolled in it.

In second grade, Ashley seemed to unleash everything she had been absorbing in kindergarten and first grade about English and Spanish. As early as September she showed great interest in adding English reading and writing to her repertoire of skills. Figure 6.1 is a sample of Ashley's second-grade Spanish writing. Translated into English and edited, it reads: "When I went to the beach my Daddy and I collected little sea shells from the sand. And I got into the big waves, and they were pushing and knocking me down in the sand. And all of us were laughing." Her writing is lyrical, creating rich visual and sensory images that capture the fun and joy of collecting shells

FIGURE 6.1: Ashley's Second-Grade Spanish Writing Sample

cuando fui a la playa mi papi y yo
juntamos conchitas. del mar en la
arena. y me meti en las olas grand
y me puchaban y me tumbavan
en la arena y todos nos reiamos

with her father as they frolic on the beach. She uses correct spelling and expresses complete thoughts, but does not follow punctuation conventions. Since she is writing in her journal (an elective Christmas break activity), which is not graded, she does not seem to attend to standard form. It is interesting to note that Ashley uses the word *puchaban* (an English/ Spanish hybrid term stemming from "push") instead of *empujaban* (Spanish for "pushing"). Her use of this word illustrates not only the influence of English on Spanish lexicon, but, more important, that Ashley has learned common colloquialism from her Mexican *American* community. This suggests at least the beginning of some sociolinguistic competence on her part.

Her English writing has the characteristics of transitional writing (Routman, 1994); that is, while much of the writing is standard, there is still use of inventive spelling and inconsistency in use of punctuation. Figure 6.2 is a sample of Ashley's English writing in second grade. These inventions rely on Spanish phonology; that is, Ashley writes them as she pronounces them: "sume gams lick sit on the chare and pop a bulun" (some games like sit on the chair and pop a balloon). She does not use grammatical conventions except for a comma between *tamales* and *posole*, but she provides a good description of her family's activities on Christmas Eve. She uses *then* as both a cohesive device to connect her ideas and a way of sequencing the events.

Up to, and through, second grade, Ashley was taught only Spanish language literacy, yet one can see that, on her own, she made great strides in writing (and reading) in English. On seeing her experiment with English writing during second grade, I often asked her which language she preferred, and her response continued to be the same: "Me gusta leer (y escribir) en dos idiomas" [I like to read (and write) in two languages]. Recognizing the importance of bilingualism, as signaled by the increase in the Mexicano/ Latino population in Colorado, her parents now encourage the development and maintenance of both languages, but the mother adds, "No quiero que se le olvide el español" [I don't want her to forget her Spanish].

Brittany: "I was born bilingual!"   For as long as she can remember, 8-year-old Brittany believes she was "born bilingual." She explained that her father spoke only Spanish to her because he knew little English, and her mother, who is bilingual, speaks mostly English to her. Brittany's Spanish language also is reinforced by her grandparents, who are Spanish speakers. Indeed, since kindergarten, when I first met her, she spoke both English and Spanish fluently. For purposes of literacy instruction, however, she was grouped with the English readers where she was learning phonics and reading easy, predictable books. Her interest in Spanish reading was not squelched. She picked up easy Spanish readers and practiced reading them

FIGURE 6.2: Ashley's Second-Grade English Writing Sample

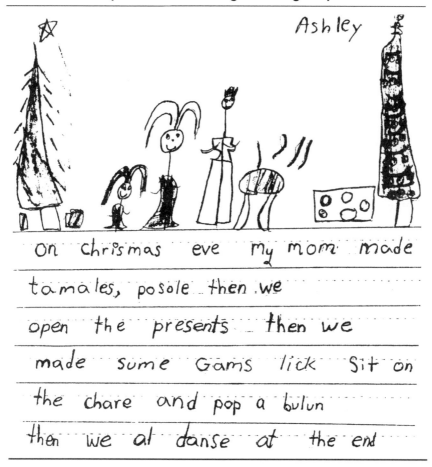

On Chrismas eve my mom made
tamales, posole then we
open the presents then we
made sume Gams lick Sit on
the chare and pop a bulun
then we at danse at the end

on her own. Brittany is bright and self-assured, always playing the role of "teacher," helping others with their reading or writing.

Brittany made no attempt to write during her kindergarten year, but in first grade she exhibited a great deal of interest in English writing. Her close friendship with Iliana, more of a Spanish-dominant speaker who was in a Spanish reading group, encouraged Brittany to experiment with writing Spanish. A couple of times I heard Iliana say, "Write it in Spanish. Yo te ayudo" [I will help you]. Here Iliana was acting as the "expert other." It wasn't so much that Brittany was not capable of writing in Spanish, but simply that she had never explored the possibility of doing it because she was assigned to an English reading group. This is an all-too-common response among bilinguals—if teachers or, in this case, more competent others don't promote a language, students simply won't attempt it. Brittany's interest in biliteracy grew because she and Iliana did everything together; they wanted to be alike in every way they could. Shortly after Brittany cut her hair, for example, Iliana followed suit. In class, they were inseparable. This close bond seemed to be of mutual benefit: Iliana acquired English at a remarkable rate and it helped Brittany enhance her Spanish writing.

By second grade, Brittany couldn't even fathom the idea of being restricted to English. In an interview she explained emphatically that she "was born bilingual." The very idea that anyone would think otherwise was preposterous to her. In spite of the fact that she had received only English literacy instruction, she took up reading in both languages, and writing in her journal and her Literature Response Booklet in English *and* Spanish, as her mood or book selection dictated. Figures 6.3 and 6.4 are examples from Brittany's Christmas break journal (a voluntary assignment) where she began her entries in English and suddenly switched to Spanish as she and her family arrived in Mexico for the holidays.

In Figure 6.3 Brittany details events that took place on the way to Mexico, such as her little sister getting locked in the car. Although her writing contains some spelling errors (i.e., "scard" for *scared*, "fier fiers" for *fire fighters*), she generally follows standard form. At the end of Figure 6.3 she writes: "Y ya llege a Mexico" [And now I arrived in Mexico]. This sudden switch from English to Spanish suggests that she has a natural instinct for appropriate sociolinguistic shifts required in different domains. In Figure 6.4, she continues writing in her journal, but it is now in Spanish. The translation of her writing is: "Today I arrived in Mexico and I play[ed] with my cousins, Liz and Chela. Liz is 8 years old and Chela is 10 years. And we played Thumb's Up [and] Seven Up."

It is evident in these examples that Brittany has already developed important literate competencies. The movement between her two linguistic worlds is fluid, almost seamless. In fact, she moves across cultural borders with so much ease, it masks the difficulty involved in mastering dual-language literacy.

Iliana: "I can read a little bit in English and a whole bunch in Spanish!" Iliana is sunshine. She is a happy, inquisitive, bright, petite girl just turning 8 years old at the end of second grade. Since kindergarten, she has identified with the Little Mermaid. In fact, when I first met her she was sitting in front of a computer doing a Spanish reading lesson. She called me over and pointed at the lower left corner of the screen where there was a picture of the Little Mermaid. She whispered to me, "Mira, ¿ves ésta

FIGURE 6.3: Brittany's Second-Grade English Writing Sample

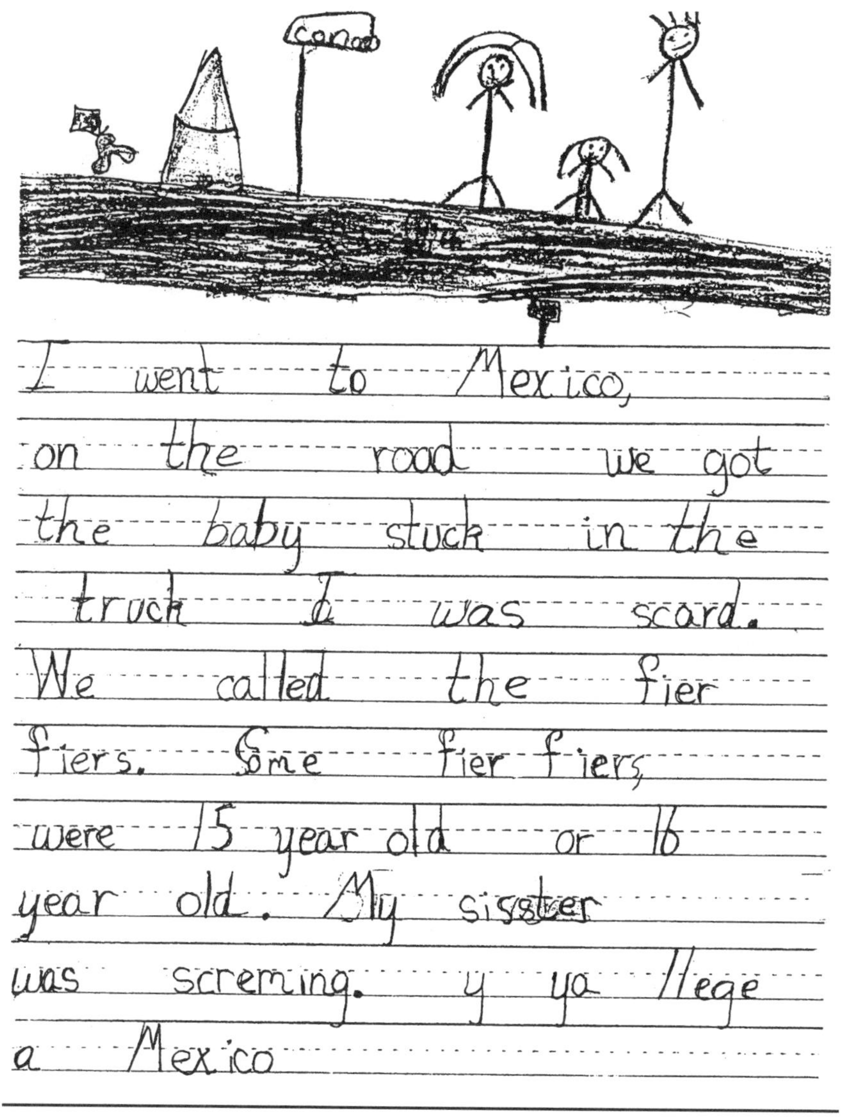

I went to Mexico,
on the road we got
the baby stuck in the
truck I was scard.
We called the fier
fiers. Some fier fiers,
were 15 year old or 16
year old. My sister
was screming. y ya llege
a Mexico

FIGURE 6.4: Brittany's Second-Grade Spanish Writing Sample

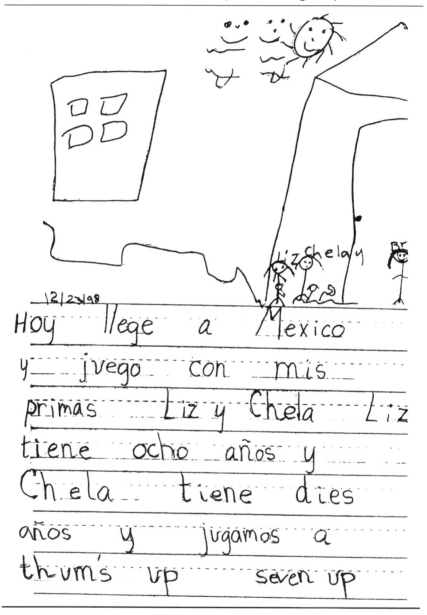

sirenita? Esa soy yo, la Little Mermaid" [Look. See this little mermaid? That's me, the Little Mermaid]. In kindergarten Iliana spoke exclusively in Spanish since she and her family had just arrived from Mexico, where she was born.

When Iliana began first grade, she showed a remarkable command of English, as if she had been storing a wealth of English knowledge during her silent period (Krashen, 1981) and it suddenly burst open. Almost overnight, she moved from being a non-English speaker to an intermediate oral English speaker with hardly a trace of a Spanish accent. She was like a little bubbly, bilingual talking machine. Iliana received literacy instruction in Spanish and continued writing and dreaming about the Little Mermaid. By December, she wrote a letter to Santa Claus (see Figure 6.5) *in English* (probably thinking that Santa might know English better than Spanish).

In this letter, Iliana tells Santa that she has been "good" because she has "obad" (obeyed) her "Ticher" (teacher). Like most girls her age, she wants a Barbie doll. Even with some errors such as "haved" (an overcorrection for past tense), and the words above, she has a good command of English vocabulary and her sentences are fluent. Iliana's writing, like Ashley's, is also transitional, but given that she was receiving no direct instruction in English whatsoever, her self-motivated efforts to be biliterate are impressive.

In Figure 6.6 we see a sample of Iliana's Spanish writing. The English translation is: "The little Mermaid, Ariel, looked and looked, looked for a ring she lost. And her father scolded her and told her. She looked for it and found it." This writing sample illustrates fluency and story line, but lacks adherence to standard form—a common practice among first graders. Iliana is still using mostly capital letters and inventive spelling. She begins the story with a capital and ends with a period, suggesting that she has some awareness of punctuation, but has not yet mastered the rules.

It is interesting to note that Iliana had a realistic view of her abilities. "I can read a little bit in English and a WHOLE BUNCH in Spanish!" she said in a first-grade interview. At school, her friendship with Brittany seemed to be a big motivating factor for her interest and gains in English. At home, she took on the role of translator for her mother, who spoke only Spanish, and her father, who spoke "some English," but was Spanish dominant. In spite of these seeming "disadvantages," Iliana not only became fluent in English and Spanish, but was also a precocious child, acquiring an impressive vocabulary in both languages and a flair for creative writing. For example, in second grade she started a "chapter book." Her story (unedited) began: "El invieron es como estar en una jaula y no me gusta estar enserada. A mi me gusta estar al aire libre . . . la casa era rojita y verdesita. Un chimenea bufaba humo . . . [Winter is like being in a cage and I don't like being locked up. I like to be out in the open . . . the house was a little red with green. A chim-

FIGURE 6.5: Iliana's First-Grade English Writing Sample

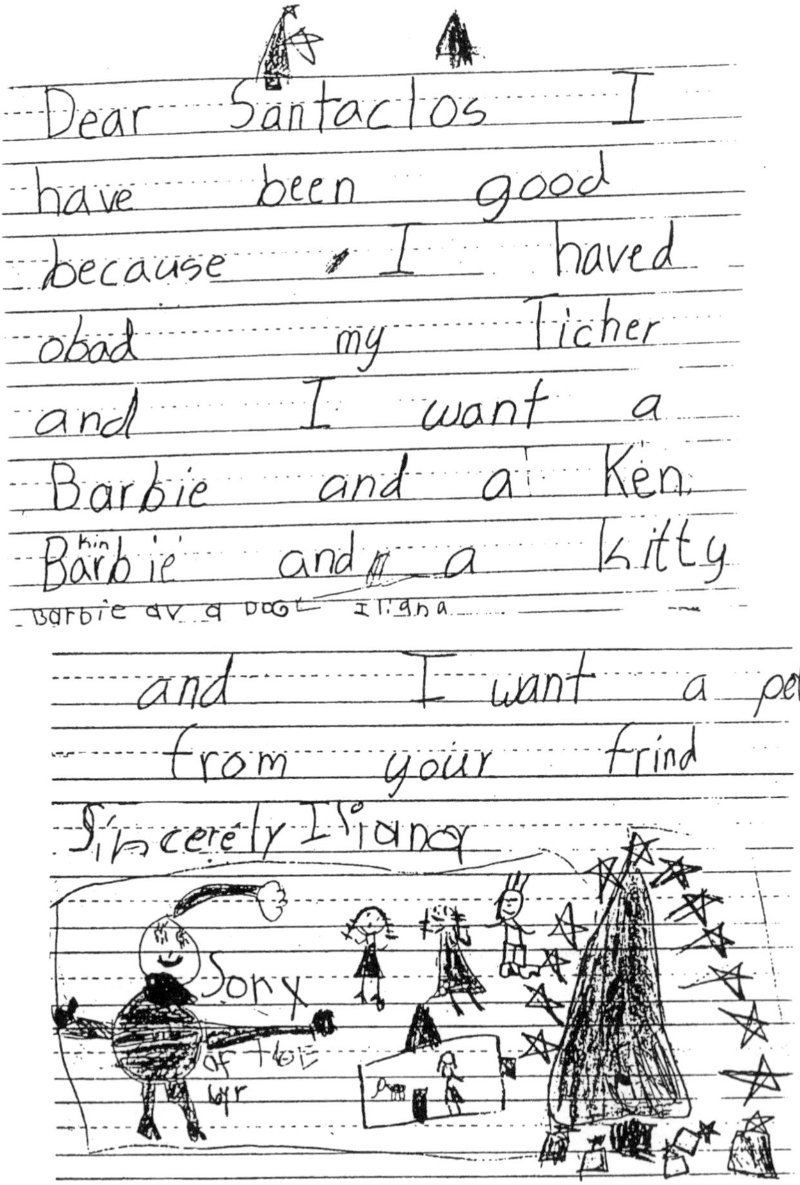

FIGURE 6.6: Iliana's First-Grade Spanish Writing Sample

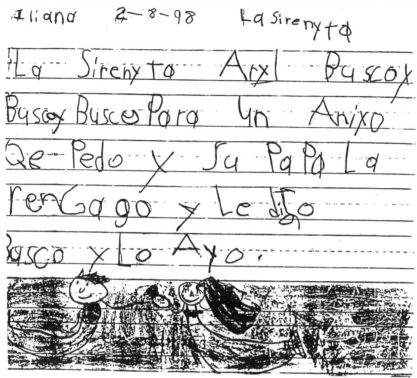

ney was puffing smoke . . .]. In this example, Iliana uses a simile, comparing winter to being locked up in a cage. She also uses descriptive words like "al aire libre" and "un chimenea bufaba." On another occasion she told my research associate that she wanted to be a writer. After being asked what she thought that would take, she responded: "I think you have to be smart and clever," adding that she wasn't sure she was clever. She ended the conversation by saying, "I think I must be wasting your time"—using English phrases not characteristic of beginning English speakers.

Lucia: "Yo leo inglés y español . . . I learned to read when I was in kindergarten." Lucia was far ahead of her class since kindergarten. At age 5 (see Figure 6.7) she was the only one who wrote a nearly perfect writing sample. In this kindergarten writing sample, Lucia uses mostly capital letters and has everything spelled correctly except that she confuses the

FIGURE 6.7: Lucia's Kindergarten Writing Sample

$$I\ Love\ MY\ To\ DoG$$

---

homonyms "to" and "two." Confusion with homonyms often continues even into the middle grades.

Lucia was placed in an English reading group although she was bilingual. This was done because she seemed to prefer English and as a way of balancing out the English and Spanish reading groups. Generally, however, children like Lucia (and Brittany) who enter United States schools with a strong bilingual background are rarely offered the opportunity to become biliterate, not even in bilingual programs. One reason is that bilingual programs are ill designed to nurture the development of biliteracy. Their primary goal is to transition students into an all-English curriculum. In the case of balanced bilinguals like Lucia, the terms "primary" and "second" languages have little meaning (see Moll & Dworin, 1996), yet they serve to restrict students to one language and doom them to becoming monoliterate for fear that instruction in two languages might lead to cognitive deficiencies. As a result, their natural potential for biliteracy frequently is squelched, stunted, or dismissed as irrelevant to their academic development.

Of all the students in the class, Lucia's parents were probably the most bilingual and biliterate. Her mother worked as a bilingual aide in the school. At home, reading and writing in English and Spanish were not only promoted and nurtured, but expected as an integral part of belonging to the family. To make sure that Lucia and her older sister would use their Spanish while they were living in the south, where few other Spanish speakers resided, their parents made it a practice to pay the girls 10 cents a day for speaking Spanish. To this day, they have retained this practice. The parents view it not as bribery, but as part and parcel of their children's socialization, like learning how to make their beds (Reyes & Costanzo, 1999).

Although Lucia was quite aware of her bilingualism and biliteracy, she seemed to prefer English. She acted as if English were large and imposing, permeating her entire universe (as indeed it does) and often showed signs of linguistic ambivalence. She would admit, "Yo leo y escribo en inglés y español" [I read and write in English and Spanish], yet frequently would describe herself as "better in English." But in first grade she reported "feeling sad" that she was not initially reading or writing in Spanish (she was, of course, placed in the English reading group). After this incident, her teacher encouraged her to feel free to write and read in the target language of the day. Lucia made giant strides in all areas of the curriculum. In fact, the results of the district's literacy assessment administered in spring of first grade showed that she was already reading at 3.2 grade level in English. (She was not tested in Spanish in first grade.)

Lucia wrote extensively in second grade, but the majority of her writing was in English. Occasionally, she wrote in Spanish. Figure 6.8 shows a sample of Lucia's Spanish writing in second grade. This Spanish sample, although impressive for her not having been taught literacy in Spanish, is less sophisticated than her English sample. Lucia, however, makes her point clear about how they will celebrate her birthday. The translation is:

> I am happy because today is my birthday and I am 8 years old. On Saturday at 5:00 me and my sister are having a party and I invited Ashley but she is going to Juarez, but my friend Brittany is going to come to my party. We are having a party at McDonalds, and the workers at McDonalds will make a cake.

Lucia confuses English and Spanish phonology, using a long *e* sound in "cumple" rather than "cumplí." She also uses the third person plural (e.g., "van" [they go]) rather than first person plural (e.g., "vamos" [we are going]) in talking about herself and her sister. Her use of "envite" [invited] is unclear as she made several corrections.

In contrast, in Figure 6.9 Lucia demonstrates her strength in English writing. It is obvious that her English writing is far beyond second-grade level. The story has a familiar ring so it is not clear whether it is based on a story or joke she read or heard. Lucia did not claim it was original. What is important is that she was able to reconstruct the entire narrative in great detail during the writing period. Not only is the narrative long and humorous, but it includes all the story elements, along with appropriate use of grammatical signals such as quotation marks, periods, capital letters, standard spelling, and so on. It is also impressive that at age 8 she understood the subtle adult humor in the story and retained it in a logical, sequential order.

Factors Contributing to "Spontaneous Biliteracy"

In analyzing these case studies, two significant factors contributing to the development of spontaneous biliteracy seemed to emerge: a learning environment that fosters and nurtures the learners' cultural and linguistic resources, and the focal students' social play. Promoting and supporting

FIGURE 6.8: Lucia's Second-Grade Spanish Writing Sample

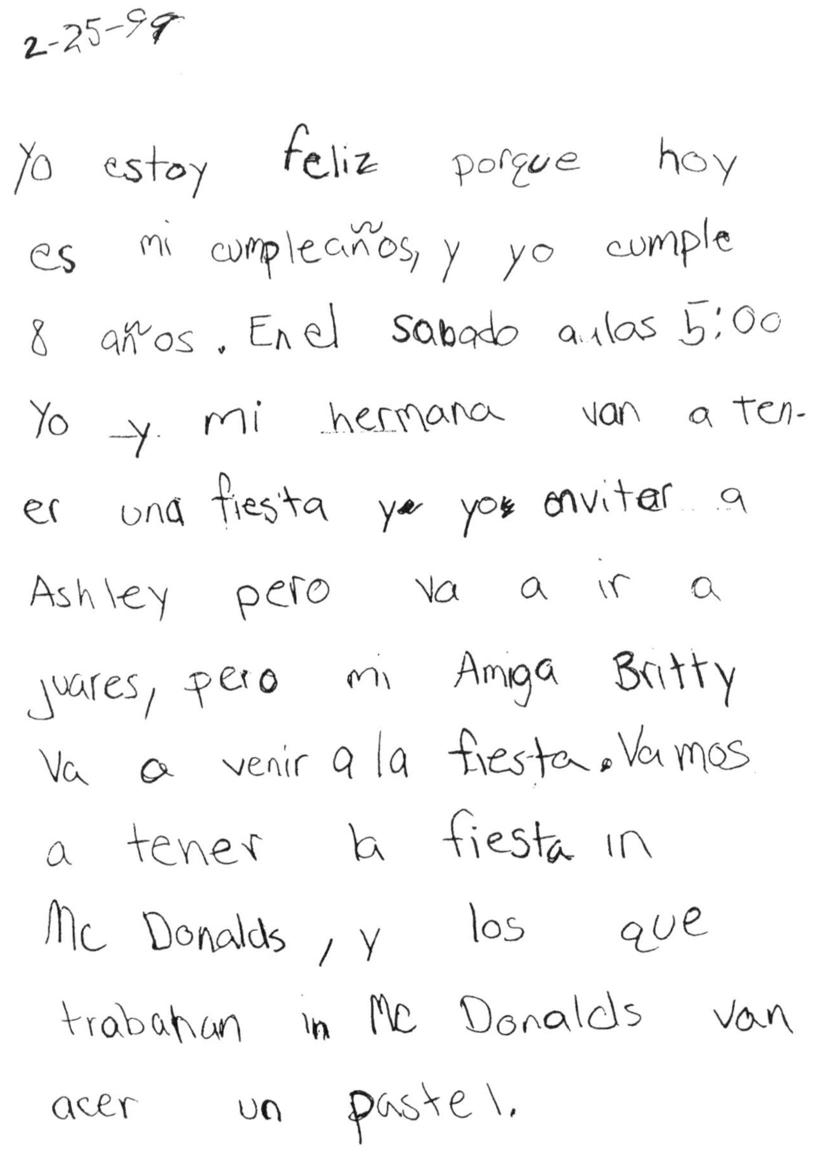

2-25-99

Yo estoy feliz porque hoy
es mi cumpleaños, y yo cumple
8 años. En el sabado a las 5:00
Yo y mi hermana van a tener una fiesta y yo envitar a
Ashley pero va a ir a
juares, pero mi Amiga Britty
Va a venir a la fiesta. Vamos
a tener la fiesta in
Mc Donalds, y los que
trabahan in Mc Donalds van
acer un pastel.

FIGURE 6.9: Lucia's Second-Grade English Writing Sample

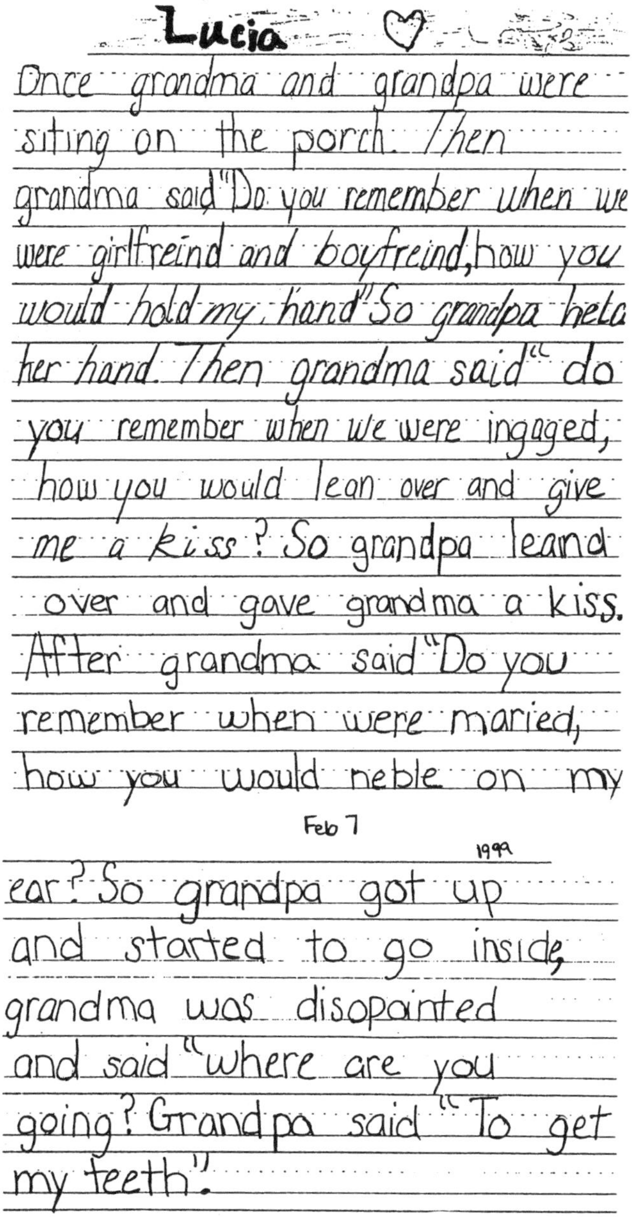

Lucia ♡

Once grandma and grandpa were
siting on the porch. Then
grandma said "Do you remember when we
were girlfreind and boyfreind, how you
would hold my hand" So grandpa held
her hand. Then grandma said " do
you remember when we were ingaged;
how you would lean over and give
me a kiss? So grandpa leand
over and gave grandma a kiss.
After grandma said "Do you
remember when were maried,
how you would neble on my

Feb 7
1999

ear? So grandpa got up
and started to go inside,
grandma was disopainted
and said "where are you
going? Grandpa said "To get
my teeth".

Mexicano/Latino students' use of their natural linguistic resources in the development of reading and writing created a learning environment conducive to biliteracy. It did so because it legitimized children's bicultural identity, unleashing their potential for bilingualism and biliteracy rather than forcing them to choose between their two cultures. As Ferdman (1990) has pointed out, "When a person loses the capability to derive and create meaning in a culturally significant way, he or she becomes *less* not more literate" (p. 199, emphasis added). There is no doubt that these students felt their languages and their culture affirmed. This allowed them to define and construct literacy in a culturally appropriate way, paving the way to biliteracy.

Although each of the girls received instruction in only one language, all their learning from kindergarten to second grade took place in classrooms where the teachers supported and nurtured their cultural and linguistic resources. Each day they heard their teachers and peers use Spanish and English. Their teachers also made great efforts to treat English and Spanish as equally as possible, valuing both languages for personal, social, and academic purposes. This treatment of both as "unmarked languages" (Fishman, 1976), as Moll and Dorwin (1996) also found in their studies, was a critical ingredient contributing to the early biliteracy of these four girls.

Social play among these four girls was another factor that contributed significantly to their development of "spontaneous biliteracy." By second grade the majority of the students had memorized the class schedule and routines of the day. Each morning the reading block began with journal writing, followed by a free reading time. It ended with Writers' Workshop where students were asked to respond in writing to what they had read, sharing it with the whole class under the direction of the teacher. During free reading time, Ashley, Iliana, Brittany, and Lucia would select one or two books, read them rather quickly, and then look for another one. To change the monotony, they would select a friend and read together. One day (in second grade) I heard Brittany and Iliana taking turns reading a bilingual book. Brittany would read the English page, and then Iliana would read the Spanish page. And, "just for fun," as they told me, they would switch again; this time Brittany reading Spanish and Iliana reading English. As they took turns, each one would read over the other's shoulder and help her if she got stuck. Soon, Lucia was reading with Ashley, taking turns and switching languages. Then they began to change partners, but keeping this biliteracy "game" primarily among themselves. They delighted in their linguistic flexibility, often laughing and giggling as other students listened to them, or as they asked the researchers to video tape their reading.

Biliteracy became a vehicle for their social play. In their play they created their own zone of proximal development (Vygotsky, 1978), challenging each other to read in the language they had *not* been taught to read.

Vygotsky (1978) wrote, "In play a child always behaves *beyond* his average age, above his daily behavior; in play it is as though he were a head taller than himself" (p. 102, emphasis added). Indeed, this seemed to be what was happening with the four girls. Their ability to read in two languages led them to attempt writing in two languages, and this seemed to be a significant source of their biliteracy development. This play–development relationship, like the instruction–development relationship (Vygotsky, 1978), became the focal children's method of advanced (bi)literacy.

These little girls were not singled out as "gifted or talented," yet their production of biliterate texts at age 8, indicates a remarkable ability to manipulate two linguistic systems. Their grade-level equivalencies for the school district reading assessment at the end of second grade were: Ashley—English 1.8, Spanish 3.6; Brittany—English 3.4, Spanish 3.0; Iliana—English 2.2, Spanish 3.0. Lucia transferred out of the district in late April before taking the post reading tests. However, her reading grade equivalent at the end of first grade was already at 3.2 in English. She was not given a Spanish reading test in first grade. It is interesting to note that, except for Ashley's English score, all four girls' reading equivalencies in English and Spanish were at or above second-grade level despite their not receiving literacy instruction in *both* languages.

The phonics instruction they received in kindergarten seems to have been sufficient to assist them in decoding both linguistic systems (Wagner & Toregeson, 1987). At the end of second grade, they demonstrated an understanding of such literate practices as abstract knowledge of the sound and structure of language, vocabulary in two languages, and knowledge of oral and written connected discourse skills (August & Hakuta, 1997).

Conclusion

The accomplishment of these four girls over the course of their first 3 years of school is impressive. It reveals a natural, spontaneous, and uncomplicated approach to bilingualism and biliteracy. Their proficiency in two languages and their ability to manipulate the two systems for their own communicative purposes stand in sharp contrast to the typical undervaluing of Latino students' potential by most schools. Because these little girls have been fortunate to be enrolled in a bilingual program where the teachers support and nurture their cultural and linguistic resources, they have not (yet) been discouraged or hampered in their individual experimentation with Spanish and English.

The findings from this study challenge the notion that Spanish hinders acquisition of English and development of literacy. Further, they contradict the argument in mainstream literature that continues to emphasize the idea that (only) children who come from literate households, who have been read to, and whose parents are educated (i.e., in English) and/or use literacy regularly are the ones *most likely to become successful readers.* Except for Lucia, this argument does not apply. In fact, the opposite is true: Most of the students are from low-income, working-class homes where not all parents speak English and some have minimal schooling, yet the children are on their way to mastering *two* linguistic systems.

Regardless of their means, these parents supported their children's education by demonstrating great interest in their academic progress, by attending school-sponsored literacy nights, and by purchasing whatever books they could afford. In some cases, the parents relied heavily on their children's English-speaking skills to access the wider English-speaking community. As they prized and valued their children's acquisition of English and supported the development and retention of Spanish, their children became even stronger bilinguals. In some cases, role reversals took place: Instead of parents reading to them, these children take on the responsibility of reading to their younger siblings—a practice that, in turn, reinforces their own literacy skills and promotes those of their younger siblings. As they read and explain the stories to their younger siblings, they learn to self-regulate their own learning (Vygotsky, 1978) and strengthen their own understanding of literacy. Furthermore, as they take on the role of "cultural brokers" (Arvizu, 1984) for their families, their confidence in English and Spanish grows and their vocabulary increases with each brokering event. In fact, a case could be made that these bilingual children may have stronger motivation to learn to read in both languages because the need is *real,* not merely contrived for the sake of instruction.

Early on, Latino children recognize that bilingualism is a commodity. Although they are young, they understand that the ability to read and write provides a key to maneuver their own, and their family's, way into better jobs, health, economic circumstances, and educational opportunities. At age 8, they display tremendous potential to "read the word and the world" (Freire & Macedo, 1987). Iliana, whose mother works in the service industry, for example, asked Lisa, my research associate, "Do you like coming here [school]?" Lisa responded, "I love coming here and being with all of you and helping you." Iliana quipped, "You wouldn't like working at McDonald's!" It seemed evident that she had already given her future some thought: She wants to be a writer.

The purpose of this chapter is not to call for *mandatory* literacy instruction in two languages in the primary grades. It is, rather, to showcase the dramatic emergence of biliteracy in the primary grades and make the case that Latino children's cognitive and linguistic abilities continue to be underestimated by schools. Although many Latinos come to school with the natural potential to become biliterate, that potential frequently is undermined, dismissed, and ignored. For example, when native-English speakers learn a phrase or two in Spanish, teachers make a "big fuss" over these small achievements. On the other hand, when fluent Spanish speakers learn to speak, read, and write *in English,* and at the same time retain their Spanish, they are still deemed "limited" English speakers. Schools label them "at-risk" as they continue to measure Latino bilinguals against a monolingual, monoliterate English-language standard that results in inaccurate and invalid assessment of their capabilities. This practice perpetuates the notion that bilingualism is a problem (see Chapters 1 and 10) and continues to promote the discourse of domination so prevalent in U.S. schools (see Chapter 4).

Our children possess the cultural and linguistic resources to become fully bilingual and biliterate. The goal of all teachers of Latino students should be to unleash students' potential by creating classrooms where English and Spanish are promoted, modeled, valued, nurtured, legitimized, and utilized. In bilingual programs, biliteracy should be a viable option for those who have the interest, ability, and motivation to pursue it.

The time has come to consider biliteracy the new threshold for literacy achievement in the new millennium. When this becomes a reality, Latino students and other bilinguals will be repositioned at the center of the curriculum rather than at the margins. To be satisfied with less than this is to accept a lower ceiling for our children's academic achievement and to force them to develop *only half* their potential.

Note

1. Throughout the chapter I keep the children's first names to match the presentation of the data on the writing of the children's own names. Any last names used throughout the chapter are pseudonyms.

References

Arvizu, S. F. (1984). *Chicano educators as cultural brokers: Case studies of innovation and problem-solving behavior in cross-cultural educational settings.* Unpublished doctoral dissertation, Stanford University.

August, D., & Hakuta, K. (Eds.). (1997). *Improving schooling for language minority students: A research agenda.* Washington, DC: National Academy Press.

Clark, M. M. (1976). *Young fluent readers: What can they teach us?* London: Heinemann.

Collier, V. P., & Thomas, W. P. (1989). How quickly can immigrants become proficient in school English? *Journal of Educational Issues of Language Minority Students, 5,* 26–38.

Cortés, C. (1986). The education of language minority students: A contextual interaction model. In *Beyond language: Social and cultural factors in schooling language minority students* (pp. 3–33). Los Angeles: Bilingual Education Center.

Crawford, J. (1997). The campaign against Proposition 227: A post mortem. *Bilingual Research Journal, 21*(1), 1–29.

Cummins, J. (1981). The role of primary language development in promoting educational success for language minority students. In California State Department of Education (Ed.), *Schooling and language minority students: A theoretical framework* (pp. 3–49). Los Angeles: California State University, Evaluation, Dissemination and Assessment Center.

Durkin, D. (1966). *Children who read early: Two longitudinal studies.* New York: Teachers College Press.

Edelsky, C. (1986). *Writing in a bilingual program: Había una vez.* Norwood, NJ: Ablex.

Erickson, F. (1996). Going for the zone: The social and cognitive ecology of teacher–student interaction in classroom conversations. In D. Hicks (Ed.), *Discourse, learning, and schooling* (pp. 29–62). New York: Cambridge University Press.

Ferdman, B. M. (1990). Literacy and cultural identity. *Harvard Educational Review, 60*(2), 181-204.

Fishman, J. (1976). *International sociological perspectives on bilingual education.* Keynote address at the annual meeting of the National Association for Bilingual Education, San Antonio, TX.

Freire, P., & Macedo, D. (1987). *Literacy: Reading the word and the world.* South Hadley, MA: Bergin & Garvey.

Giff, P. R. (1980). *Today was a terrible day.* New York: Penguin Books.

Giroux, H. (1987). Introduction. In P. Freire & D. Macedo, *Literacy: Reading the word and the world* (pp. 1–27). South Hadley, MA: Bergin & Garvey.

Hudleson, S. (1984). Kan yu ret an rayt en Ingles: Children become literate in English as a second language. *TESOL Quarterly, 18*(2), 221–238.

Krashen, S. (1981). *Second language acquisition and second language learning.* London: Pergamon Press.

Legaretta, D. (1979). The effects of program models on language acquisition by Spanish speaking children. *TESOL Quarterly, 13*(4), 521–534.

Moll, L. C., & Dworin, J. (1996). Biliteracy development in classrooms: Social dynamics and cultural possibilities. In D. Hicks (Ed.), *Discourse, learning, and schooling* (pp. 221–246). Cambridge: Cambridge University Press.

Reyes, M. de la Luz. (1998, March). *Learning in two worlds: Primary students negotiating meaning.* Paper presented at the National Council of Teachers of English Spring Conference, Albuquerque, NM.

Reyes, M. de la Luz, & Costanzo, L. (1999, April). *On the threshold of biliteracy: A first grader's personal journey.* Paper presented at the annual meeting of the American Educational Research Association, Montreal.

Reyes, M. de la Luz, & Laliberty, E. A. (1992). A teacher's "pied piper" effect on young authors. *Education and Urban Society, 24*(2), 263–278.

Routman, R. (1994). *Invitations: Changing as teachers and learners K–12*. Portsmouth, NH: Heinemann.

Shaw, J. (1986). *Meet Kristen: An American girl.* Middleton, WI: Pleasant Company Publications.

Skutnabb-Kangas, T. (1981). *Bilingualism or not: The education of minorities.* Clevedon, Avon, England: Multilingual Matters.

Tripp, V. (1997). *Así es Josefina* [This Is Josefina]. Middleton, WI: Pleasant Company Publications.

Vygotsky, L. S. (1978). *Mind in society: The development of higher psychological process.* (M. Cole, V. John-Steiner, S. Scribner, & E. Souberman, Trans. & Eds.). Cambridge, MA: Harvard University Press.

Wagner, R. K., & Toregeson, J. K. (1987). The nature of phonological processing and its causal role in the acquisition of reading skills. *Psychological Bulletin, 101,* 192–212.

Wong-Fillmore, L., & Valadez, C. (1986). Teaching bilingual learners. In M. C. Wittrock (Ed.), *Handbook of research on teaching* (3rd ed.; pp. 648–685). New York: Macmillan.

Zentella, A. C. (1997). *Growing up bilingual.* Malden, MA: Blackwell.

CHAPTER 7

Literacy as Hybridity

Moving Beyond Bilingualism in Urban Classrooms

KRIS D. GUTIÉRREZ, PATRICIA BAQUEDANO-LÓPEZ, AND HÉCTOR H. ALVAREZ

Much has been written about the positive social and cognitive consequences that result from group learning (see reviews by Good, Mulryan, & MacCaslin, 1992; Slavin, 1990). Specifically, prior research on student groups has shown that cooperative learning increases learning for individual children, improves student attitudes toward school, and decreases racial tension (Chiu, 1996). This is of particular significance to educators and researchers concerned with improving the educational circumstances of urban schools with high racial tension, and student populations with low achievement.

In this chapter, we present a view of collaborative learning that is grounded in a cultural-historical or sociocultural view of learning and development. Vygotsky (1978) contributed much to our understanding of these terms. As Scribner (1990) notes:

> Vygotsky's special genius was in grasping the significance of the social in things as well as people. The world in which we live in is humanized, full of material and symbolic objects (signs, knowledge systems) that are culturally constructed, historical in origin and social in contents. (p. 92)

Traditional understandings of groupwork or co-participation in learning activities have focused on the individual, on what individuals do in a group, and on coordinating individuals' actions to accomplish a task. Learning from this perspective is organized at the individual or group level, without explicit focus on how the larger context influences and organizes learning in the cooperative learning activity. We make a distinction between these traditional commonplace notions of cooperative and collaborative learning and, instead, utilize the concept of *joint activity* to describe particular processes of co-participation and co-learning.

In contrast, a cultural-historical view of learning reconceptualizes the nature and purpose of cooperation and collaboration. The process of coordinating actions, or joint activity, with others is a socially mediated process that can be understood not only in terms of the "more capable other assisting the less capable one" but in terms of how human beings "use social processes and cultural resources of all kinds" to construct potential zones of proximal development (Scribner, 1990, p. 92; see also Griffin & Cole, 1984). The zone of proximal development is defined as "the distance between the actual developmental level as determined by independent problem solving and the level of potential development as determined through problem solving under adult guidance or in collaboration with more capable peers" (Vygotsky, 1978, p. 86). Collaboration here is understood as a process in which participants acquire knowledge through co-participating, co-cognizing, and co-problem solving with linguistically, culturally, and academically heterogeneous groups throughout the course of task completion. The goal is learning, and joint activity facilitates or mediates learning for the participants. Too often the distribution of roles and subtasks in more traditional forms of cooperative learning becomes the focus and thus precludes the ongoing joint activity needed for the moment-to-moment sharing of linguistic and cognitive resources.

From a cultural-historical perspective, individual development must be understood in the context of the larger social milieu (Cole, 1996; Engeström, 1987; Moll, 1998; Rogoff, 1990; Vygotsky, 1978). Becoming competent, then, is more than an individual process; it is a socialization process that is mediated by a number of circumstances, including: (1) social interactional processes; (2) cultural resources, and (3) the social context of development (Gutiérrez & Stone, 1997). In this way, learning to collaborate with others takes place at multiple levels of activity: at the community level (the social practices of the larger context of development), the interpersonal level (the ways in which people relate, talk, and interact with one another in the moment-to-moment activity), and the individual level (the ways in which the individual person responds to the task) (Gutiérrez, Baquedano-López, & Alvarez, 1998; Gutiérrez & Stone, 1997; Rogoff, 1990). As Rogoff (1990) argues, these three levels of activity do not exist independent of one another.

Accordingly, we argue that for collaboration to serve as a resource for learning in moment-to-moment interaction among students in dyads or other group configurations, collaboration must be a central characteristic of the larger activity system, the classroom or learning context. In other words, for productive collaboration to occur at the local level (dyads and groups), it must be an ongoing feature of the normative practices of formal and nonformal learning contexts. It is through participation in routine activities that utilize collaboration as a commonplace strategy that students begin to see co-learning as the normative way of participating and learning in everyday activities. In this way, the micro and macro processes of the learning environment influence one another in important ways. The important point here is that individual learning cannot be separated from the ways in which the larger learning context is organized. In other words, there is a relationship between what is learned and the social contexts of development. The goal, then, is to create rich zones of development in which all participants learn by jointly participating in activities in which participants share material, sociocultural, linguistic, and cognitive resources.

Although we focus on one group observed over time, our data illustrate our case across many different learning group configurations. More specifically, we present the notion of "hybridity" to illustrate how diversity functions as a resource for building collaboration and promoting learning. Also, we emphasize the importance of language as a central mediating tool in fostering productive joint activity, its goals, and its learning outcomes.

Creating Cultures of Collaboration

Productive collaboration among participants in learning contexts does not just occur. These cultures of collaboration sometimes are known as communities of learners or communities of practice (Gutiérrez, 1993; Gutiérrez & Meyer, 1995; Gutiérrez & Stone, 1997). Robust learning contexts are characterized as cultures of collaboration that afford multiple opportunities for both teachers and students to take on a variety of roles in learning activity, to receive a variety of forms of assistance, and to utilize a full repertoire of material and ideational tools, including skills and strategies. The structure, organization, and goals of learning are organized in particular ways in these cultures of collaboration. Specifically, there are ongoing opportunities to participate with others and receive a range of forms of assistance to push students beyond their current levels of competence. Both teachers and students are learners in this learning environment. In this way, there are ongoing shifts in responsibility for teaching and learning for both students and teachers.

Language and Literacy as Mediating Tools

We view language and literacy as a set of practices that we use to make sense of our various experiences and to communicate a variety of different meanings as we participate in different contexts; language is a tool for social interaction and a tool that transforms our thinking (Cole, 1996; Gee, 1990; Ochs, 1992). Language and literacy are inseparable parts of the sociocultural context of development. In this way, literacy development should be not only a learning goal, but also a central means of appropriating knowledge. From this sociocultural perspective, individuals can use their literacy skills, including language, to clarify their own emergent understandings of the task and its goals, to share knowledge, to assist one another, and to shift roles in the learning process. To illustrate these principles, we include the following example of how productive joint activity is fostered at multiple levels of activity in a collaborative community.

The Case

For the past 2 years, computer-mediated game activity has become the basis for collaboration among Los Angeles elementary-aged children; UCLA undergraduates, graduates, and professors; and urban school educators who come together to create and nurture productive learning experiences for children and adults alike. In a lively after-school computer club, children participate in educational activities organized around several dimensions of play. This after-school club, Las Redes [Networks], is simultaneously a playful world and a collaborative culture that brings play and learning together. Las Redes, located at a port-of-entry urban elementary school near Los Angeles International Airport, is a flexible adaptation of the general principles around which Michael Cole conceptualized the Fifth Dimension projects (Cole, 1996; Griffin & Cole, 1984). This system-wide collaborative constitutes the University of California's response to recent legislative and regential initiatives that virtually truncate the educational pipeline for diverse and qualified students from elementary school through postdoctoral levels in communities throughout the state. The model links after-school K–12 activities with intensive undergraduate coursework combining classroom theoretical study with practice in community settings, in this case, Las Redes.

Guided by our long-term ethnographic work in urban schools (Gutiérrez, 1992, 1993, 1995), and motivated by the current political context in California where initiatives against immigrants, affirmative action, and bilingual education have been widely passed (see Chapter 4), Las Redes is a conscious effort to promote cognitive and social development and foster collaboration among a cross-generational and diverse group of participants. The children at Las Redes reflect the population of the elementary school, comprising mainly Latinos, African American, and Tongan students. The UCLA undergraduate and graduate students, known as *amigas* and *amigos*, represent a balance of Euro-American, Asian American, Latino, and African American students from a variety of academic disciplines. In the playful environment of computer-mediated learning at Las Redes, participants draw from their own as well as each other's linguistic and sociocultural resources to collaborate in problem-solving activities, creating robust zones of development. These diverse and hybrid repertoires and practices, as we will illustrate, become the tools for mediating literacy learning.

While hybridity in learning contexts is ubiquitous, few scholars and practitioners consciously discuss or use it as a resource for enhancing joint activity and productive learning. Las Redes is an ecological system that fosters and utilizes hybridity as integral to the social organization of learning. Of importance is that learning in this context requires participants to negotiate their roles and understandings as they co-participate in various problem-solving activities. Thus, participation in these activities requires both the development of shared rules as well as the voluntary acceptance of those rules. However, the culture of the Fifth Dimension is not just the sum of interactions. It is an activity system that uses hybridity strategically in the way its artifacts, division of labor, and semistructured tasks are conceptualized and then used locally (Engeström, 1987, 1993). In this chapter, we will illustrate the ways in which hybridity is central to creating and maintaining this culture of collaboration and how it serves as a resource for learning for all participants in the after-school learning context.

The Theory

Our emergent understanding of hybridity is informed by a transdisciplinary body of work in cultural-historical theory (Cole, 1996; Engeström, 1987; Gutiérrez, Baquedano-López, & Alvarez, 1998; Rogoff, 1990; Vygotsky, 1978) and cultural and postcolonial studies (Anzaldúa, 1987; Arteaga, 1994; Becquer & Gatti, 1991; Bhabha, 1994; Gómez-Peña, 1996; Lipsitz, 1994, 1998). Our understanding of hybridity also builds on earlier work across several fields, most notably Chicana/Chicano and ethnic studies. Parallel constructs such as *mestizaje*, borderlands, or marginality also have been used to describe hybrid forms of being (Gutiérrez, Baquedano-López, & Tejada, 1999; hooks, 1990, 1994). For example, Anzaldúa (1987) first proposed the notion of borderlands for those inhabiting the margins of discourse communities. The construct of borderlands counters the idea of the "pure" origin of elements as fixed, essential identities prior to their hybridization (Becquer & Gatti, 1991, p. 66). Subsequently, the construct of hybridization has been expanded in other cultural studies work, particularly in discussions of postcoloniality (Bhabha, 1994; Gomez-Peña, 1996). Hybridization, from this perspective, focuses on the dialogic nature of alternative and dominant discourses (Arteaga, 1994). Of significance to our work is the adaptive, strategic, and paradoxical nature of hybridity (Valle & Torres, 1995).

Following Shohat and Stam (1994), we too see hybridity as the ubiquitous and unmarked form that exists within, across, and between social and discursive spaces. Hybridity from this perspective is "an unending, unfinalizable process . . . [that] is dynamic, mobile, less an achieved synthesis, or prescribed formula than an unstable constellation of discourses" (Shohat & Stam, 1994, p. 42). An expanded view of hybridity also recognizes the power-laden and asymmetrical potential of hybridity, as well as its transformative potential.

McLaren (1997), drawing on the work of Pieterse (1995), however, cautions us about the productivity of working with the notion of hybrid cultures/identities (and contexts) when all cultures result from mixtures and contact. One way to avoid such flat views of culture and identity, then, is to use hybridity to counter forms of essentialism and static views of culture, language, and human development. In our ongoing work, we hope to extend these notions by re-examining hybridity in situated practice and, thus, reversing its valence by illustrating how it is a resource for literacy development and transformation.

We first conceptualized hybridity as a resource for learning in our work on the third space (Gutiérrez, Baquedano-López, & Turner, 1997; Gutiérrez, Rymes, & Larson, 1995). The third space is a discursive space in which alternative and competing discourses and positionings transform conflict and difference into rich zones of collaboration and learning. In this way, the third space provides the mediational context and tools necessary for future development. We will argue that transformation, in this case in literacy learning, is stimulated by the hybrid nature of Las Redes, most notably the culturally mediated co-construction of activity. In turn, we will explore how hybrid language and literacy practices that are part of the everyday routines of this setting foster sustained participation and productive learning.

Following Bakhtin (1981), we will argue that "what is vital [here] is that the languages [used] be viewed from each other's perspectives, that they be 'hybridized' so that an 'interminable' dialogue is created among them. Such hybridization demands enormous effort, it is stylized through and through, thoroughly premeditated. This is what distinguishes it from the frivolous, mindless and unsystematic mixing of language" (Morson & Emerson,

1990, p. 314). For us, then, hybrid language use is more than simply code-switching as the alternation between two codes. It is more a systematic, strategic, affiliative, and sense-making process among those who share the code, as they strive to achieve intersubjectivity.

The Practice

Hybridity is also more than the sum of its parts. The larger context of Las Redes is itself conceptualized as a hybrid activity system. Organized as both a playful and learning context, the computer club reflects the spontaneous character of a play environment, as well as the institutional nature of the elementary school of which it is a part. In this way, the linguistic and sociocultural repertoires, various forms of knowledge, and practices of the school's diverse communities and participants necessarily become part of the after-school learning community.

However, for hybridity to serve as a resource for learning in moment-to-moment interaction among participants in the ensembles that *amigas/os* and children constitute, hybridity must be present in the way the activity system and, thus, learning are organized. The notion of ensembles, rather than cooperative and collaborative groups, is used not only to capture the participants (the children, the undergraduates, and other adults), but also to include the way learning and space are organized in interaction, as well as the tools or resources used in the learning activity. The ensembles, then, organize the social context of development of the computer-mediated learning activity (Granott, 1996; Stone & Gutiérrez, 1998). Ensembles in this context can assume a variety of configurations, depending on the nature and goal of the problem-solving activity, and on the availability of human and material resources (computers, board games, etc.). For example, on any particular day, we observe ensembles that include children co-participating in computer or board games, or children and *amigas/os* co-learning. Dyads comprising a child and an *amiga/o* are also common. The variable and flexible nature of ensembles contributes to the hybrid character of this learning context.

As Cole (1996) argues, however, "it is insufficient to describe the artifacts of the culture without saying something about the social relations they mediate" (p. 297). In these goal-oriented interactions, the dynamic relations of knowledge exchange among participants in the ensembles allow for the ongoing constitution and transformation of the roles of expert and novice. Learning, then, is evidenced in these shifts in participation in learning activity. For example, in one particular interaction at Las Redes, a child's knowledge of games and an undergraduate's knowledge of learning strategies can facilitate the sharing of expertise and skills as they co-cognize and co-problem solve in the various learning tasks. In this problem-solving activity, the opportunity to negotiate the presented problem locally allows both the children and adults to utilize their funds of knowledge and ways of knowing (Baquedano-López, Alvarez, & Gutiérrez, 1998; Stone & Gutiérrez, 1998). Further, the changing dynamics of the interaction help create and sustain this special relationship between the children, the undergraduates, and other participants. Such shifts, however, would not easily be accomplished, if it were not for the playful environment in which these learning activities are embedded.

Play provides the environment for natural learning to occur, because the division of labor is based on participants' authentic competence, rather than on traditional school criteria such as age, education, or ability (Cole, Olt, & Woodbridge, 1994). Thus, participants draw freely on their linguistic and sociocultural repertoires to solve a variety of problems together. Further, play allows the participants to go beyond their everyday worlds and assume new perspectives. In the context of play, artifacts such as task cards guide participants through different levels of difficulty and mastery as they complete each level of the game. As detailed in other accounts of the Fifth Dimension, "a task card [or adventure guide] is an artifact designed to promote reflection and create opportunities for getting children to generalize principles they have encountered in the games in a different medium" (Cole, Olt, & Woodbridge, 1994, p. 4). The productive tension between play and learning creates zones of development otherwise not evident in traditional classrooms.

To sustain both the playful and learning character and goals of this setting, an ambiguous entity called "El Maga" resides in cyberspace and is accessible through electronic mail. Even Maga's name, a combination of the masculine article with a feminine noun in Spanish, symbolizes its hybrid identity. Of significance is how El Maga helps sustain the culture of collaboration and promotes meaningful participation, socialization to the culture of the setting, and affiliation among participants through ongoing and highly personalized dialogue. Thus, the larger culture of collaboration is reconstituted continually by an ever-present ensemble compring of the children, the undergraduates, and El Maga.

El Maga, utilizing personal knowledge of the children's everyday practices in the after-school club and the children's linguistic and cultural repertoires, co-participates with the children to create zones of proximal development in a routine literacy activity (Vygotsky, 1978). This literacy activity encourages the children, often in collaboration with their *amigas/os*, to describe their various experiences at Las Redes each day. In particular, children are asked to recount to El Maga the ways in which they accomplish the various computer learning tasks and solve problems and to describe any difficulties they encounter playing the games. In addition to its role of sustaining the culture of this Fifth Dimension, Maga's mischievous and ambiguous qualities serve to motivate the children to solve what they believe is the central question of the Fifth Dimension: the identity and personal characteristics of El Maga.

The children and El Maga continually engage in problem-solving exchanges in which they pose questions to one another, hoping to achieve their own individual and shared goals. For example, El Maga often asks questions to help the children elaborate on statements made in previous e-mail texts. The children, in turn, often hypothesize about who El Maga is, ask questions to help them resolve issues or conflicts that emerge in the club, or narrate events in their lives as members of larger communities. Often these exchanges occur with the assistance of an *amiga/o*. However, the extent and nature of assistance provided are dynamic and adaptable because of the ongoing dynamic assessment that occurs in the moment-to-moment interaction between the children, the undergraduates, and El Maga (Stone & Gutiérrez, 1998).

This multipurpose writing activity utilizes mixed genres, that is, letters and narratives, and mixed discourses, including problem-solving, narrative, and academic discourse. Further, because no one single language or register is privileged in this activity and setting, the larger linguistic repertoires of participants become tools for meaning making. Such language practices certainly challenge current English-only policies that privilege one particular language and minimize learning. In a Bakhtinian sense, hybridity increases the possibility of dialogue—and thus the possibility of collaborating and learning in the third space (Gutiérrez, Baquedano-López, & Turner, 1997; Gutiérrez, Rymes, & Larson, 1995).

Moreover, this routine literacy event helps the children reflect on the day's activities by narrating and, thus, externalizing their thoughts in writing. The problem-solving nature of the narratives in the form of letters, in turn, helps children clarify their own understandings and formulate explanations for their own learning. Such interaction often leads to higher levels of learning. In other words, this literacy activity creates a Zoped for language and literacy learning, because participants in the ensemble at certain moments have to provide some assistance in order to jointly accomplish the various tasks. In doing so, El Maga and the child (and other members of the ensemble) provide a very natural environment for language acquisition and development.

As Griffin and Cole (1984) point out, "Adult wisdom does not provide a teleology for child development. Social organization and leading activities provide a gap within which the child can develop novel creative analyses" (p. 62). Citing Emerson (1983), they propose the Zoped as a metaphor for describing this key or leading activity of the Fifth Dimension: "A Zoped is a dialogue between the child and his future; it is not a dialogue between the child and an adult's past" (p. 62). The focus of the interaction and assistance in the Zoped is on learning for all participants. In other words, the goal is to stimulate learning and development through the strategic use of all the resources and forms of assistance available.

Productive Joint Activity

In this section, we will illustrate through four e-mail exchanges how El Maga and the ensembles interactionally constitute a dynamic space for learning. Note that the bidirectionality of the linguistic and sociocultural exchanges does not privilege the adult as sole teacher and knowledge bearer. Utilizing mixed genres, discourses, and codes, El Maga and a young third-grade bilingual Latina, Martha, share experiences and knowledge over a series of exchanges, the contents of which have not been edited.

E-mail Exchange #1:
E-mail from Martha to El Maga: 1/28/97
Dear El maga,
This afternoon, I played Reader Rabbit 2. I could play all the game because I am a smart girl. The game was too easy for me. My favorite game was the Alphabet Dance. It was fun how the animals danced.
Are you married? How many kids do you have?
Sincerli, Martha

As shown above, Martha begins her narrative by embedding it in a letter marked by the conventional greetings and closings of that genre ("Dear El maga," and "Sincerli"). She continues her text by narrating her game-playing activities for the day, in this case that she played a game called Reader Rabbit 2. Consistent with the narrative genre, she provides an evaluation of her own participation in the events she describes. She reasons that she could play the first game because, in her own words, "I am a smart girl" and also because "the game was too easy." Moreover, she writes that her favorite game was Alphabet Dance and that she especially enjoyed seeing the animals dance. As so many other children do in their letter-writing activity, Martha ends her e-mail with personal questions to El Maga ("Are you married?" "How many kids do you have?").

The above text illustrates how Martha commingles genres to complete the literacy task. However, it is El Maga's subsequent responses that ulti-

mately motivate Martha to draw on her larger linguistic repertoire, not only
to accomplish the required literacy task but also to engage in sustained
and increasingly complex written communication with the mythical
Wizard.

> E-mail from El Maga responding to Martha: 1/28/97
> Dear Martha,
> Thank you for writing to me. I know that you are a very smart
> girl. Your teachers at Moffett, and my assistants at Las Redes have
> told me that you are very, very, very smart. I was also told that you
> have a nice smile. Keep smiling amiguita.
> Congratulations on doing so good on Reader Rabbit. So, the
> game was too easy for you, huh? Did you try all three levels—begin-
> ner, good, and expert??? When you play any game at Las Redes, if
> one level is too easy, you should try the other levels.
> Also, when you write me remember to tell me some of the things
> that you did to finish the game. I want you to teach me how to play
> the games, o.k? I am interested how the animals danced. Can you
> describe the animals and how they danced for me?
> To answer your questions—I am married and I do have chil-
> dren. I consider all of the kids at school my children. I love chil-
> dren!!! So I have thousands of children.
> Write back soon, amiguita. Keep that sonrisa bright.
> Hasta Pronto,
> El Maga

El's response also employs the conventional openings and closings of
the epistolary genre; however, here Maga uses an English greeting ("Dear
Martha") but ends with a conventional Spanish closing (*"Hasta Pronto"*
[Until next time]). Maga's response personalizes Martha's letter and reinforces her self-evaluation of her performance. El does this by providing
commentary from her teachers and other members of Las Redes to validate her ability and contribution to the club. Since affiliation is a leading
activity in a child's development, Maga's use of Spanish terms of endear-
ment such as *"amiguita"* [little friend], as well as the personal reference
to her smile, helps create a more intimate relationship between them,
especially because Spanish is one of Martha's languages. Moreover, the
use of personal knowledge of Martha lends credence to El Maga's existence and presence in the after-school club. These strategies increase the
potential for elaborated dialogue between them.

Further, Maga not only reinforces Martha's accomplishments but also
assists her future performance by suggesting that she challenge herself to

play more difficult levels of the game ("Did you try all three levels—beginner, good, and expert???"). At the same time, El begins to socialize Martha about the nature of expected participation in future games ("When you play any game at Las Redes, if one level is too easy, you should try the other levels"). Here Maga introduces Martha to problem-solving discourse, that is, how to talk about and define problems and how to describe problem-solving strategies, including their effectiveness and consequences.

El also asks Martha to expand on her narrative by suggesting that she share more explicit discussion of the strategies she used and of what the game entailed ("tell me some of the things that you did to finish the game"). In this interaction, El Maga is strategically positioned as a learner and Martha is asked to share her expertise so that Maga may learn how to play the game ("I want you to teach me how to play the games. . . . Can you describe the animals and how they danced for me?"). This shift in roles helps constitute Martha as an expert and opens the possibility to change the nature of her participation in future exchanges.

Finally, in response to Martha's personal queries about El Maga's life, Maga informs her that all the children of Las Redes are Maga's children (including her). In closing, Maga refers once again to Martha as a little friend ("*amiguita*") and to her bright smile ("*sonrisa*"). The repetition of such friendly terms in Spanish legitimizes and encourages the use of Spanish and personal knowledge in the literacy event.

In the following week, Martha and Maga communicate again. Consistent with Martha's previous narrative, she describes her game-playing activities and accomplishments, as well as the assistance she receives from one of the UCLA *amigas* when she encounters difficulties playing the game. Maga corroborates her frustration in playing the game and attributes part of the difficulty to the prankishness of the frog, the central character of the game.

E-mail Exchange #2:

    E-mail from Martha to El Maga: 2/4/97

    dear El Maga, are are you? the pond was little bit harder. I couldn't understand the game and Christina helped me figure it out. In the end, I passed the first level and I was surprised. thanks for writing to me.

    E-mail from El Maga responding to Martha: 2/4/97

    Dear Martha,

    I am doing pretty good, thank you for asking!!! How are you?? I hope you still have that big smile!!! The pond was difficult to figure out, huh? That frog causes many of us problems. It has a mind of its

own and sometimes it does not want to do what we program it to do.
Que ranita . . .
    I am glad that Christina helped you figure out the game. What
kinds of things did you both do?? Did the frog do every thing you
told it to do???
    Write back,
    El Maga

Note how El Maga's use of English and Spanish in the responses to
Martha exemplifies how biliteracy is promoted in this setting. Of significance
in the above rather routine e-mail exchange is Maga's strategic use of a single
Spanish phrase ("*Que ranita*" [That mischievous, little frog]) in an otherwise English text. While this is not a new strategy utilized by Maga, it is the
use of the phrase *que ranita* that requires not only shared linguistic knowledge but also sociocultural knowledge, in this case humor, that ultimately
signals to Martha the appropriateness and usefulness of using Spanish in
this problem-solving arena.
    In a letter written 6 days later, there is a dramatic change in Martha's
text, evidenced in the language she chooses to narrate her activities, in the
register she employs, and in the way she now begins to relate to El Maga.

E-mail Exchange #3:
    E-mail from Martha to El Maga: 2/10/97
    Querido/a
    Yo no sabia que era bilingue. Usted es mujer o hombre? haora
juque boggle, y un rompe cabesas de batman. y Bertha nos ayudo
armarlo.
    adios, Martha.

    [Dear, I did not know that you were bilingual. Are you a man or
a woman? Today I played boggle, and a Batman puzzle. And Bertha
helped us put it together.
    goodbye, Martha.]

Martha's use of Spanish in this text allows her to employ a formal register to demonstrate her biliterate skills and also to demonstrate her proficiency in Spanish. Central to this and subsequent responses is Martha's
recognition that Maga is bilingual; this recognition and her biliteracy are
instantiated in her production of a fluent Spanish text. Although she
maintains the genre in Spanish, Martha's salutation and closing are more
affiliative and personalized ("*Querido/a*" and "*adios*") and are indices of a
more intimate and familiar tone. Simultaneously, her use of a more formal

register ("*que era bilingue*" and "*usted*") in Spanish indicates both respect and an attempt to build a relationship with Maga. This hybrid text provides Martha an opportunity to draw from her larger linguistic and cultural repertoires.

Martha's text also motivates the production of a Spanish text from Maga, presented below. In doing so, Martha defines the conditions for language use and participation in this and subsequent texts, and stimulates a change in participant roles.

> E-mail from El Maga responding to Martha: 2/10/97
> Martha,
> Claro que si amigita. Soy bilingue. Tu que crees que soy, hombre o mujer?? Como se juega Boggle, y como era el rompecabesas de batman?? Me gustaria que me escribas como juegas los juegos en Las Redes para que me enseñes a mi como juegar.
> Espero tu proxima carta,
> El Maga
>
> [Martha, Of course little friend. I am bilingual. What do you think I am, a man or a woman?? How do you play Boggle, and what was the batman puzzle like?? I would like you to write how to play the games at Las Redes so that you can teach me how to play.
> I look forward to your next letter,
> El Maga]

Here Maga explicitly identifies as a bilingual and produces a sustained response in Spanish; consequently, Maga indexes co-membership in a Spanish-speaking community. Consistent with previous e-mail responses, El responds to all of Martha's queries and requests an elaboration of her game-playing strategies. Martha again is provided an occasion to share her expertise.

Over a span of a few weeks of communication, Martha and Maga continue their collaboration in cyberspace. Martha once again exhibits her bilingual, bicultural, and biliterate knowledge and skills, although in this text she chooses English as the predominant medium of communication. Martha displays not only her fluency in both languages but also her ability to be humorous and play with language across cultures and codes.

> *E-mail Exchange #4:*
> E-mail from Martha to El Maga: 3/12/97
> Dear La Maga
> Don't you like tortillas? Today I played La Corrida de Toros. The game was too easy for me, but in the hard level I was too con-

fused because I didn't read the word list because I was too floja
[lazy]. My brother gave me some candy. The candy was so delicious.
Quiere probar some candy? [Would you want to try some candy?]
You could . . . . . buy it in the store! ha, ha, ha! I make you laugh.
I'm funny today because today my boyfriend gave me a kiss. But
in a picture! ha, ha, ha . . . La Maga, I decided that you are a girl
to me because I am a girl and Oscar de la Hoya told me El Maga
is mi admirador preferido [my biggest fan] . . . . . . see you later
alligator! ha, ha, ha. I'm soooo happy . . . . . because I'm scooby-
dooooooooooooooooooooooo! Where are you?!!! I'm right here!!
ha, ha, ha,
     Martha

Martha's linguistic repertoire is sophisticated. Each switch from Spanish to English and vice versa is a conscious and strategic choice to accomplish
several goals: (1) to complete the required literacy task of reporting on the
day's activities, (2) to use this literacy text as a vehicle for self-expression,
and (3) to build a sustained relationship with El Maga.

Martha's text is complex both linguistically and pragmatically. Key linguistic constructions range from words to complete units of thought. Her
use of the word *floja* in her explanation of why she had difficulty with the
more advanced game level (instead of the English word *lazy*) serves as an
emphatic assessment of her uncharacteristic performance playing the game.
Martha is not limited to switches at the lexical level. She also engages larger
units of text in Spanish, for example, the clause "*mi admirador preferido*" [my
biggest fan]. Some of these larger units are grammatically complex, such
as, "*Quiere probar* some candy?" [would you want to try some candy?], which
uses a formal register in a complex syntactic structure.

Her text also presupposes shared knowledge of cultural norms and practices, the "funds of knowledge" Moll (1998) discusses in his work. For example, Martha alludes to a well-known Chicano boxer, Oscar de la Hoya,
who she claims offers testimony to Maga's admiration of her. Similarly, she
draws on the larger popular culture by playing with familiar cartoon lyrics,
"scooby-doo, where are you?", in the creation of a humorous text in both
Spanish and English.

These new texts also begin to reveal characteristics of Martha that are
consistent with her face-to-face interactions in Las Redes. As documented
in field notes and video tapes taken by the adults, Martha is an outgoing,
playful, and witty child who regularly shares jokes with those she trusts.
Through the dynamic exchange of knowledge and role shift promoted in
the culture of collaboration of Las Redes, Martha is socialized, over the
course of 3 months, to use her complete repertoire to participate more fully

in this playful, yet challenging environment. The socialization here, though, is bidirectional.

From a language socialization perspective, children are socialized both to use language and through language (Ochs, 1988). Thus, this literacy event serves a socializing practice in which children can appropriate sociocultural knowledge about the culture of Las Redes, its forms of participation and rules, and its academic, social, and personal goals. Participants also receive explicit and implicit instruction about literacy, including the nuances of language use, spelling, vocabulary, sentence structure, and language play. In the context of their e-mail exchanges, they also learn how to write a letter, how to request assistance, and even how to generate a complaint about a practice of the after-school club. Simultaneously, El Maga and the other adult participants of Las Redes are socialized to children's linguistic, sociocultural, and academic experiences.

> E-mail from El Maga responding to Martha: 3/12/97
> Hi Martha,
> Are you kidding—I love tortillas. I make my own. My mom taught me how to make them. Do you know how to make tortillas? If you do we must exchange "recetas" [recipes].
> You do make me laugh with your e-mail. Keep up the good work and please write me more like you wrote me today. Ha Ha Ha!
> Hay nos vamos, vimos, viendo,
> [We'll be seen/seeing each other]
> El Maga

In the above example, Maga mirrors Martha's linguistic strategies and writes a playful, informal, and predominantly English text. Maga again signals co-membership in a shared community by suggesting that the making of tortillas is an activity of Maga's home and a skill appropriated from El's mother. Maga also validates Martha's humor and encourages her to continue writing her playful e-mails. Finally, Maga utilizes cultural humor by closing with a well-known phrase from the Mexican comedian Cantinflas ("Hay nos vamos, vimos, viendo"). Simultaneously, Maga builds on shared cultural knowledge and challenges Martha to extend her linguistic abilities and knowledge of Spanish by introducing her to sophisticated sentence structure and meaning.

Both of these last examples represent the kind of hybridity that serves to stimulate learning and development. These findings support the empirical work of others, including Moll and Díaz (1987) who documented the dramatic gains in learning of bilingual students who engaged in literacy learning practices that made use of their larger linguistic repertoires, including their home language. In both cases, the object was learning.

Conclusion

In this chapter, our analysis of collaborative literacy learning in the Fifth Dimension has focused on how hybridity in the larger activity system and in the moment-to-moment interactions of Las Redes stimulated joint participation and learning for all learners. The dynamic nature of participation, assistance and assessment strategies, language use, and cultural exchanges motivated sustained collaboration across time and tasks, and thus increased the potential for learning. By examining hybridity in situated practice, we have been able to see hybridity as a resource for literacy learning. Moreover, the dialogic nature of hybridity allowed the use of alternative discourses, their conflict and tensions, and the contradictions usually inherent therein. Hybrid zones of development are characteristic of what we have called the third space, where alternative, competing, and even shared discourses and positioning and/or roles mediate literacy for experts and novices (Gutiérrez, Baquedano-López, & Turner 1997; Gutiérrez, Rymes, & Larson, 1995). In this way, the third space provides the mediational context and tools necessary for future social and cognitive development. Such rich contexts for learning are particularly critical in a time when English-only, anti-immigrant, and anti-affirmative action sentiments influence, if not dominate, educational policy and practice. This playful and stimulating learning environment provides a model for understanding how meaningful collaboration can be created and sustained and how difference and diversity can serve as resources for learning.

References

Anzaldúa, G. (1987). *Borderlands/La frontera: The new mestiza.* San Francisco: Aunt Lute Books.

Arteaga, A. (1994). *An other tongue: Nation and ethnicity in the linguistic borderlands.* Durham, NC: Duke University Press.

Bakhtin, M. (1981). *The dialogic imagination* (M. Holquist, Ed.; M. Holquist & C. Emerson, Trans.). Austin: University of Texas Press.

Baquedano-López, P., Alvarez, H., & Gutiérrez, K. (1998, December). *Negotiating fairness at an after-school club.* Paper presented at the ninety-eighth annual meeting of the American Anthropological Association, Philadelphia.

Becquer, M., & Gatti, J. (1991). Elements in vogue. *Third Text, 16/17,* 65–81.

Bhabha, H. (1994). *The location of culture.* London: Routledge.

Chiu, M. (1996). *Building mathematical understanding during collaboration.* Unpublished doctoral dissertation, University of California, Berkeley.

Cole, M. (1996). *Cultural psychology: A once and future discipline.* Cambridge, MA: Belknap Press of Harvard University Press.

Cole, M., Olt, A., & Woodbridge, S. (1994, April). *Documenting children's problem solving behaviors using fieldnotes of participant observers.* Paper presented at the annual meeting of the American Educational Research Association, New Orleans.

Emerson, C. (1983). Bakhtin and Vygotsky on internalization of language. *Quarterly Newsletter of the Laboratory of Comparative Human Cognition, 3*(1), 9–13.

Engeström, Y. (1987). *Learning by expanding: An activity-theoretical approach to developmental research.* Helsinki, Finland: Orieta-Konsultit Oy.

Engeström, Y. (1993). Developmental studies on work as a test bench of activity theory: The case of primary care medical practice. In S. Chaiklin & J. Lave (Eds.), *Understanding practice: Perspectives on activity and context* (pp. 64–103). Cambridge: Cambridge University Press.

Gee, J. (1990). *Social linguistics and literacies: Ideology in discourses* (2nd ed.). Bristol, PA: Taylor & Francis.

Gómez-Peña, G. (1996). *The new world border: Prophecies, poems, and locuras for the end of the century.* San Francisco: City Lights Books.

Good, T., Mulryan, C., & MacCaslin, M. (1992). Grouping for instruction in mathematics: A call for programmatic research on small-group processes. In D. Grows (Ed.), *Handbook of research on mathematics teaching and learning* (pp. 165–196). New York: Macmillan.

Granott, N. (1996, April). *How to analyze the co-construction of knowledge? A dynamic approach.* Paper presented at the annual meeting of the American Educational Research Association, New York.

Griffin, P., & Cole, M. (1984). Current activity for the future: The Zo-ped. In B. Rogoff & J. Wertsch (Eds.), *Children's learning in the zone of proximal development: New directions for child development* (pp. 45–63). San Francisco: Jossey-Bass.

Gutiérrez, K. (1992). A comparison of instructional contexts in writing process classrooms with Latino children. *Education and Urban Society, 24,* 224–262.

Gutiérrez, K. (1993). How talk, context, and script shape contexts for learning: A cross-case comparison of journal sharing. *Linguistics and Education, 5,* 335–365.

Gutiérrez, K. (1995). Unpackaging academic discourse. *Discourse Processes, 19,* 21–37.

Gutiérrez, K., Baquedano-López, P., & Alvarez, H. (1998, April). *Building a culture of collaboration through hybrid language practices.* Paper presented at the annual meeting of the American Educational Research Association San Diego.

Gutiérrez, K., Baquedano-Lopez, P., & Tejada, C. (1999). Rethinking diversity: Hybridity and hybrid language practices in the Third Space. *Mind, Culture, and Activity, 6*(4), 286-303.

Gutiérrez, K., Baquedano-López, P., & Turner, M. G. (1997). Putting language back into language arts: When the radical middle meets the third space. *Language Arts, 74*(5), 368–378.

Gutiérrez, K. & Meyer, B. (1995). Creating communities of effective practice: Building literacy for language minority children. In J. Oakes & K. Quartz (Eds.), *94th NSSE Yearbook: Creating new educational communities* (pp. 32-52). Chicago: University of Chicago Press.

Gutiérrez, K., Rymes, B., & Larson, J. (1995). Script, counterscript, and underlife in the classroom: James Brown versus Brown v. Board of Education. *Harvard Educational Review, 65*(3), 445–471.

Gutiérrez, K., & Stone, L. (1997). A cultural historical view of learning and the learning disabilities: Participation in a community of learners. *Learning Disabilities Research & Practice, 12*(2), 123-131.

hooks, b. (1990). *Yearnings: Race, gender, and cultural politics.* Boston: South End Press.

hooks, b. (1994). *Outlaw culture: Resisting representations.* New York: Routledge.

Lipsitz, G. (1994). The bands of tomorrow are here today: The proud, progressive, and postmodern sounds of Las Tres and Goddess 13. In S. Loza (Ed.), *Musical aesthetics and multiculturalism in Los Angeles* (Vol. 10; pp. 139–147). Los Angeles: University of California, Department of Ethnomusicology and Systematic Musicology.

Lipsitz, G. (1998). *The possessive investment in whiteness: How white people profit from identity politics.* Philadelphia: Temple University Press.

McLaren, P. (1997). *Revolutionary multiculturalism: Pedagogies of dissent and the new millennium.* Boulder, CO: Westview Press.

Moll, L. (1998, February). *Funds of knowledge for teaching: A new approach to culture in education.* Keynote address at the Illinois State Board of Education, Twenty-First Annual Statewide Conference for Teachers of Linguistically and Culturally Diverse Students.

Moll, L., & Díaz, E. (1987). Change as the goal of education research. *Anthropology & Education Quarterly, 184,* 300–311.

Morson, G., & Emerson, C. (1990). *Mikhail Bakhtin: Creation of a prosaics.* Stanford: Stanford University Press.

Ochs, E. (1988). *Culture and language development: Language acquisition and language socialization in a Samoan village.* Cambridge: Cambridge University Press.

Ochs, E. (1992). Indexing gender. In A. Duranti & C. Goodwin (Eds.), *Rethinking context: Language as an interactive phenomenon* (pp. 336–358). Cambridge: Cambridge University Press.

Pieterse, J. N. (1995). Globalization as hybridization. In M. Featherstone, S. Lash, & R. Robertson (Eds.), *Global modernities* (pp. 45–68). London: Sage.

Rogoff, B. (1990). *Apprenticeship in thinking: Cognitive development in social context.* New York: Oxford University Press.

Scribner, S. (1990). Reflections on a model. *The Quarterly Newsletter of the Laboratory of Comparative Human Cognition 12*(3), 90–94.

Shohat, E., & Stam, R. (1994). *Unthinking Eurocentrism: Multiculturalism and the media.* New York and London: Routledge.

Slavin, R. (1990). *Cooperative learning: Theory, research & practice.* Boston: Allyn & Bacon.

Stone, L., & Gutiérrez, K. (1998). *Problem finding as distributed intelligence: The role of changing participation in mathematical problem-solving activities in an after-school learning community.* Unpublished manuscript.

Valle, V., & Torres, R. (1995). The idea of mestizaje and the "race" problematic: Racialized media discourse in a post-Fordist landscape. In A. Darder (Ed.),

Culture and difference: Critical perspectives on the bicultural experience in the United States (pp. 139–153). Westport, CT: Bergin & Garvey.

Vygotsky, L. S. (1978). *Mind in society: The development of higher psychological process* (M. Cole, V. John-Steiner, S. Scribner, & E. Souberman, Trans. & Eds.). Cambridge, MA: Harvard University Press.

CHAPTER 8

Hooked on Writing

Linking Literacy to Students' Lived Experiences

ELOISE ANDRADE LALIBERTY

Reflecting on my elementary years in school, I remember sitting in the back of a third-grade classroom, feeling on the verge of tears. Mrs. Taylor had put me in the back of the room to redo a homework paper filled with red marks. It was in English, so my parents had not been able to help me. The material in front of me seemed foreign and difficult to grasp. I was thinking to myself, "Am I the only third grader that doesn't understand how to tell time? What does 'half past the hour' mean or 'quarter after'? This way of telling time doesn't make sense in Spanish . . . I must be really dumb."

This feeling of inadequacy would stay with me for many years, even after high school graduation. The irony is that in spite of this, and for as long as I can remember, I wanted to be a teacher! I wanted to help students like myself who struggled with language and low self-esteem. Looking back over my years in school, I realized that not *one* teacher in elementary, junior high, or high school ever recognized my potential to be a teacher. Instead, the school placed me in a traditional noncollege track, destined for secretaries, bookkeepers, and sales clerks.

For this reason, I vowed to make a difference for children struggling academically. As a result, I have always taken my teaching seriously, believing that I could positively influence students, especially Mexicano/Latino children with whom I share similar experiences. Although I realize I cannot change each student in my class, I know I can have a positive influence on who they are and what they believe about themselves by the expectations I set for them. I feel fortunate to be able to say that, for the most part, the students I have taught have been successful. This is especially true in literacy because I *expect* my students to accomplish whatever they set their minds to learn. In this chapter, I describe what I think led to my students' love of writing and how I organized my literacy instruction for intermediate-grade students. Finally, I conclude with some reflections about teaching children from our own community.

How My Students Got Hooked On Writing

Two events were significant in getting my students hooked on writing. One, which I will describe first, was implementing Olivier Dunrea's (1990) writing method, and the other was sharing a personal narrative about my father.

In the summer of 1991 I attended a Whole Language Institute that changed the way I taught writing. I learned about writing that focused on process rather than product, about the reading and writing connection, and about literature-based instruction. This was exciting and interesting to me; I was anxious to try these new ideas. In fact, I found the Institute so interesting and challenging that I didn't even notice that no one discussed how we could adapt the group writing approach to students learning English (SLE). As a result, I tried the ideas only with my English-speaking students. Another reason was that my Spanish-dominant speaking students were in a pullout program with a bilingual resource teacher where they received language arts instruction in Spanish.

Dunrea's Method

At the Institute I was introduced to Dunrea's book *The Writing Process* (1990), which showed a step-by-step approach to getting the whole class involved in writing stories. Essentially, this method calls for the teacher (i.e., the editor) to help students (the writers) select the *who* (characters), *where* (setting), and *what* (plot) of a group story. The teacher then gets students to brainstorm some ideas for the *who*. Only three ideas or suggestions are selected. The writers vote on each choice. The suggestions that get the most votes become the characters in this group story. This same procedure continues with the setting and the plot. This is how I began the group stories that set my students on fire about writing.

However, this method created a logistical problem of finding a way to involve *all* my students. To solve this, I had the students keep a writing folder.

The lefthand side of each page was labeled *My Ideas* (in Spanish, *Mis Ideas*), and the righthand side, *Group Story* (*Cuento del Grupo*). I gave students time to write down their thoughts. If students were absent, it was easy for them to catch up with the story because it was written on easel paper or on a transparency in Spanish and English. This kind of group story allowed even my reluctant writers to participate because there was no risk in making spelling errors (the teacher does all the writing).

This method also created a great deal of frustration among the students. Frustration arose because not all the students' choices were selected by the group. Dunrea describes this frustration as an important part of the process because it serves to prepare students for other writing projects. The frustration built momentum for students to want to write their own stories.

For a bilingual class, the beauty of this kind of writing is that the story develops at a slower pace, allowing students time to process the information from Spanish to English. Everything that is shared is translated into the second language. For example, if a student offered his or her idea in Spanish, it would be written in Spanish, but also translated into English so the students would know how to continue, and vice versa. In spite of this pace, the students were still very excited. Many did not want to stop when writing time was over. What is amazing was that they would plead to write "just one more sentence" or stay in at recess to finish writing, typing, or illustrating their stories.

In late October of the year, my English language arts class completed its first "big book" project. This project was the in-class published group story in large format like a big book. It was illustrated by each of the students who helped write it. The students' excitement over this book was contagious and evident to all who walked into my classroom. One afternoon, when the SLE returned from the bilingual resource teacher's classroom, Elvira approached me and asked, "Maestra, ¿nosotros vamos a hacer libros como esos?" [Teacher, are we going to make books like those?] Her question seared my heart because it was not until that moment that I realized I had been *excluding* the very students who needed the rich and exciting activities I was offering to the English-speaking students. As a result of this incident, and after examining ways I could make it better, I took a risk to include *all* students in the writing activities. Although I was not technically responsible for teaching language arts to the SLE, it was a choice I made. Consequently, I changed my teaching schedule so language arts could begin when all my students were present, including the students learning English. This change required a rethinking on my part of how I would manage teaching two language arts groups concurrently, knowing that I might not have a bilingual aide to assist me in this new endeavor. I was convinced, however, that this was the only way to involve *all* my students in challenging and creative writing activities (see Reyes & Laliberty, 1992).

Sharing Personal Narratives

The second event that occurred in my classroom was the one that hooked my SLE on writing. One afternoon I shared with my students a story I was writing about my father. I explained to them that my writing was based on a true story but that I had changed it, adding a happier ending. In my explanation, I made a point of telling them that authors have the "power" to change whatever they want to make their stories come alive. As I was finishing the part describing a reunion between my father and his father, I was filled with so much emotion that I was unable to continue reading. My aide took over for me and finished the story.

> Dusk was setting on the old pueblo and the night was so quiet you could hear the stars twinkling. Suddenly, Guadalupe [my father] heard a faint sound from the cliffs below, an old rumbling noise that got louder as he gazed toward the river. Guadalupe's young heart began to pound, pounding faster as the noise got closer. Memories flooded his thoughts and he remembered the sound. He waited breathlessly until he saw the old rumbling, fuming truck. He couldn't believe his eyes. He was certain it was his father! A gray haired man, aged and thin, emerged from the truck and Guadalupe recognized the man as the father that had abandoned him many years before. Guadalupe had pictured and rehearsed this day in his mind many times. Father and son gazed at each other without speaking. They each took small steps toward each other and embraced with silent tears streaming from their eyes. It was the most joyous reunion of father and son.

It was evident that my students could visualize the scenes I described about the "rancho" where my father lived and the "río" that had to be crossed in order to arrive at the "pueblito," because their eyes were also brimming with tears. Maybe it was just that on seeing their teacher overcome with emotion, they couldn't help but be affected by it. Nonetheless, this incident showed my students the power of writing that is based on our lived experiences (Fránquiz & Reyes, 1998).

From then on, my bilingual students reached into their "funds of knowledge" (see Chapter 1) as a source for writing their own poignant stories about their lives in Mexico and about their families. It was almost as if I had given them the "key" to unlock their writing potential. Once they realized that there was no great mystery about writing, my students couldn't find enough time to write all the stories they wanted to share.

I believe that sharing my father's story with my SLE was the turning point for their writing success. Taking some cues from me, they wrote their own powerful stories.

Sandra, a fourth grader, chose to write a chapter book, *Daniel y su Abuelo*, about a boy and his grandfather. Below is her unedited story:

> Una mañana Daniel y su abuelo fueron a dar un paseo a un rio muy bonito llamado "Pajaritos." Luego dijo el abuelo a Daniel. Ven sientate, te voy a contar una historia. Era una vez un conejo y una coneja. En eso interumpe Daniel. "Espera quiero que me digas donde estan mis padres."
>
> "Pues no te puedo contestar ahora porque ya es hora de irnos. Te contare en la casa," dijo el abuelo. Cuando llegaron ala casa se sentaron en un sillon y luego insistio Daniel a su abuelo, "Cuentame donde estan mis padres."
>
> "Pues no quisiera contarte," contesto el abuelo muy triste. "Pero si tu insistes te voy a contar. Tus padres te abandonaron cuando tu estabas chico. Ellos se fueron porque no te queria tu papa. Tu mama decidio dejarte y se fue con tu papa. Ella lloraba, pero tu papa se la llevo.
>
> [One morning, Daniel and his grandfather went for a walk to a beautiful river named "Pajaritos." Then the grandfather told Daniel. Come and sit down, I will tell you a story. Once there was a boy rabbit and a girl rabbit. Suddenly, Daniel interrupts him, "Wait, I want you to tell me where my parents are."
>
> "Well, I can't answer you right now because it is time for us to go. I shall tell you at home," said the grandfather. When they arrived home they sat on an easy chair and Daniel insisted, "Tell me where my parents are."
>
> "Well I don't really want to tell you," answered his grandfather sadly. "But if you insist I will tell you. Your parents abandoned you when you were young. They left because your father didn't want you. Your mother decided to leave you and go with your father. She cried, but your father took her."]

Sandra's story relates the search for Daniel's parents and ends with a happy reunion. Notice how she selects emotional and personal themes that elicit pathos. This story, along with the illustrations, also shows how a student was able to take her own experiences and develop them into a story using important events in her life. Other students in my class also followed the same themes. Their themes often made me wonder if they were influenced by the "tele novelas" they watched at home, or whether the theme of abandonment made a significant impression on them. A common practice among low-socioeconomic Mexican families permits children to be left in the care of grandparents or other relatives. Young children may view this as abandonment.

Sandra and all the other students in my class felt like real authors. And, like authors, they began their books with a dedication and ended them with a short biography about themselves. Giving my students the freedom to write about their own lives, using their native language, had a transforming effect on them. For me, this was an important lesson in understanding how their lived experiences improved the quality of their writing. The choice of writing in English or Spanish expanded their repertoire and their audiences.

Book Covers and Story Recipes

I discovered another strategy that helped my students become more independent writers. This happened one day when I was spending time at the local library. I saw a box of free book covers/jackets. Instantly, I realized that using these colorful book covers was a perfect way for my students to continue their writing by utilizing the pictures on the covers.

The story recipe project involves each student selecting a book jacket, then writing a story that reflects the illustrations on the jacket. When I began this project, I developed a worksheet labeled "Story Recipe" in Spanish and English. I modeled how to fill out the sheet by taking a book jacket and showing the students a story plot that would be appropriate for the illustrations on the book jacket. My students were excited about this because the cover illustrations provided them with ideas for the *who, where,* and *what.* I also showed them a book that had been published as an example of a finished product. Jiménez (see Chapter 9) also discusses the importance of modeling assignment expectations, especially for bilingual students. I had each student choose a book cover. The book covers were placed all around the classroom and the students went from one area to another trying to choose a favorite one. Students would take a book cover, then put it down to take another one. Many of them could not decide which one to use because they were enthralled with more than one colorful book cover. I remember two Spanish-speaking girls brought me two book jackets and said, "Maestra, ¿puede guardarme éste para cuando termine el primer cuento [entonces] puedo comenzar con éste?" [Teacher, can you save this one so when I finish my first story, I can start on this one?] How could I refuse such motivation and eagerness for writing? To my delight, many of these students took book jackets home over the summer so they could publish and continue with their writing.

When the stories were finished, students bound them using the book jackets as the covers. Covering the author's name with a "post it" strip, and writing in the name(s) of the new author(s), changed the books and made them the students' own.

A Celebration of Literacy

At the end of the year, I decided to hold an Authors' Celebration, an idea that was inspired by Padak (1988). I wanted (1) to showcase the extensive work my students had done during the year, (2) to have parents share in the special event as a way of acknowledging their support of their children, and (3) to let the administrators and the larger community witness my students' success. Additionally, I wanted everyone to experience the excitement we all felt about writing and how this affected and helped the student's confidence and self-esteem. The students published an average of five books; two students published more than 10 books. Anticipation and excitement filled the classroom as we prepared for the evening event. Special invitations were mailed to parents, the principal, and the superintendent. I made personal phone calls to follow up and encourage parent participation. Preparation took many hours. Students struggled deciding which book they wanted to share at the celebration night. They practiced and timed the stories they would read. Students made special nameplates for their published books that would be displayed in the cafeteria. Parent volunteers helped make corsages for the girls and bow ties for the boys.

On the evening of the Authors' Celebration, students arrived in their best attire. As they arrived each was given a name badge to wear and was assigned to a room. Concurrent sessions were held in different rooms. The students read their stories to a mixed audience of English- and Spanish-speaking parents. Parents rotated to various classrooms where five to six students waited nervously for their shining moment. Some stories were read in English and some in Spanish, all without translation. There was no evidence of discomfort or intolerance for the "foreign language" not understood by one linguistic group or the other. Parents listened with a great deal of sensitivity and interest even when they did not understand the students' language. Booklets/comment sheets were prepared ahead of time for those attending to write comments to the students as they listened to their stories (see Reyes & Laliberty, 1992, for more details).

This event provided the parents a chance to observe their children's academic work. It was evident from their responses that they felt a great deal of pride in their children's success. After an hour of rotation among the classrooms, everyone assembled in the cafeteria where my students were honored with a special certificate of accomplishment. Afterward parents browsed through the children's "published" books while enjoying refreshments. For all involved, it was truly a memorable night but also a night that would recognize my students' success as writers.

Reflections and Lessons About Students' Needs

During my first year of teaching, I had two students learning English enrolled in my classroom, but they were never physically in my room. They would enter my class in the morning with the other students, gather their materials, and go to the ESL resource teacher who was in charge of all their instruction. At the end of the day, they would return to my classroom, put their materials away, and wave "Adios" to a homeroom teacher who hardly knew them.

During the past few years as the population in our district changed and the number of SLE increased, the ESL pullout program continued to be the most economical method of addressing the linguistic needs of SLE in our school district. However, I am not sure this was best for all students learning English. It is easy to overlook second-language learners and place the responsibility on the resource teachers. In my case and as I mentioned earlier, I initially did not feel I needed to change what was already in place. I did not realize, however, the effect the pullout program was having on the Mexicano/Latino students in particular. It wasn't until one of them pointed it out that I realized that I was excluding them from the rich activities that were taking place in my room. This incident served as the catalyst for deciding to include all my students in the language arts activities that they were yearning for. In making that change I also did not realize the impact it would have on their ability to produce the kinds of stories that sprung from their heads.

The changes that I implemented were difficult at first because I was not fully aware of the implications they would have on the structure of my class and the hoops I had to jump through to conform to the system. I had to scrounge for materials to teach language arts in Spanish and spend extra time translating materials to meet the needs of the 12 students who would now be a part of the group. The decision to change my schedule to accommodate the SLE would have an impact on all my students and especially benefit my Mexicano/Latino students.

In this chapter I have described how students in a bilingual classroom were inspired to become excellent writers and how powerful writing can be when they integrate their own experiences into their writing. What can we, as educators, glean from these findings? Can teachers inspire students to write the kinds of stories that emerge from their minds and hearts? I believe it is possible to inspire even reluctant writers. The key to success lies not in what a teacher does to promote prolific writers, but in how the teacher sets up the environment for learning (see Chapter 6) as well as how she guides and directs instruction. A critical start is classroom activities that foster cultural awareness and value all students for who they are. A crucial component of effective instruction for bilingual students is the activation of their prior knowledge and culture to ensure their academic success. Cummins (1998) states that "the development of reading and writing skills can only occur in an instructional context where students are actively engaged. However, students will enthusiastically immerse themselves in these literacy activities only when both the process and products of these activities are affirming of their developing academic and personal identities" (p. 17).

There is no magic to great writing, just the magic that teachers create when, as stated in Chapter 2, they teach to students' potential, setting expectations and challenges the students can meet. I believe this is what occurred in my classroom and how my students got "hooked on writing."

References

Cummins, J. (1998, March). *Linguistic and cognitive issues in learning to read in a second language.* Paper presented at the Conference on Reading and English Language Learner, California Reading and Literature Project, Sacramento.

Dunrea, O. (1990). *The writing process: One writer's approach to writing with children.* Conestoga, PA: Stonetrow Studio.

Fránquiz, M. E., & Reyes, M. de la Luz. (1998). Creating inclusive learning communities through English Language Arts: From chanclas to canicas. *Language Arts, 75*(3), 211–220.

Padak, N. D. (1988). *Writing should be read: Encouraging and celebrating young authors.* Monroe, NY: Trillium.

Reyes, M. de la Luz, & Laliberty, E. A. (1992). A teacher's "pied piper" effect on young authors. *Education and Urban Society, 24*(2), 244–262.

PART III

Reading the Word
by Reading the World

CHAPTER 9

Strategic Reading for Language–Related Disabilities

The Case of a Bilingual Latina Student

ROBERT T. JIMÉNEZ

Sara was a student in a self-contained special education classroom for bilingual Latina/o students with learning disabilities when I first met her. At that time, she was 13 years old, of Mexican origin, and in grade 7. When I visited her classroom, Sara usually could be found sitting quietly at her desk. She was almost always nicely dressed and carefully groomed. Her teacher shared with me that Sara suffered from severe auditory, visual, and memory problems and that she lagged behind most of the other students in her classroom. Her teacher appreciated the fact that Sara could be counted on to deliver messages to other teachers or water the plants in the classroom; in her teacher's words, "she is a responsible person." As a former bilingual teacher, and now a bilingual literacy researcher, I was concerned that I seldom observed Sara being encouraged or provided with opportunities to read, write, or speak in either of her two languages. In this chapter, I will explore Sara's literacy development and her response to what I call culturally relevant, cognitive strategy instruction that is linguistically sensitive.

Sara intrigued me from the very first time I met her. She was born in the United States and had been in the same district since preschool. Her schooling experience, however, included no fewer than 10 moves to different school buildings. She began school in an all-English, general education kindergarten class. After kindergarten, she was referred to what the district called a bilingual developmental first-grade classroom. Children referred to these classrooms are considered to be at-risk for referral to special education. In fact, she was referred for a full evaluation while in this setting. Placement in special education was not recommended at that time. Sara continued in general bilingual classrooms during grades 2 and 3; in grade 3 she was referred for another evaluation. She was diagnosed as having a reading and writing learning disability, and she was placed in a self-contained bilingual special education classroom for grade 4. She continued to receive the majority of instruction in this type of classroom while this research was conducted.

Sara's Total Reading Battery score on the Metropolitan Achievement Test (MAT) was 67 out of a possible 223. Her grade equivalent score was 3.0 (test date, February 1995). The MAT is an English-language, group-administered test. Sara also completed the Woodcock Achievement Battery in Spanish, an individually administered test, and scored a grade equivalent of 2.4 on the Reading Achievement Cluster. As I mentioned earlier, at that time she was 13 years old and in grade 7. The psychologist who administered this test concluded that Sara was 4 years below current grade placement.

Sara's scores on tests of language proficiency were also revealing. For example, she received a receptive English-language age score of 10.2 months and an expressive English-language age of 9.6 months. Her receptive Spanish-language age was 11.8 months and her expressive Spanish-language age was 6.6 months (test date, May 1994). In other words, Sara's oral English and English-language comprehension skills were just a bit lower than one might expect considering her age. Her Spanish-language proficiency was stronger in the area of listening comprehension than in speaking, a not uncommon phenomenon for students from language-minority communities in the United States.

Not surprisingly, Sara repeated to me that she did not like to read, but she also expressed a strong desire to learn to read and write at higher levels. In her classroom, I observed that her literacy instruction consisted almost entirely of reading aloud in round-robin fashion from materials such as high-interest, low-vocabulary, teen-type magazines. Sara's oral reading was torturous. She stopped frequently within almost every sentence, often struggling with each word. The teacher continually provided Sara with the pronunciations of words, seemingly with no noticeable improvement. Sara seldom volunteered to answer her teacher's questions.

When I asked her to read from texts at different levels, Sara demonstrated the same problems with word recognition and reading fluency that I had observed earlier in her classroom. She was unable to choose any materials from her classroom that she could read with ease. Even when she successfully read a sentence written at about the third-grade level, she found it very difficult to discuss its meaning. In addition, Sara very rarely implemented reading strategies known to enhance comprehension. Clearly, Sara *behaved* like a student with a learning disability, especially with respect to literacy. Sara's classroom placement, the literacy instruction provided to her, and the manner in which her unique linguistic and cultural identity was systematically ignored by her instructors and omitted from the curriculum all seemed to conspire against the possibility of any real academic achievement, particularly literacy learning.

Sara is representative of many Latino students at the middle school level who are experiencing major problems with literacy. Students like Sara can be challenging even to veteran teachers with training and experience in bilingual education and/or special education. In addition, middle school students who read far below grade level are at major risk for school failure and for not completing their high school education (García et al., 1995). Students like Sara have difficulty transforming their justifiable resistance to meaningless curriculum, lack of effective instruction, and negation of their Latino identity into a starting point for truly "reading the word, and . . . continually reading the world" (Freire & Macedo, 1987, p. 35).

In the sections below, I discuss research findings that I believe are relevant for promoting or hindering the reading comprehension of Latina/o students (Jiménez, García, & Pearson, 1996). The overall theoretical framework I have adopted is captured in the words of Freire and Macedo (1987), who described literacy as an activity that is "grounded in critical reflection on the cultural capital of the oppressed," and who further see literacy as "the vehicle by which the oppressed are equipped with the necessary tools to reappropriate their history, culture, and language practices" (p. 157).

One very specific and concrete means for achieving this vision of better equipping those who have been marginalized in the process of literacy learning can be extrapolated from the work of Sonia Nieto (1992), who very insightfully identified dull and insipid pedagogy as one of the major structural barriers to the academic achievement of culturally and linguistically diverse students. In previous research, my colleagues and I identified many strategic processes used by successful and less successful bilingual readers (Jiménez et al., 1996). I have used these research findings as the basis for working with students like Sara. It is important to point out, however, that my previous research (Jiménez et al., 1995, 1996) was grounded in a framework that was informed primarily by an information processing approach. As such, the examples are not as powerful as they might have been had culturally familiar text been used or had critical reflection been promoted. Even so, the examples provide hints of how such a combined approach might be used in a more instructionally robust manner.

In that previous research, we identified three overlapping and interrelated domains of knowledge and strategic deployment used by successful bilingual Latino students: student response to unknown vocabulary, the ability to integrate prior knowledge and textual information for the purpose of drawing inferences, and the ability to ask questions and find answers. I use examples produced by successful Latino readers to illustrate how this information can promote the comprehension of students learning English as a second language. Some discussion of how a strategic approach might be enhanced by drawing from a more critical theoretical perspective also is included. Finally, I demonstrate how Sara responded when she was taught selected key strategic reading processes, and I use this information to flesh out a broader instructional approach to literacy development.

Key Reading Strategies for Bilingual Latino Students

Reading strategies are conscious and flexible plans that readers apply and adapt to particular texts and tasks (Pearson, Roehler, Dole, & Duffy, 1992). In other words, reading strategies have been described as all-purpose tools that readers use to unlock the meaning of stories and content-specific materials such as science or social studies texts.

Determining the Meanings of Unknown Words

Research focused on mainstream students indicates that vocabulary knowledge is a potent predictor of reading ability (Anderson & Freebody, 1981). Specifically, the ability to quickly access the meanings of a wide range of printed words is a vital component of skilled reading (Golinkoff, 1975–76). In other words, students who know a lot of words and recognize them quickly when they appear in print tend to be successful readers.

As one might expect, students for whom English is a second language frequently encounter unfamiliar words when they read English-language texts (García, 1991). When tested, Sara, for example, experienced her greatest difficulties in the verbal domain. She scored at a grade 2.1 level on the vocabulary subsection of the MAT. Successful Latino readers of English have linguistic resources to help them figure out the meanings of new words (Jiménez et al., 1996). By making decisions as to which unknown words need attention, and then developing a plan for figuring out what these words mean, these readers often make sense of the materials they read.

In contrast to the efforts made by more successful bilingual readers to construct meaning, Sara's chief preoccupation with words was to pronounce them correctly. But Gilda, a successful Latina reader of English, made use of several strategies when she encountered unknown words. For example, when she came across the word *wantonly* while reading a short science fiction story titled *The King of the Beasts* (Farmer, 1982), she used the strategies of focusing on vocabulary, monitoring her comprehension, using context, and making inferences. She stated: "Want, wan tan ly. What is that?" Her comment, "Well, I don't know the meaning of a word," demonstrated her interest in this vocabulary item. Her determination led her to specify the item's grammatical function: "They're talking about a kind of way they were killed." Gilda resolved her understanding by assigning the word *wantonly* the meaning of mean and stupid, a close approximation of its sense as malicious.

> Because the next sentence, it says that, . . . I'm trying as it were to make . . . Oh! OK, so he wants to do this because people, he thinks people were like really mean and stupid and everything; now I know.

In addition, successful Latino readers use other strategies when they see words they do not know, such as searching for cognates and translating. Cognates are vocabulary items that are related across languages because of common ties to an ancestral language. Cognates in Spanish and English are often similar in spelling and meaning. Some false cognates exist such as *exito* in Spanish [success] and *exit* in English, or *actualmente* in Spanish [currently] and *actually* in English, but students can be taught to avoid this potential pitfall by monitoring their comprehension (García, 1998). Pamela, another highly successful bilingual Latina reader, demonstrated how this strategy can enhance comprehension.

> Like carnivorous, *carnívoro*. OK, some [words] like, I know what it is in Spanish. Some words I go, what does that mean in Spanish?

Students with English- and Spanish-language proficiency appreciate and take advantage of opportunities to search for cognate vocabulary (Jiménez, 1997). In effect, one simple technique teachers can use to clearly communicate the message that students' Spanish-language abilities are a valuable and worthwhile body of knowledge is to encourage them to access cognate vocabulary knowledge, as well as to translate judiciously and in paraphrase, and to reflect on text in either or both of their languages. McKay and Wong (1996) argued in their research on Chinese-speaking students that teachers who ignore these students' knowledge of the Chinese language and its writing system reduce them to a status that is "rather ignorant and pitiful, indeed infantile" (p. 590). For students who speak a cognate language of English, in this case Spanish, such an omission is without a doubt a waste of linguistic resources and probably reflects a deficiency-oriented ideology (see Chapter 3).

The Importance of Inferential Reading Processes

Another important strategic activity used by successful Latino readers of English is that of making inferences, otherwise known as drawing conclusions or integrating prior knowledge with textual information. The ability to make inferences is crucial for comprehending text, perhaps even its essence (Anderson & Pearson, 1984). Yet, the instruction that typically is provided to students like Sara is seldom designed to help them improve this ability. In Sara's case, I noted little to no comprehension instruction during classroom observations that began in November and ended in April. Sara herself provided little indication that she could make inferences on her own when she was observed during reading instruction or when interviewed individually.

Class time devoted to reading typically involved the students bidding for turns to read orally from a text selected by the teacher. Discussion of the text, and even teacher-directed questions, were rare. Most of the students experienced difficulty with oral reading, although few demonstrated as many problems as Sara. When questions did occur they followed the ubiquitous I–R–E pattern, with the teacher initiating a question, a student responding, and the teacher evaluating the response. Even controversial topics, which might have led to spirited discussion, were handled in this fashion. For example, after reading a text on U.S. military involvement abroad, and reading the question, Should U.S. armed forces be a world police force? one student answered, "They should help our own. Take the poor off the streets." Unfortunately, no further discussion ensued nor was it encouraged.

On the other hand, Lisa, another successful Latina reader of English, was able to explicitly identify her prior knowledge of relevant topics while reading. Her prior knowledge laid the foundation for making inferences. For example, while reading a science text in Spanish, she discussed what she knew about solar energy.

Y en Chicago me acordé que vi en las noticias que hay un laundrymat, una lavandería, donde ellos no meten dinero, la energía lo obtienen del sol . . .

[And in Chicago I remember that I saw on the news that there is a laundromat, where they don't insert money. They get the energy from the sun . . .]

Lisa had figured out, perhaps on her own, the importance of making connections between experience and information found in text. It seems sensible to find ways to provide low-performing Latino readers of English with opportunities to learn this strategy. Research studies suggest that this ability can be taught (Hansen, 1981; Harris & Pressley, 1991). A potentially important means of helping students see the relevance of their lived experience is to provide them with culturally familiar text (Barrera, 1993; Jiménez, 1997) and then to discuss the relationships between the two.

Asking Questions While Reading

The ability to ask pertinent self-directed questions and then to find or generate answers has been shown to enhance the reading comprehension of students with learning disabilities (Palincsar & Brown, 1984). More important, asking questions can be the starting point for engaging in critical reflection.

By combining the cognitive approach with culturally relevant content, as well as a critical approach to literacy learning, we can provide students with opportunities to engage in genuine critical reflection. Freire and Macedo (1987) critiqued a stand-alone cognitive approach to teaching students literacy by pointing out

> Since students' cultural capital, i.e., their life experience, history, and lan-
> guage—is ignored, they are rarely able to engage in critical reflection, regard-
> ing their own practical experience and the ends that motivate them in order,
> in the end, to organize the findings and thus replace mere opinion about facts
> with an increasingly rigorous understanding of their significance. (p. 147)

Successful Latino readers of English ask themselves relevant questions while reading narrative and expository text. These students are able to determine the importance of this activity to their comprehension of text. The following questions asked by Gilda set the stage for her to understand the gist of the science fiction story, *The King of the Beasts*, by realizing that "they" were not human beings at all. The main characters were extraterrestrial aliens, but this information was not explicitly stated in the text itself.

> Well, why are they making a man, aren't they people? They're
> biologists, aren't they? Why would they be scared if it was a man?

Sara and the other Latino students with learning disabilities who were involved in this research project rarely, if ever, asked themselves questions while reading. Again, it makes sense to find ways to teach students like Sara the question-asking behavior of more successful readers. Providing these students with texts that portray culturally familiar information may facilitate this process. In addition, such behavior fundamentally alters the existing socially constructed contexts of which these students are a part (Moll,

Estrada, Díaz, & Lopes, 1980). It provides them with a learning environment where their prior knowledge, linguistic strengths, and community-derived skills are recognized and valued.

Teaching Latino Students with Learning Disabilities

The instructional outline presented below provides a sequential list of events and activities used to teach Sara and some of her classmates.

I. *Generate Student Language*
   - Present students several items of Mexican food—corn flour (*masa harina*), corn on the cob (*mazorca, elote*), package of tortillas.
   - Stimulate discussion—for example, "tell me about these things, when are they used, for what purpose?"
   - Language experience—write down student-generated language and distribute written text to students
   - Use student-generated text as basis for initial modeling of think-aloud procedure
II. *Teach, Demonstrate, and Continually Review Think-Aloud Procedure*
   - Present culturally familiar tradebooks
   - Support students' initial attempts at thinking aloud
   - Work on reading fluency—multiple rereadings of texts, silent and oral reading
   - Discuss first of three major reading strategies—integrating prior knowledge
III. *Emphasize Three Major Domains of Strategic Processing*
   - Approach unknown vocabulary, make inferences, monitor comprehension, and ask questions
   - Model the think-aloud procedure for each of the three strategies multiple times
   - Have students practice thinking aloud; ask students to reflect on their comprehension

First, students were encouraged to talk by presenting them with the Mexican food items. In essence, the language experience approach was used for the purpose of creating a shared experience. Students were presented with three items commonly found in traditional Mexican cuisine (corn on the cob, tortillas, and corn flour), and then they were prompted to tell all that they could about these items. After students' statements were recorded in the form of a continuous narrative, the resulting text was typed into a computer and then distributed to the students.

In addition, a thematic strand of literature was selected for the purpose of building on and taking advantage of the previously described language experience. Three of the books used for this purpose were: *Quetzalcóatl, A Tale of Corn* (Parke & Panik, 1992), *The Day It Snowed Tortillas* (Hayes, 1985), and *Aztec, Inca and Maya* (Baquedano, 1993). All three of these books included stories that involved corn, corn flour, tortillas, and many other food items commonly used in Mexican cuisine, or they discussed these items in an expository text format.

The instructional approach adopted emphasized learning of three of the strategies already described in the first part of this chapter—*approach unknown vocabulary, make inferences,* and *ask questions.* The following is an example of how students were taught these strategies:

Sara: "The people of the Earth will starve unless they get food," said Quetzalcóatl.

Researcher: What does that mean, "the people of the Earth will starve"?

Sara: I don't know, well, they don't have any food, they will starve.

Researcher: Starve means what?

Sara: They don't have food, they don't eat food.

Researcher: What happens if you don't eat?

Sara: You die.

Researcher: Exactly, so that's what it makes you think about. See, you're using what you know, you're integrating it with what you're reading here. You know that if people don't eat they're going to die, they will starve, that's making an "inference," OK? Putting together what you know with what you read.

Instruction Designed to Improve Reading Fluency

Low-literacy students who are learning English as a second language often experience major difficulties with word recognition and reading fluency. This was certainly the case for Sara. As a result, it made sense to pursue the goal of helping Sara achieve what Samuels (1988) calls *automaticity.* Automaticity refers to the ability of successful readers to effortlessly recognize words quickly and accurately. The problems these students were experiencing with word recognition and fluency did not become apparent until after I began to work with them. Because I had employed a formative experiment as a component of this research project, I adjusted my approach to working with the students and added this aspect of literacy instruction (Jiménez, 1997; Reinking & Watkins, 1997).

In the past, instruction on building reading fluency generally consisted of repetitive and dull exercises. This work can, however, be embedded within an overall context of meaningful, culturally relevant text, student-generated language, and instruction designed to promote comprehension. Students should, for example, be given opportunities to read text silently at first. Then, on occasion, individual students can be asked to read orally. Building reading fluency is a means of helping students monitor their reading comprehension more carefully.

Care should be taken to limit the number of interruptions when students read orally. When students cannot pronounce a word or struggle inordinately to do so, assistance should be provided. When students demonstrate difficulty with word recognition and overall reading fluency (overly slow, choppy, meaning-altering miscues), they should be asked to reread specific phrases orally. At times, rereading a phrase two to three times may be necessary. Embarrassment can be avoided by asking other students to occasionally read chorally as a group. The purpose of rereading should always be focused squarely on the larger goal of comprehension.

Reading fluency also should be viewed as a means to comprehension, not an end in itself. Students need to understand that a consequence of poor reading fluency is an inability to understand. The following example provides an indication of how Sara began to respond to instruction designed to improve her reading fluency after 6 days of instruction. In this example, Sara indicates some monitoring behavior (I don't remember what that word is . . .). Sara had not previously provided any evidence that she was concerned with accurately decoding text either in her classroom or during a pre-intervention interview.

> *Sara:* OK. Quetzalcóatl asked the ants for some . . . I don't remember what that word is . . .
> *Researcher:* Kernels
> *Sara:* kernels of corn to which they replayed
> *Researcher:* Replied
> *Sara:* Replied, Maize is food for the gods, why do you want it?
> *Researcher:* OK, now read it again nice and smooth.
> *Sara:* Quetzalcóatl asked the ants for some kernels . . . Right? To which they replied, Maize is food for the gods, why do you want it?

Sara's Response to Instruction

After receiving 2 weeks of instruction characterized by an emphasis on learning reading strategies, use of culturally relevant text, linguistically sensitive instruction, and reading fluency, Sara made a statement (see below) that appeared to reflect added confidence in her ability to read and in her desire to read. Statements made by other bilingual students with learning disabilities also reflected increased metacognitive knowledge about themselves as readers and about useful strategies for increasing comprehension of text (Baker & Brown, 1984).

> *Researcher:* Yesterday, Sara was telling me what she used to think about reading.
> *Sara:* I didn't like it.
> *Researcher:* What was it that you didn't like?
> *Sara:* [It was] hard.
> *Researcher:* Hard, it was very hard for you to read, OK. How about now?
> *Sara:* I kind of like it.
> *Researcher:* How come?
> *Sara:* Because it makes a little more sense, sort of, and I can read better.

Encouraging students to reflect on the activity of reading is an excellent opportunity to review important information concerning cognitive and metacognitive reading strategies. The following two examples indicate that bilingual students with learning disabilities can begin to discuss reading in ways similar to more experienced or successful readers (Jiménez et al., 1996). Their statements are encouraging.

> *Researcher:* What do you think you need to do to become a really good reader?
> *Adán:* Read a lot.
> *Researcher:* Yeah, read a lot. What else do you have to do when you're reading?
> *Sara:* Picture things in your head.
> *Researcher:* Yeah, you have to picture things in your head and what else?
> *Sara:* Try and look for clues for words you don't know.
> *Researcher:* Look for clues . . .
> *Sara:* Try the words out in Spanish.
> *Researcher:* Try it in Spanish, yeah, that's really smart. What else, Victor, what do you do to become a good reader? These are good answers because the first time I talked to you guys . . .
> *Victor:* Imagine it and ask yourself questions. [They make] pictures in their head.

Sara: They ask questions.

Researcher: They ask questions, they make pictures in their head, and they do what . . .

Victor: Mix what we know . . .

Researcher: Mix what they know with what they're reading about, mix it together and they understand.

These opportunities for more critical reflection on the activity of reading appear to be not only intriguing but perhaps also necessary to help students become aware that reading involves thought and that comprehension is the end product. By and large, Latino students do not receive sufficient opportunities for this type of reflection (Moll et al., 1980; Reyes, 1992).

Conclusion

The underlying structure of the instructional approach used for working with Sara was threefold: an emphasis on key comprehension strategies, use of culturally relevant children's literature, and provision of opportunities to build word recognition and reading fluency abilities. This is the sort of comprehension-based literacy program that teachers will find useful for students from linguistically diverse backgrounds. The basis for this instruction was grounded in both cognitive and critical theoretical views of literacy learning (Anderson & Pearson, 1984; Freire & Macedo, 1987; Harris & Pressley, 1991).

Sara's statements about reading indicated some positive changes, and some of her responses to instruction were encouraging. Initially she was quite dubious of efforts to teach her reading. It required substantial time to win her confidence. Sara repeatedly stated, "I don't know," or "I can't think of anything" during initial instructional efforts. These responses stand in marked contrast to her later utterances where she described and discussed reading strategies in a manner similar to that employed by successful bilingual Latino readers of English (Jiménez, et al., 1995, 1996).

These responses also may indicate that the use of culturally familiar topics can facilitate the development of students' voices. In his Introduction to Friere and Macedo's (1987) work, Henry Giroux contends that literacy learning should adopt this development as one of its goals.

At its best, a theory of critical literacy needs to develop pedagogical practices in which the battle to make sense of one's life reaffirms and furthers the need for teachers and students to recover their own voices so they retell their own histories and in so doing "check and criticize the history [they] are told against the one [they] have lived." (Giroux in Freire & Macedo, 1987, p. 15)

Even more striking than Sara's potential for growth, indicated by her description of cognitive strategies, was her willingness and desire to work hard, to listen to instruction, and to try out the focal reading strategies that were presented. In other words, Sara was motivated to improve her knowledge of literacy. McKay and Wong (1996) prefer the term investment to motivation. They argue that students who traditionally are marginalized and described as unmotivated do, on occasion, become actively engaged in their learning. They further argue that this engagement can be accounted for by how the students are positioned by their teachers, their classmates, and the curriculum, whereas motivation as a construct usually is viewed as either present or absent. One possible conclusion is that Sara became invested in her learning when the instructional context was such that she felt valued and accepted for who she was, a bilingual Latina student with learning disabilities who could, nevertheless, perform well at reading.

Sara and her classmates seemed to crave instruction that was comprehensible and that allowed them to do something they had been only marginally successful at previously: read with understanding. Both Lipka (1991) and McCarty, Wallace, Lynch, and Benally (1991) have shown that students from minority communities will talk and actively engage in their learning when they are provided with a culturally relevant context and activities.

More work is needed to determine fully the effectiveness of an instructional intervention for bilingual Latino students that emphasizes cognitive strategies, makes use of culturally familiar text, and is linguistically sensitive. In particular, a longer period of time devoted to an instructional intervention would provide students with sufficient information and practice to allow for more traditional types of measurement, such as the use of academic achievement tests. Of course, the real test of the efficacy of these strategies will occur when teachers can implement a similar approach with whole classrooms of students.

References

Anderson, R. C., & Freebody, P. (1981). Vocabulary knowledge: A state of the art survey. In J. J. Guthrie (Ed.), *Comprehension and teaching: Research reviews*. Newark, DE: International Reading Association.

Anderson, R. C., & Pearson, P. D. (1984). A schema-theoretic view of basic processes in reading. In P. D. Pearson (Ed.), *Handbook of reading research* (pp. 255–292). New York: Longman.

Baker, L., & Brown, A. L. (1984). Metacognitive skills and reading. In P. D. Pearson (Ed.), *Handbook of reading research* (pp. 353–394). New York: Longman.

Barrera, R. (1993). Ideas a literature can grow on: Key insights for enriching and expanding children's literature about the Mexican-American experience. In

V. J. Harris (Ed.), *Teaching multicultural literature in grades K–8* (pp. 203–242). Norwood, MA: Christopher-Gordon.

Freire, P., & Macedo, D. (1987). *Literacy: Reading the word and the world.* South Hadley, MA: Bergin & Garvey.

García, G. E. (1991). Factors influencing the English reading test performance of Spanish-speaking Hispanic children. *Reading Research Quarterly, 26*(4), 371–392.

García, G. E. (1998). Mexican-American bilingual students' metacognitive reading strategies: What's transferred, unique, problematic. In T. Shanahan & F. Rodríguez-Brown (Eds.), *National Reading Conference Yearbook 47* (pp. 253–263). Chicago: National Reading Conference.

García, G. E., Stephens, D. L., Koenke, K. R., Pearson, P. D., Harris, V. J., & Jiménez, R. T. (1995). *Reading instruction and educational opportunity at the middle school level* (Tech. Rep. 622). Champaign–Urbana: University of Illinois, Center for the Study of Reading.

Golinkoff, R. M. (1975–76). A comparison of reading comprehension processes in good and poor comprehenders. *Reading Research Quarterly, 11*(4), 623–659.

Hansen, J. (1981). The effects of training on inference training and practice on young children's reading comprehension. *Reading Research Quarterly, 16*(3), 391–417.

Harris, K. R., & Pressley, M. (1991). The nature of cognitive strategy instruction: Interactive strategy construction. *Exceptional Children 57*(5), 392–404.

Jiménez, R. T. (1997). The strategic reading abilities and potential of five low-literacy Latina/o readers in middle school. *Reading Research Quarterly, 32*(3), 224–243.

Jiménez, R. T., García, G. E., & Pearson, P. D. (1995). Three children, two languages, and strategic reading: Case studies in bilingual/monolingual reading. *American Educational Research Journal, 32*(1), 31–61.

Jiménez, R. T., García, G. E., & Pearson, P. D. (1996). The Reading strategies of Latina/o students who are successful English readers. *Reading Research Quarterly, 31*(1), 90–112.

Lipka, J. (1991). Toward a culturally-based pedagogy: A case study of one Yup'ik Eskimo teacher. *Anthropology and Education Quarterly, 22,* 203–223.

McCarty, T. L., Wallace, S., Lynch, R. H., & Benally, A. (1991). Classroom inquiry and Navajo learning styles: A call for reassessment. *Anthropology and Education Quarterly, 22,* 42–59.

McKay, S. L., & Wong, S.-l. C. (1996). Multiple discourses, multiple identities: Investment and agency in second-language learning among Chinese adolescent immigrant students. *Harvard Educational Review, 66*(3), 577–608.

Moll, L. C., Estrada, E., Díaz, E., & Lopes, L. M. (1980). The organization of bilingual lessons: Implications for schooling. *The Quarterly Newsletter of the Laboratory of Comparative Human Cognition, 2*(3), 53–58.

Nieto, S. (1992). *Affirming diversity: The sociopolitical context of multicultural education.* New York: Longman.

Palincsar, A. S., & Brown, A. L. (1984). Reciprocal teaching of comprehension-fostering and comprehension-monitoring activities. *Cognition and Instruction, 1*(2), 117–175.

Pearson, P. D., Roehler, L. R., Dole, J. A., & Duffy, G. G. (1992). Developing expertise in reading comprehension. In S. J. Samuels & A. E. Farstrup (Eds.), *What research has to say about reading instruction* (pp. 145–199). Newark, DE: International Reading Association.

Reinking, D., & Watkins, J. (1997, December). *Balancing change and understanding in literacy research through formative experiments.* Paper presented at the National Reading Conference, Scottsdale, AZ.

Reyes, M. de la Luz. (1992). Challenging venerable assumptions: Literacy instruction for linguistically different students. *Harvard Educational Review, 62*(4), 427–446.

Samuels, S. J. (1988). Decoding and automaticity: Helping poor readers become automatic at word recognition. *Reading Teacher, 41*(8), 756–760.

Children's Books

Baquedano, E. (1993). *Aztec, Inca and Maya.* New York: Knopf.

Farmer, P. J. (1982). *The king of the beasts.* In I. Asimov, M. H. Greenberg, & C. Waugh (Eds.), *Mad scientists* (pp. 8–9). Milwaukee: Raintree.

Hayes, J. (1985). *The day it snowed tortillas: Tales from Spanish New Mexico.* Santa Fe: Mariposa.

Parke, M., & Panik, S. (1992). *Quetzalcóatl, A tale of corn.* Carthage, IL: Fearon Teacher Aids, Simon & Schuster Supplementary Education Group.

CHAPTER 10

Reflections on the Power of Spanish

Confessions from the Field

CARMEN I. MERCADO

During the past decade, I have collaborated with teachers to address the unequal access to literacy that limits the learning opportunities of Latino youth. Literacy, as we know, plays a vital gatekeeping function in creating or limiting access to postsecondary education, which is essential to increasing the life chances of these students. Ours was a modest effort: to craft a version of quality instruction that addressed concerns associated with being a member of this stigmatized "minority" during their vulnerable middle school years. In these activities, literacy constituted a way of thinking and learning and therefore an important cultural tool for human development. It played a critical role in self-formation, enabling undervalued youth to understand better who they are and what they are capable of becoming. Literacy also enabled students to access a broad range of intellectual and emotional resources by relating to adults and peers beyond the walls of their segregated classroom existences.

Specifically, we offered students an opportunity to engage in interesting and important work (in our estimation) through an inquiry approach in which literacy was applied to understanding their lived experiences rather than being merely another "boring" subject in the curriculum (in students' estimation). First- and second-generation children of Spanish-speaking immigrants from the Dominican Republic, Ecuador, El Salvador, and Honduras, and second- and third-generation Americans of Puerto Rican ancestry drew on local knowledge to understand social issues of concern. They collected data as they went about daily activities such as hanging out, going to medical appointments, visiting an ailing relative, running errands, attending church services, or watching television. In effect, "doing research" legitimized students' realities in the curriculum and required students to relate to family members, friends, and other youth and adults in qualitatively different ways.

Although we should not delude ourselves into thinking that we can make up for years of undereducation in the few brief months of the academic year, we have documented the dramatic and impressive gains, on standardized measures of reading and writing, that challenge myths about the intellectual, communicative, and moral inferiority of these students (Mercado, 1998). These debilitating myths, which many students come to believe, impede their progress in school and rob them of precious opportunities to learn in ways that only schools can provide (see Chapter 1). Through their activities, Latino students began to develop strategic uses of literacy to shape the kinds of human beings they wanted to become, and to address social and educational injustices that affected them as individuals and as members of identifiable communities. Some of these students now believe that doing "college work" in middle school was decisive in helping them go on to college.

What I have come to realize as I reread narratives written over a 9-year period (1990–1999) is the relatively minor significance I have attributed to the role that Spanish has played in these activities. Did I allow the anti-Spanish, anti-Hispanic attitude that is so pervasive in Anglo America, as Mark Falcoff (1996), resident scholar of the American Enterprise Institute, acknowledges, to color my perceptions and interpretations of these experiences? Possibly, but it would be more accurate to acknowledge that educational research on literacy in bilingual contexts is complex and requires cross-disciplinary knowledge. Because of the urgency to take action for the benefit of our youth, we are often compelled to embark on cross-disciplinary projects before we have full access to the complex knowledge they require. Consequently, I could not see what I did not fully understand. In the interest of a more complete, if not accurate, retelling, I will take this opportunity to reflect on what I have learned about the vitality of Spanish in Latino communities. I also discuss how it may have played out in the development of English literacies among Latino youth in one middle school setting and the potential for using Spanish for social and economic mobility at this historical juncture.

Spanish: A Vital Language Among Our Youth

Much has been said about the hegemony of English over Spanish and the undervaluing of Spanish among Latino children and youth. I do not doubt that that is true. We also have found that Spanish, in its infinite varieties, *is* a vital presence in the lives of Latino youth. It cannot be denied. When Latino youth enter the schoolhouse door, so does the language that introduced them to the world, which for most (but not all) is some variant (or possibly several) of Spanish, even when intertwined with English. Consequently, in spite of the low social status that Spanish has in institutional settings such as schools, its influence is ineradicable, in the same way that the influence of English is pervasive. For those of us who have been socialized in bilingual/multidialectal settings, Spanish is in our English, as English is in our Spanish, and both are an inextricable part of who we are. Sometimes both languages are intertwined in complex ways and sometimes they have distinct identities, and many variants are possible within the same person. These interlingual realities present interesting possibilities to Victor Hernandez Cruz (1991) as he muses from the stance of a Latino writer.

> Let us look at it with clear eyes in the trajectory from one language (Spanish) to another (English). . . . Is there an inner flower which passions its fragrance despite its being clothed in English words? I believe that this is happening in much U.S. Hispanic literature; the syntax of the English is being changed. . . . Of course we must strive for an English that is standard and universal, a language that can be understood by as many people as possible, but why lose the Spanish in the process. We should change the English and give it spice, Hispanic mobility, all this can be done within the framework of understanding, whether the reader is Anglo or Latin. (pp. 88–89)

Presently, the phenomenal growth and diversification of the Latino community in the United States are strengthening the influence of Spanish in our lives. Each new wave of immigrants from Latin America introduces new varieties of Spanish into established communities. Circular migration combined with the social and linguistic isolation that comes from the residential segregation that many Latinos experience contribute in unexpected ways to the revitalization of Spanish. Falcoff (1996) argues that "in raw statistical terms, the United States is more important in the constellation of Spanish-speaking countries than Uruguay, Ecuador, or Chile or the five Central American republics and Panama combined" (p. 14).

New York City, which historically has been the destination for large numbers of immigrants, has evidenced dramatic changes over the past decade in the growth and diversification of its Latino population, which now constitutes 25% of the total population and 38% of the school-aged population. It is noteworthy that a full one-third of the city's school-aged population has been Latino, primarily Puerto Rican, for the past 30 years. Puerto Ricans have outnumbered all other Latino groups since the turn of the twentieth century. However, the influx of immigrants from the Caribbean and Central America, overwhelmingly from Santo Domingo and in large numbers from Colombia, Ecuador, and Mexico, over the past 2 decades is changing the face of the city.

Because of the power of English and the revitalization of Spanish, New York City has a distinctive "Latinized" bilingual character, unlike Miami, which appears to be decidedly Cuban in its bilingualism. Puerto Ricans, who constitute 50% of the Latino population, are possibly the most bilingual, even after three generations of living in the United States. Scholars at the Center for Puerto Rican Studies at Hunter College in New York City indicate that the bilingualism common among Puerto Ricans reflects a history of migration between Puerto Rico and the United States, a pattern that is beginning to characterize more recent arrivals from the Caribbean and Central and South America.

When Latinos live within geographical proximity in barrios or neighborhoods that form distinct sociolinguistic communities, as many do, the resulting mutual influence and accommodation produce variations or hybridizations in cultural practices, language, and resources. Zentella (1997) documents how this dynamic affects the use of Spanish and English found in these heterogeneous communities, which she describes as a "bilingual/multidialectal repertoire." By this she means, "a spectrum of linguistic codes that range from standard to non-standard dialects in English and Spanish, one of which an individual may speak the best and others which s/he may speak with specific interlocutors or for specific purposes" (p. 41). Zentella identifies at least seven dialects of English and Spanish as constituting this bilingual/multidialectal repertoire in the Puerto Rican community she studied, which suggests that an even broader range of dialects is arising from the Latinization of New York. Among the dialects Zentella found in the Puerto Rican community of East Harlem are popular Puerto Rican Spanish, standard Puerto Rican Spanish, English-dominant Spanish, Puerto Rican English, African American vernacular English, Hispanicized English, and standard New York City English. She cautions, however, that these dialects are more overlapping than a discrete listing conveys, thus leading to her use of the term *multidialectal repertoire.* More important, Zentella adds that this repertoire is dynamic and in constant flux to reflect the influence of kinship, friendship, and collegial networks in our lives. Simply put, our language changes as a result of the company we keep.

This linguistic diversification has been characterized as problematic by the "language police" on both sides of the border: English-speaking extremist groups, such as advocates of U.S. English, and those self-appointed members of the Academia Real de la Lengua who are dedicated to the preservation of the "mother tongue" have very narrow views as to what constitutes standard (high-status) Spanish and standard (high-status) English. The problem is that this type of thinking adds to the confusion and uncertainty of mainstream as well as bilingual educators who have not been oriented to understand how the history of a community is reflected in the language of its speakers. Language is a powerful marker of identity, particularly among adolescent learners, which explains the resilience of Spanish among Latino youth even when it is not the official language of instruction. These realities need to be understood if we are to broaden in strategic ways the intellectual and communicative resources that our youth bring into the classroom, as the profiles of Latino youth presented below illustrate.

Latino Youth in Mainstream Settings

Latino youth in mainstream settings are a very diverse group, but within their uniqueness what is common to all is the presence of the language of primary socialization, Spanish. Their bilingualism is not always apparent, although it becomes evident in school, as it does in settings outside of school, when the need arises to accomplish personal and social goals. Specifically, in different ways, the Latino youth who became my researchers/collaborators used Spanish in combination with English to establish social and pedagogical relationships, to access information, and to represent themselves through the written and spoken word. (Luis Moll, in Chapter 1, also talks about the use of Spanish and English in conducting research in bilingual communities.) Students' use of Spanish, which never detracted from the primacy of English, was evident in face-to-face interaction with peers and adults and in the substantive body of writings that were collected over a 4-year period from different groups of students. The written texts produced by students as they engaged in inquiry were, in effect, a means of representing themselves within the various social worlds in which they interacted, and in all of these worlds Spanish had an undeniable presence. Moll also points out how bilingualism and the use of a combination of Spanish and English are vital elements in conducting research in Latino communities.

It must be understood, however, that this self-representation does not reside in the written word alone, because the written and spoken word are seamlessly interwoven, as Hornberger (1989) describes. Further, although Spanish may be more transparent in the presence of others who are similarly bilingual, it is always present in ways that are more difficult to discern. It must be read in the symbolic representations that are products of students' expressive capabilities, even of those who are long-time Americans. The Latino youths who are profiled next evidenced surprising levels of biliteracy in the sense that Hornberger (1990) uses the term: "any and all instances in which communication occurs in two or more languages in or around writing" (p. 2).

Indio

Indio was 12 years old when I first met him in the fall of 1989. He was born in Puerto Rico of a New York City-born mother. He entered school in New York City at the age of 5. However, it was only after he was held back in the first grade that his mother agreed to place him in a bilingual program. He says with a tinge of anger that he was held back "because he was Spanish." Even so, by way of introducing himself in one of his first writings, he tells me that his "favorite school subjects are reading and Spanish." Indio relates that he has four brothers and three sisters and that he often spends his summers with his grandfather in Puerto Rico. This constant contact with the island is evident in the "Hispanicized English" he speaks, which, according to Zentella (1997), is marked by a transfer of Spanish phonology and grammar, "common among those who have been reared in Puerto Rico" (p. 47).

It is characteristic of Indio to use his bilingualism to learn and to create relationships. This is, in part, a reflection of a very sociable and resourceful personality and, in part, a reflection of a life shared between New York and Puerto Rico. He is confident and equally comfortable interacting with adults, peers, and children, possibly because he plays "teacher" to younger siblings (and nephews) at home. What is especially distinctive about Indio is that he accomplished complex relational work through writing, as he discovered its potential to elicit the attention, approval, and encouragement of respected adults. However, because Indio often wrote in response to face-to-face conversations, the spoken word (often in Spanish) was always intertwined with the written word (usually in English). In speaking as in writing, Indio was a gifted, imaginative storyteller. My colleagues and I grew to depend on him to preside over conference presentations because of his oratory virtuosity and his confidence in addressing large groups in settings that are intimidating even for adults.

The oratory skills that are evident among Latino youth are a reflection of social practices valued in bilingual/multidialectal communities but undervalued in school. While the majority of our conference presentations were in English, Indio harnessed his expressive abilities in Spanish as the need arose. This occurred when, in the spring of 1991, my colleagues and I were asked to address, *in Spanish*, the Parent Institute of the State Association for Bilingual Education (SABE) conference. Addressing an audience of about 600 people was, perhaps, our most challenging experience as a group. It brought to the surface the incredible potential that resides in Indio, and in all of our students, but that remains an uncultivated and untapped resource for learning and for augmenting career opportunities at this historical juncture. Thus, while I recognized that Indio shifted easily into Spanish to hold casual conversations with peers and adults, to explain ideas to others, and to discuss his writings, I did not realize that he was capable of far more sophisticated uses of Spanish. His notes on the SABE conference, which was conducted in Spanish, were written *in English.* This suggests that Indio had an advanced knowledge of Spanish enabling him to summarize in English, as evidenced below.

> The "Save" Conference was very nice. . . . Before we went to the presentation, Dr. M. show us some of her researcher friends. In the conference, the student researchers were doing fine and spoke so professional. . . . After the questions, the researchers went to another one but the difference was that the conference was in Spanish. That conference was nice and experenceful to me. C.M. did lovely in her speech the only thing I remember was the word "L.E.C.T.U.R.A." I also forgot what it meant. After CM finish, Lisa's mother went up to talk. She had said to the parents in the audience that when parents hear and let their kids talk and express themselves that the parents then will understand their kids problems. . . . At the end Indio took the stand and talk to the parents about how the program "Research" has help him and his mother get closer. . . .
>
> *Comments:* CM you did great!!! Mrs. G. I think you did a wonderful speech! I love it! . . . Student researchers you all did wonder, marvelous, great . . . !!!!
>
> (Indio's field notes, 03/09/91)

Although we found no evidence that Indio wrote in Spanish (possibly because the situation never required it), the influence of Spanish is evident in his English orthography. For example, he writes, "C.M. did lovely in her speech." It is very likely that he thought, "C.M. hizo su presentación muy bonito," and translated it literally into English. The use of "lovely" in this way is uncommon in English, suggesting the sociolinguistic influence of Spanish in his English. For Indio, Spanish remains an underutilized potential because it is used primarily as an adjunct text that gives rise to, or enhances, the written word.

Izzy

I met Izzy in September 1990 when he was 12 years old. He was a first-grade holdover, which he angrily attributes to the fact that he is a Spanish speaker. He introduced himself in one of his earliest pieces by highlighting the fact that "his heritage is from the United States" (he was born in the Bronx) and that his family comes "from someplace else." Although his mother was born in the Dominican Republic and his father in Puerto Rico, it is clear that Izzy identifies himself as "American." He lives with his mother and two younger sisters and considers himself responsible for their well-being in his father's absence, which in his case means negotiating the world for an adult who speaks little English. Although Izzy has a good sense of humor and an easy relational style, he has the maturity and seriousness of one who bears the responsibility of being "the man of the house." During our moments together in school and during travels to conferences, Izzy is thoughtful and curious about learning from others, which may explain why he sometimes seeks out *consejos* [advice] and information from esteemed adults. Although respected and liked by teachers and peers, on occasion Izzy also lacks confidence in his own abilities, possibly the result of having had schooling experiences that robbed him of his confidence.

Izzy emphasizes, as the situation warrants, that he "speaks two languages," but it might be more appropriate to say that he is multidialectal in the sense that Zentella (1997) uses this term. His English reflects the influence of family and peer socialization, with traces of Spanish and African American phonology and lexicon. His Spanish reflects ever so slightly the phonological influences of Dominican Spanish along with Puerto Rican Spanish. Clearly, Izzy's speech, like Indio's, reflects a distinct set of family and friendship networks, suggesting the uniqueness of each student's language use. Like Indio, Izzy shifts easily between English and Spanish during casual conversations, in a manner that illustrates the importance of Spanish in establishing and marking personal relationships among Latinos. Spanish is also the language of the home, and the language he uses to help his mom learn English. He teaches her by writing English words on a blackboard at home. Although most of his school writing is in English, it is clear that for Izzy Spanish and English are intertwined in interesting ways, most evident in his life outside school.

While Izzy does not rely on talking to compose, nor is he as consistent a writer as Indio, he has a distinctive clean, clear narrative style that transforms the ordinary into the extraordinary. What to other students might be factual chronicles of our travels on Amtrak, Izzy turns into fascinating adventure stories, possibly the influence of the media or of social practices in his community. His lexicon also reveals the influence of a broadening social network that is the result of our activities together (e.g., "We mingo [mingled] with Dr. Mercado's students"). Izzy was among the students who participated in the SABE conference. I suggested he share with the group his interview of the ESL educational assistant who accompanied us on one of our trips. At this conference Izzy found himself, once again, helping an adult (this time a paraprofessional) make her comments in Spanish. Also, as was characteristic of Izzy, he later expressed appreciation (in writing) to Lisa's mother for the "beautiful ten page speech" she delivered (in Spanish) at the conference, "the best speech" he ever heard. Although the instructional contexts establish the primacy of English, Izzy experiments with writing in Spanish as the need arises. This occurred when Izzy's class was invited by the bilingual social studies class to a lecture on AIDS presented by a Spanish-speaking epidemiologist. Izzy's notes, which were translated into English (an appropriate choice for a mainstream class), are an impressive display of the intellectual gymnastics and linguistic capabilities that Latino youth harness to broaden their learning possibilities when the situation arises. Izzy uses his understanding of Spanish to gain access to technical information from an expert on an important topic (probably the type of information that is unavailable to students in English). Then he uses his communicative competence in English to translate what he has learned to present it within the genre of lecture notes. In this particular set of notes, Izzy uses Spanish to refer to important terms that may be unfamiliar in English (e.g., *fiebres* [fevers], *diarreas* [diarrhea] *pulmonía* [pneumonia], *trastornos del sistema central* [upset stomach], etc.). This situation made transparent the vital role that Spanish plays in augmenting the learning opportunities of a student who was born and raised in the Bronx. It illustrates, as well, how deceptive it is to assume that Izzy's English competence will be on a par with native-born speakers of English who do not live bilingual lives.

Lisa

Lisa was one of the youngest students in her class (i.e., 11½) when I met her in September 1990. She was born in the Dominican Republic, as were her parents and older brother. For reasons related to their inability to obtain a visa for her, Lisa's family left her in Santo Domingo when they first ventured to New York City. It was her uncle who brought her to New York at the age of 2½ to reunite her with her family. Lisa's schooling thus far has alternated between the Dominican Republic and New York City. She attended bilingual programs in kindergarten through second grade in New York City. As a result of a death in the family, she returned to the Dominican Republic for third grade in a school where the principal was a close friend of her mother. She came back to New York for fourth grade where, once again, she was placed in a bilingual class because she "needed to learn more English." This is her second year in a mainstream class, and the first with a bilingual teacher.

Lisa is often hesitant and shy to speak in class (even in small groups), but her writing reveals a playful personality, sharp wit, and independent thinking, depending on her mood. Her writing also evidences heightened metalinguistic awareness as a tool for thinking, unusual in comparison to her peers, and possibly a reflection of her strong bilingual background. In one of the first writings she produced, she felt free to code switch into Spanish to describe a favorite meal (*arroz con mollejaz*) in a letter to an unknown pen pal. Her personality is reflected in her soft-spoken manner, and her bilingualism is revealed in her softly accented speech in English. She uses fairly standard Spanish phonology and grammar in speaking, perhaps the product of her mother's background in education. What is distinct about Lisa's situation in comparison to her peers, however, is that she probably has had the greatest exposure to literate Spanish at home. This is because her mother loves to read and to write in Spanish, even though Lisa may not fully understand or appreciate its potential as yet. Lisa was as surprised as we all were to learn about her mother's oratory and writing skills in Spanish at the SABE conference, which she wrote about in English in the same way that she wrote about her experiences at the AIDS lecture in English.

David

David was born in Ecuador and came to the United States in 1987. He returns to Ecuador "once a year to visit." When I met him in the fall of 1990, he had turned 11. This was David's first year in a mainstream class, having just passed the school's English proficiency test in September. In one of his first writings, he shares that he lives with his mother, aunt, brother, and little cousin, and relates that he learned English from his uncle and the kids. David speaks what I assume is a standard Ecuadorian Spanish. In his research portfolio David reports that he loves coming to school, "specially on Mondays because we get fun classes like French," the designated foreign language, an indicator of the low status that Spanish has in this institutional context. However, his favorite subjects are science and social studies because, as he writes, he loves maps because he wants to be a scientist when he grows up.

I first met David through his writings, where his voice came out clearly and distinctly; he seemed more expressive and detailed when compared with native speakers in the class. I was surprised by how "quiet and shy" (his words) he was in person. Because it takes a while to get to know him, I was unsure whether he had limited communication skills in English (what Valdés, 1991, refers to as incipient bilingual), or he feared that others would mock his accent, or both. As his comfort level increased, however, he revealed himself to be a soft-spoken young man who had clear opinions about right and wrong in accented, but comprehensible English. David feared going to presentations because he did not feel "prepared," by which he meant that he did not know enough about his topic to talk about it. Although we did not want to pressure him into participating in communicatively challenging situations, David eventually was able to participate in two major presentations in the late spring before the end of the school year. Although initially these were intimidating experiences, they contributed immensely to boosting David's self-confidence, a result of meeting the challenge. He wrote that he was very proud of himself for what he had done. Like Lisa's mother, David's mother joined us at the second conference, where she, too, surprised us by addressing a graduate course on methods of teaching reading at Hunter College. Even though David has just exited out of a bilingual class, it is evident that Spanish continues to be an important intellectual resource and David continues to write in Spanish on his own. Unfortunately, many of these documents, which his teacher had seen, were lost during a cab ride, thereby leaving us with few examples of David's writing in Spanish. His notes from the AIDS lecture, which are written in English and Spanish, were an exception.

Daniel

Daniel was 13 years old when I met him in January 1992. A mistake led to a premature transfer out of the bilingual/ESL program and into Ms. Torres's mainstream class. After several weeks of uncertainty, Daniel was allowed to remain in the class because he had already established a close bond with his teacher and because of her influence on his behalf. Ms. Torres was a veteran teacher with 10 years experience (at the time) and held a master's degree in bilingual education. In his autobiography, Daniel relates some of the loneliness he experienced in making the journey with his father from the Dominican Republic to the United States in 1987. His separation from his mother, who remained in the Dominican Republic, has been emotionally affecting, as he describes in his writing. He entered school in New York City in grade 3, after having completed the first 2 years of schooling in the Dominican Republic. Daniel repeated the third grade, and we assume this occurred while he was enrolled in the school's bilingual program. He remained in the bilingual program until grade 5.

I met Daniel in January as the class was preparing for their first conference presentation. At the time, writing was his primary mode of communication in English, although he used Spanish to explain himself to bilingual adults. Interestingly, he used the written text in English to guide his speech at his first presentation. When I observed Daniel in this setting, in the midst of a great deal of informal socializing, I was impressed with his seriousness and his focused attention on writing. Like David, Daniel used his writing skills in Spanish when the situation made it appropriate. Thus, when a professor from the University of Puerto Rico came to visit, Daniel planned, conducted, and wrote up his interview of her in Spanish, the likely influence of a teacher who valued students' bilingualism.

> [D:] Que le interezo venir ala clase? [What interested you in coming to the class?]
>
> [Prof.:] Para saber como son las escuelas. [To know about the schools.]
>
> [D:] Como usted serelaciono con este programa? [How do you relate to this program?]
>
> Eya conocio un hombre en connetticot que staba aciendos [She met a man in Connecticut who was doing]
>
> [D:] Que uste cree aserca del programa? [What do you think about the program?]
>
> Ella cree que es una oportunida vien bonita. . . . [She believes it is a beautiful opportunity.]
>
> (Daniel, 04/92)

In this excerpt of the interview, we get glimpses of Daniel's expressive capabilities in Spanish, which suggest that he has had little formal study of his primary language. This is most evident in his segmentation problems (*serelaciona* for *se relaciona*) and his lack of familiarity with a basic lexicon (*eya* for *ella, vien* for *bien*). This is not surprising considering that he left school in the Dominican Republic after completing grade 2 and perhaps the bilingual program he attended in the Bronx gave little attention to writing in Spanish. This is, nevertheless, a situation that instruction may readily change, particularly since Spanish is a valued language for Daniel. This is evident in a number of different ways, including his willingness to teach Spanish to Patty, the student teacher who, through her activities with Latino students in the middle school, has come to realize just how important Spanish is for a future teacher.

The Role of Spanish in Creating Responsive Learning Environments for Latino Youth

In our activities, Spanish was vital to creating and broadening community and narrowing the social distance between people so that they could learn and form new social identities. However, it was in valuing and respecting each student that we created a safe haven where each was able to use Spanish to broaden his or her intellectual and expressive possibilities in a setting where Spanish was not the official language of instruction. That may explain why in thinking about our activities, it was easy to overlook the influence of Spanish, as our concern was not with the language but with the well-being of our youth. As I now see, they are inseparable.

Using Spanish to broaden community is evident in Daniel's observation during one of our research celebrations that "everybody is welcoming the parents in Spanish." Not unlike what occurs outside school, students assumed the role of translators to enable family members "who spoke a little bit of English" to participate in celebrating their children's accomplishments. However, because Spanish was always interwoven with English (the target language in the mainstream program), it was never used to exclude, although English often did. On one occasion, Ms. Torres willingly served as Maya's personal translator because this English monolingual student wanted to attend the AIDS lecture, an activity organized to allow Spanish-dominant students in the school to gain access to expert knowledge on a topic of vital concern to them. (The Bronx has one of the highest incidences of AIDS nationally.)

Using Spanish was also a vital means of lessening the social distance between Latino students and teachers. It allowed us to make discoveries about the strengths and capabilities of learners that would not have been as readily transparent in English. In their study of community-based organizations for Latino and African American youth, Heath and McLaughlin (1993) found that creating a sense of belonging or community "depends much more on how those in one's immediate environment ask questions, give directions, frame time and space, and reflect expectations than it does on verbal declarations of collectivity or acceptance" (p. 8). It is evident that creating community occurs in subtle ways during ordinary, face-to-face interactions, and in our community both Spanish and English played important roles in accomplishing this sense of belonging, as Daniel's quote suggests.

However, separate from its use to create social/pedagogical relationships, Latino youth had exposure to learning in Spanish in ways that served to elevate the status of Spanish among youth for whom Spanish is often a disparaged language in school settings, even in bilingual programs. For example, when a Latino epidemiologist was invited to give a lecture on AIDS-related diseases, it gave access to expert knowledge provided by an authority on the subject, but far more was accomplished. This also might elevate the status of Spanish among students who had little exposure to Latino professionals who use their bilingualism to help others learn. Similarly, when students attended the SABE conference in Rye, New York, and the National Association for Bilingual Education (NABE) conference in Washington DC, they had exposure to a large professional community who use Spanish in their personal and professional lives to learn and to connect to others, and to improve the conditions for learning in schools. In effect, Latino youth gained entry into a social network that made clear the value of bilingualism by example, not by mere rhetoric.

As important, students had exposure to non-Latinos who valued the importance of Spanish, such as Carolyn and Monique (pseudonyms), the graduate students who learned from and worked with the students. Although Monique was initially more fluent in Spanish than Carolyn, eventually Carolyn's resolve to learn Spanish led her to gain sufficient competence in Spanish to give a talk about her experiences in the middle school to faculty from the School of Education at the University of Puerto Rico. For both of these young women entering the profession, the valuing of Spanish went far beyond empty platitudes and the students knew it. It is for this reason that Daniel felt responsible for helping Carolyn learn Spanish, as did several other students in the class. Needless to say, these important experiences, which are unusual for Latino youth in U.S. schools to have, serve to illustrate how students' attitudes toward Spanish surface (and are changed) during ordinary activities when the language that defines the students also is valued in school.

Newkirk (1997) tells us that all forms of "self-expression," all of our ways of being personal, are forms of performance, in Erving Goffman's terms, "a presentation of self" (p. 3). Although I have already indicated that students in the middle school actually did little writing in Spanish, their writings invariably revealed their Latino selves, in what they said about themselves and how they packaged these ideas, as evident in Indio's notes presented earlier.

Conclusion

We embarked on this research project to enable young adolescents to harness the power of literacy, to take control of their own development, and go beyond the limitations schooling may impose. Although the dominant ideology has characterized linguistic diversification as problematic and persists in its emphasis on the negative impact that the vernacular (in this case Spanish) has on school achievement and the learning of English, our experiences suggest otherwise. Latino youth continue to harness their bilingualism to gain access to knowledge and information and to create positive social relations with esteemed adults, even when Spanish is not the official language of instruction. Furthermore, all this is accomplished as the valuing of English also is strengthened.

However, while we valued and respected the variations of Spanish and English that the middle school students brought into the classroom, we missed important opportunities to broaden students' use of their bilingualism in strategic ways as intellectual, social, and economic resources. We need to go beyond valuing Spanish to become more strategic in our efforts if we are to broaden the communicative repertoires as well as the learning and career opportunities of Latino students. This also means that all educators, including researchers, need to understand the vital connection between language, community, and identity—that language has deep affective roots. In emphasizing the role of language in learning from purely psychological models, bilingual and mainstream teachers are not being prepared to understand the important role that language plays in the formation of self, and we perpetuate existing social and educational inequalities. This constitutes a serious problem at a time when Latino youth, especially males, are an endangered species.

These understandings are especially important at this historical juncture when there are signs that the growing Latino presence is altering the dynamics of power in interesting ways. In our free-market economy, producers of goods and services are paying close attention to the Latino community, and the competition for the huge profits that are at stake is affecting access to print in Spanish. This is evident in the strategic (instrumental) use of Spanish in the media and the wide assortment of products and services specifically targeted at Latinos.

> Some of the most important television and radio transmissions in the Spanish language originate in the United States. There is a vigorous daily, weekly, and monthly Spanish-language press. The importance of books in Spanish is growing rapidly, and some major American publishers are starting to print Spanish-language novels, essays, and works of nonfiction. (Falcoff, 1996, p. 14)

This surprising change in the treatment of Spanish in the media, and therefore in the public domain, may already be affecting the status and economic value attached to Spanish (and bilingualism) among both those who are members of the Latino community as well as those who are not. Because schools are the mirrors of society, attention to the Spanish language in out-of-school settings has implications for the use of Spanish in schools. For students who typically do not recognize themselves in school texts, the societal curriculum may yet emerge as a powerful and positive learning vehicle in ways that we have yet to imagine. This may play a decisive role in the use of Spanish in schools, particularly in mainstream English settings.

References

Falcoff, M. (1996, May 17). North of the border: The origins and fallacies of the "Hispanic" threat to the United States (Commentary). *The Times Literary Supplement, 4859*, 14–15.

Heath, S. B., & McLaughlin, M. (Eds.). (1993). *Identity in inner-city youth.* New York: Teachers College Press.

Hernandez Cruz, V. (1991). *Read beans.* Minneapolis: Coffee House Press.

Hornberger, N. (1989). Continua of biliteracy. *Review of Educational Research, 59*(3), 271–296.

Hornberger, N. (1990, Spring). Creating successful learning contexts for biliteracy. *Penn Working Papers in Educational Linguistics, 6*(1), 1–20. Philadelphia: University of Pennsylvania.

Mercado, C. I. (1998). When young people from marginalized communities enter the world of ethnographic research: Scribing, planning, reflecting, sharing. In A. Egan-Robertson & D. Bloome (Eds.), *Students as researchers of culture and language in their own communities* (pp. 69–92). Cresskill, NJ: Hampton Press.

Newkirk, T. (1997). *The performance of self in student writing.* Portsmouth, NH: Boynton Cook/Heinemann.

Valdés, G. (1991). *Bilingual minorities and language issues in writing: Toward profession-wide responses to a new challenge* (Tech. Rep. No. 54). University of Berkeley, Center for the Study of Writing.

Zentella, A. C. (1997). *Growing up bilingual.* Malden, MA: Blackwell.

CHAPTER 11

Reading Adolescents/ Adolescents Reading

Toward Critically Literate Latino Youth

ROBERTA MALDONADO

A few days ago I directed my eighth-grade Title I reading students to choose one of several options for how to spend their 45-minute period. They could work on their end-of-the-year research papers on U.S. society or complete a webbing and writing activity describing the five main characters in the play we had just completed, *A Raisin in the Sun* (Hansberry, 1958). If they were already caught up with these, they could ask for help with any other content area reading, writing, or studying they needed to do for finals week. One student called out, "Miss, can I get help with *anything* I need to write?" Something in his tone prevented me from what might have been a knee-jerk response that I was quite certain he wasn't yet finished with the required class assignments, but that once he was I would be glad to help him with something extra.

Instead, I took a breath and asked, "What is it, Carlos?" A motion of his head signaled that he wanted to speak to me in confidence. When I got to his desk, he silently pointed to the paperwork for a court hearing, indicating a section of the page outlining the terms of his participation in the city's "diversion" program, an alternative to lockup in juvenile detention. We spent the next 20 minutes drafting a formal letter of apology for his having stolen a camera, wherein we covered letter-writing conventions, the use of transition words, how to avoid redundancy by the use of synonyms, and even how to create a voice expressing sincerity and integrity. A pretty full lesson, I'd say, but would it fulfill district standards?

I am a middle school Title I literacy teacher in a suburban school district that, like many other districts around the country, is experiencing a growth spurt in its ethnic minority population due to ongoing immigration, both documented and undocumented, from Mexico. Some of the city's Mexican immigrant residents have been here for as many as 17 years, or long enough to see their grandchildren reach school age. However, most of the children born in the United States have close relatives across the border, and they commonly travel with their families to and from Mexico several times a year. As Mexican students achieve English proficiency, they maintain their Spanish language with the support of the district's dual-literacy bilingual program. The students have strong emotional ties to Mexico and enjoy their visits there. Nonetheless, if asked, many of my students will say they identify as both Mexican and Chicano.

As someone who plays the dual role of middle school literacy practitioner and doctoral student-researcher, and who in both cases focuses on issues of educational equity, I've been privy to the latest buzzwords, paradigms, and shake-ups that schools and the academy, respectively, promote. It is significant, I think, that my experience and knowledge as a Chicana fail to win me any extra credibility or authority, let alone status, in either the school system or the academy. Nonetheless, my cultural identity is a ballasting constant, in teaching as in life. Spread across two decades, three states, two countries, and eight elementary and secondary schools, my teaching experience coalesces with my ethnic worldview, sociolinguistic background, and subsequent political stances they have helped shape over 44 years of living. Brought together, these inform an eclectic teaching philosophy that picks and chooses, sifts through the experientially tried-and-true, and culls the district teaching standards for what I believe my predominantly Mexican immigrant and Chicano students need *at that moment.*

Foundations, Scaffolds, and Constructivism

In this chapter I discuss how and why my approach to literacy often diverges from that of mainstream teachers or school district curricula. There may very well be something about being a Chicano culture member that gives me greater confidence and independence—the inner permission, or even the arrogance, some surely would say—to be true to my own standards, to listen to my conscience, and to trust my personal and professional experience before I go into a tailspin about the latest Latino educational crisis or jump on the newest theoretical bandwagon (Reyes, 1992). Whereas sometimes I find it is appropriate to favor the pragmatic over the fashionable, at other times a more radical approach is necessary. However, I have never operated on the principle that because my students are poor and Mexican, they "have nothing to lose," as it was put to me by a mainstream doctoral student defending an experimental "critical" curriculum (Giroux & Simon, 1988). I was appalled to hear this fresh version of the deficit theory (Flores, Cousin, & Díaz, 1991); the new liberal view characterizes poor urban and minority students as possessing so little of value that some so-called progressives feel they are performing an act of charity by making them guinea pigs (Delpit, 1988).

The presently favored constructivist model of teaching is one example of an egalitarian and pedagogically sound theory that can be applied casually with little productive effect. Self-described constructivist educators strive ideally to integrate school literacy experiences with students' real-world lives in meaningful and authentic ways. In this model, language development is assumed to naturally emerge out of a combination of old and new knowledge, encouraging and validating diverse notions of what it means to be literate. My concern is that in today's heterogeneous classrooms constructivist curriculum risks haphazardness unless we remember that any sound construction also requires careful evaluation of the times, locations, and opportunities to build. Similarly, our students' skill levels need to be evaluated, the timing of instruction cannot be arbitrary, the classroom environment should be appropriately organized to facilitate learning, and teachers must be watchful for those "teachable moments" that indicate that a perfect learning opportunity is near at hand. Vygotsky (1978) termed this careful ordering of thoughtfully chosen parts, pedagogical "scaffolding." His mediating concepts address what common sense and physics dictate about structures being built from the ground up, with each level having the capacity to support greater and greater weight. I've found that my students need individual help building the weight-bearing connections between the familiar and the strange. They require firm guidance if they are to successfully negotiate the many possible dimensions of meaning, and they need direct instruction about how to handle the more complicated kinds of expressive tools useful for explaining complex new experiences.

There is good reason that so many of our educational metaphors refer to how things are built. To extend the metaphor even further, educators, like builders, should strive ultimately toward structural integrity, the prerequisite of which is laying a firm foundation. Any builder worth her salt must know the full range of the trade's methods, materials, and conditions in all their possible combinations. In this way, teaching and learning, like construction, proceed in what I term an "organically systematic" way.

Two-Way Background Knowledge

Being competent and current regarding the most effective teaching methodologies and materials is insufficient, then, without an attendant understanding of the "conditions" that underlie a student's potential for learning. Ironically, while literacy teachers direct their students to activate their background knowledge to help them make sense of text, they themselves often lack sufficient background knowledge about the text of their students' daily lives. It is simply imperative that *two-way* background knowledge exist between classroom teachers and their adolescent students of color (see Chapter 1). I hope that for Carlos I managed to seize a teachable moment and mediate a literacy experience that was both authentic as well as skill building. I was able to make what might seem like a spontaneous decision, having worked with this particular student and his family for 3 full years. But perhaps to an even further extent, I made it based on my own experience of seeing nephews and Chicano/a friends' children ensnared in the juvenile court maze. Over the 5 years that I've taught at my present site, I've learned that almost all of my students presently have or have had brothers, uncles, cousins, and fathers involved in the penal system. It is not a reassuring statistic, but ignoring it to give children pep talks about how we are preparing them for the inevitability of college and career only heightens their sense of futility and mistrust. Better that we make every effort to acknowledge the disturbing but pivotal facts of students' actual lives (Giroux, 1987).

Living Literacy

I recently taught a critical literacy unit based on several adapted and leveled versions of Victor Hugo's *Les Misérables* (1862/1989) and discovered a rich vein for students' reading, discussion, writing, and reflection. Again, my curriculum went against the popular "best practices" grain of letting reluctant readers choose their own reading material (Reyes, 1992). Instead, I granted myself the role of "expert" because I had a good idea and a strong hunch that the right approach would engage the children. I suggested to them that after we read the novel, we might be able to see a professionally mounted production of the play at the most elegant theater in Denver, and I promised that we definitely would watch the recent movie based on the story. They took up the challenge. I never made the goal of the unit to finish reading the novel, although many of the students did. Truthfully, I didn't talk much about reading at all. Instead, I approached

Les Misérables thematically, probing questions of good and bad choices, of morally defensible social transgressions, of the possibility of reform, of the development of personal integrity, of social justice.

We were able to go see the play, thanks to the city's Youth Services Division and the help of my school's community liaison, and the majority of the students returned from the excursion glowing. They felt great that they had been able to follow the musical (and that they had sat in $40 seats!). They recognized the Broadway version of Jean Val Jean as overly prissy and not true to the complexity of the character they'd gotten to know through the novel, while the stylized barricade scene where Gavroche was killed and the unexpectedly humorous portrayal of the despicable Thenardiers met with their approval. These they compared with the treatment given them in the movie, further showing their appreciation of the stylization inherent in theater as opposed to the stark realism possible in film. For example, they were impressively alert to how the set designers produced the visual effect of the churning river Seine where Javert leapt to his death. Of course, they would not have caught any of this without having first understood what they had read. In other words, in addition to merely "reading the word," they evolved into enthusiastic, sophisticated critics fully capable of "reading the world" (Freire & Macedo, 1987).

Despite a supervisor's concern that the students were probably just "picking up on my enthusiasm" about a novel that was over their heads, and that they might be better served by focusing on explicit reading strategies, I consider this unit to have been a success. What are the chances an adolescent will voluntarily pick up a Victor Hugo novel, given the tempting options of countless easy, photo-studded celebrity biographies, or 30 thin books in R. L. Stein's popular "Goosebumps" series? How could such a layered literacy experience as the one we had possibly be compared with an equal amount of time spent on cloze exercises and other "direct" reading instruction? Which activity provides for the most authentic and holistic understanding (Goodman, 1992) of the purposes, ways, and kinds of reading in which highly literate people engage? And in the end, which will render the most transferable skills to the widest possible spectrum of living and learning circumstances? (See also Chapter 12.)

Classics, Culture, Content, and Critique

Designing the *Les Misérables* unit, I was fully conscious of its potential for expanding the students' cultural capital (Bernstein, 1990) as well as for boosting basic literacy skills. In fact, I do not believe that they can or should be separated in our literacy curricula. The background knowledge that students are told to apply to text is, in effect, the use of cultural capital. Only with large amounts of cultural capital are we able to buy our passage through accurate and efficient textual interpretation, from properly defining a single word, to vividly visualizing descriptions of setting and character, to grasping the thematic sweep of a book.

Ethnic- and linguistic-minority children often are wrongly assumed to lack the cultural capital/background knowledge necessary for deciphering more difficult texts, when the reverse is logically true. As bicultural, bilingual, and biliterate persons, they may indeed have at least twice as much knowledge to bring to bear on their narrative and expository reading (see Chapters 1, 6, and 10). A large part of my work as a literacy teacher is recognizing connections and anticipating gaps between what students and authors know. Authors have the prerogative of addressing a universal audience— themselves, their contemporaries, their enemies (real and imagined) or their beloved—but young students bring only themselves and their personal trunk full of still rather fresh memories to the text. I need to understand the time and setting of, as well as the author's intention for, whatever I have my students read. In this way I may not only help them make meaning of the text before them, but help guide that meaning to the greater demands of life's more elusive and convoluted text. That is why it seemed best to read aloud and discuss a challenging but beautifully insightful chapter in *Les Misérables* describing some seedy underworld characters. With some contextualization, the students were able to see that these were a nineteenth-century French version of today's gangbangers, and they could easily relate to the staggering social pressures under which Jean Val Jean labored to genuinely reform and become his own man. In her teaching, Ciriza Houtchens (see Chapter 12) also found the "homies" capable of thematically relating to a character as unlikely as Heathcliff of *Wuthering Heights*.

If I have struggling students reading "classics," it is hardly because I subscribe to hegemonic notions of "cultural literacy" (Hirsch, 1987). Today cognitive domains, all with their own specialized lexicon, are multiplying exponentially and clamoring for our attention. Which representatives from what fields should legitimately determine what must count as essential knowledge for the new millennium? To me, the question is not so much what must be included in the new canon, but rather what can we afford to exclude? When I teach *Les Misérables* I know that my students are getting important insights into world history and European culture—topics they are bound to revisit later in high school. I have nothing against fortifying students' cognitive networks in the hopes of improving their chances of future academic success (Chamot & O'Malley, 1994). However, just as important as our discussions of post-

Napoleonic France are those about the social construction of an unwed mother.

I also have students read the play and view the original movie, *A Raisin in the Sun*, at roughly the same time they are studying the civil rights period in eighth-grade U.S. society class. Briefly, this masterfully crafted play (a contemporary "classic," many would argue, which happens to have been written by a Black playwright, Lorraine Hansberry) is about an extended family whose members have a variety of sometimes conflicting dreams about how to improve their life conditions. It beautifully highlights the intersection between the personal and the political. An interesting side note is that the playwright came under fire from more radical Black nationalist groups for her moderate, acculturated views—unfair criticism that no doubt was expressed most loudly by those who had failed to read or understand Hansberry's multiple messages, and aggravated by a Black power movement dominated by males.

Thus, I use the play to illustrate the era's salient topics of segregation versus integration, the Black power movement, and the growing ethnic pride of diverse cultural groups (which not too surprisingly remain quite abstract notions to students, despite numerous readings, discussions, and films in U.S. society class). I also use the more nuanced concepts of assimilationism, minority upward mobility, sexism within radical parties, standard English forms versus ethnic dialects, cultural worldview, and early minority exclusion from the arts and entertainment industries. In addition, I use the play to teach the ostensibly benign but insidious forms of racism that people of color must prepare themselves to encounter whenever we attempt to shatter the glass ceiling. I take the opportunity to speak of my own family's difficult history of integrating schools and neighborhoods, of my father's monumental and ultimately successful effort to become a doctor, and of my personal battle against my family's and my culture's limiting gender roles during the 1950s, 1960s, and 1970s.

Of course, I don't cover this much terrain expecting that the students will memorize or even understand it all. But along with supporting their content learning, teaching them how to approach a new written genre, giving them a better idea of characterization, and allowing me to coach their oral reading, the unit exposes students to important vocabulary, vital ideas, and interconnected events that eventually should became part of any well-educated citizen's academic as well as life understanding. While I do use literature that fits acceptably into the canon, at every opportunity I point out how the text inherently subverts and questions, and how it upholds dominant ideas of manifest destiny and meritocracy.

The "Other" Skill: Reading Critically

An enjoyable activity that I like to plan around the Thanksgiving holiday familiarizes more recent immigrants with the occasion's historical roots, while it allows explicit modeling of critical literacy strategies. I bring to class volume "T" from several encyclopedias published over 3 decades. We do a comparative reading, picking out descriptive words and observing the semantic structures that lend each version a different emphasis. Through the years of editorial revisions, Native Americans' role in the first Thanksgiving has become increasingly foregrounded, illustrating how perceptions of "self" versus "other" (in this case, "other" being the Native Americans written about by White scholars) are historically embedded. We discuss the awesome power of language and how subtle shades of meaning can be used to direct our learning and manipulate our thinking. I complete the period by reading from the children's book *Guests*, by Native American writer Michael Dorris (1994). In this lovely telling of the first Thanksgiving from the Native American point of view, an angry adolescent boy, Moss, resents the preparations and accommodations being made by his tribe for the arrival of their English guests. He nags his parents to explain why they tolerate such an intrusion and feel obligated to help the awkward strangers. He is answered by his father:

> "Because. They are hungry." He wiped his forehead with the back of his hand and looked around, hoping someone would come by to interrupt us.
>   "We've been hungry before," I reminded him. "Nobody invited us to come ruin *their* only-once-in-a-whole-year special day."
>   "Don't you wish that during those times someone *had* invited us? Moss, it's simply the proper thing to do."
>   . . . I tried one last appeal to my father. "These people are not our relatives. . . . We can't talk with them because they speak a language no one but they understand. They make me uncomfortable with their oddness." (pp. 8–9, 11)

Good teachers will see no end of built-in chances for teaching minilessons here, including rule-breaking stylistic literary devices, dialogue, the use of italics and hyphens, contractions, synonyms, homonyms, and so on (see Chapter 8). However, the chance to point out the relativeness of "other" is, to me, irresistible. Reading literature is ideally a multidimensional experience, and, in my perception, skills are merely the means for accessing the deepest levels of meaning. Children learn to perform the act of reading competently by absorbing and applying a long list of necessary conventions. They fall in love with reading and choose to do it again and again because something they have read intrigued, thrilled, awakened, mystified, or scared them (Coles, 1989; McGinley et al., 1997; Nussbaum, 1991; see also Chapter 12). Finally, by being directed to and guided through carefully chosen texts and by having critical reading of those texts explicitly modeled for them by sociopolitically conscious teachers, they gain metacognition of literacy's powerful ripple effect in their lives.

The Stealthful Strategist

I should clarify that I often use only excerpts from longer works of literature, selecting for interest, narrative continuity, and thematic relevance. While teaching *Les Misérables*, for example, I was careful to have students skip parts of the novel that I knew would be too confusing or boring, and that would not necessarily add to their overall comprehension or appreciation of the story. Similarly, *A Raisin in the Sun* has scenes that for more mature readers add detail and texture, but that would be frustrating and superfluous reading material for my students.

Using this strategy, last year I had my seventh-grade students read portions of Victor Martínez's prize-winning novel, *Parrot in the Oven: Mi Vida* (1996), paying special attention to a chapter entitled "The Rifle" that I compared with pieces of a Gary Paulsen novel, *The Rifle* (1995). Martínez's largely autobiographical novel tells the straightforward coming-of-age story of Manny, a young adolescent Chicano in northern California. "The Rifle" is the novel's climax, relating what happens following the arrest of the protagonist, Manny's father, for domestic violence and possession of a firearm. Curious as to why his father, now released from jail, would have spent $150 on legal fees to win back a $50 rifle and wondering "why he loved it so much" (p. 99), Manny takes the loaded rifle out of the closet where it's hidden. The rifle accidentally goes off, coming within inches of killing the little sister Manny is supposed to be baby-sitting.

I scheduled this novel around the time that Victor Martínez would be coming to a local book fair to do a reading and arranged for my students to attend the event. During the reading, which was held in a noisy, bustling convention center, the antsy children talked, fidgeted, flirted, signed to children from other schools, and did what middle schoolers do best: They made a point of deliberately ignoring all the adults, including Martínez. After the reading, I made my own point of letting the students see me approach Martínez just to chat casually with him and to have him autograph two books, one each for my personal and class libraries. I knew they were watching me. Then I collared a boy who lately had been getting in loads of trouble at school and asked him in Spanish, "Hey, do you want to meet a real writer?"

He was astounded, suddenly shrinking several inches and turning into a meek, shy child. "Can I really do that?" he asked. So I introduced the writer and the student, and they proceeded to have a conversation, the boy asking Martínez questions in his dominant language of Spanish, while Martínez visited pleasantly with his boyish admirer in English. When the student rejoined me, he had a dreamy look in his eyes, and his exact words were, "I've never met a *Mexican* writer before."

One year later, during a free reading period, another "trouble-making" student who had attended the same book fair and seemed not to have paid much attention to the author's reading, asked if he could borrow the signed class copy of *Parrot in the Oven*. I was amazed that he remembered I had it. Something about the way he held that paperback book during free reading time throughout the weeks gave me goose bumps. Attention is as attention does. What we expose children to matters in the long run, although sometimes it takes a patience-taxing eternity to see any results.

Discussion

I have shared some things I do and will try to continue doing in my classroom because, by my standards, they work. I say, "will try to do," as I feel increasing pressure from all sides to align my personal standards to those of norm-referenced tests and state-mandated curricula. I'm expected to devote myself to reducing dropout rates, and to transform problematic youth into eager, academically acculturated students, or "school boys and girls" in their own typecasting language of resistance.

As a Chicana, I've been disregarded, condescended to, and feared in educational and employment settings. These experiences only make me more anxious to hasten Latino adolescents' acquisition of much beyond basic literacy skills. After all, despite always having been one of the better English readers and writers in my classes from kindergarten through graduate school, the simple fact of my being literate has never shielded me from racial and gender discrimination. If anything, it has been through reading that I've learned why institutionalized inequities will remain a ubiquitous presence in my lifetime. Only with the personal guidance of many enlightened thinkers and by becoming a *critical* reader with the help of a few teachers, have I learned the language, concepts, and theories that give shape and purpose to my anger, that renew my faith in pressing forward no matter what. There can be no doubt that given all this, I teach differently. I would like to think that with each passing year I instruct from a position of greater "political and ideological clarity" (see Chapter 3). Fueled by my belief that education is not a neutral proposition, many of my goals for the students are bound to diverge from those of my mainstream peers, even those who consider themselves especially culturally sensitive.

In my district there are a number of non-Latino teachers who are, to their great credit, completely bilingual in English and Spanish. But to their claims that they are bicultural just by virtue of their dual-language abilities and their work with Latino students, I once emotionally blurted out, "No, you are not." One woman defensively complained, "You seem to be saying that we need to have suffered to be bicultural." Although I would never recommend gratuitous suffering as a means of gaining cultural access, the very word "minority" confirms that firsthand experience of marginalization is part and parcel of being one. Being a person of color is not an intellectual exercise but a lifetime of hurts and offenses suffered in a country historically wrested from or forced upon us. Being a person of color is about finding ways to survive with dignity during the long forced march to the less bountiful edges of this land of plenty.

Authentic cultural membership in any group is achieved through initiation and invitation, and the privilege it affords is extremely explicit and bounded. Although I spent over a year living and working in Colombia, South America, where I spoke only Spanish dotted with local idioms, socialized exclusively with Colombians, and learned to do the cumbia like a native, I am in no way Colombian. If anything, what I learned during my time immersed in Colombian culture is how very Mexican I am. However, whenever I go to Mexico, I'm reminded how Chicana I am. I began to learn about such subtle cultural distinctions among Latinos as a child traveling across the border, where I first heard the disparaging word *pocha* applied to me as a limited-Spanish-speaking, American-born Mexican. Ironically, when I lived in South America I became a *gringa*, a term that I had grown up thinking had racial rather than national significance. Working through confusing issues of identity was just one aspect of the complicated rite of passage I survived in order to *evolve* into a Chicana.

I do confidently declare bicultural status, yet I realize that being a lifelong product of U.S. public schools and having English as my first language, having had a family that achieved the American dream of residence in middle-class neighborhoods and attendance at elite colleges and universities, and having been a student who possessed an unusual passion for all things language-related, I am sometimes incomprehensible to my students and their parents, much as I may look like one of them. I can attribute it to generational, class, national, or regional peculiarities, or simply to the mongrel mix of Spanish that I speak. The point is that even possessing all the hallmarks of a genuine Chicana, I am always painfully aware of needing to constantly qualify and earn my cultural standing in what has become an increasingly amorphous, complex "community" of Hispanos. I must account for and accommodate some undeniable differences between me and many of my students, most of whom are recent immigrants from rural or border-town Mexico during the mid-1980s. Of course, I recognize a great deal of myself in them, physically, linguistically, and culturally, but perhaps an even greater number of differences beg to be noticed.

Specialized teaching credentials merely give us tools and, hopefully, a more compassionate outlook about all students' diverse educational needs. Yet endorsements alone will not magically transform individuals who are at core ethnocentric and fearful of baring themselves to the unknown. I have heard too many alarmingly ignorant statements coming out of the mouths of "well-prepared" teachers to believe that. I continually make mistakes myself. We do not learn a new culture in the classroom or between the pages of a book, but in homes, at dinner tables, while doing the hard work of becoming functioning parts of dynamic communities. Still, more than ever it seems incumbent upon students and their families to adjust to the school's needs, not the other way around.

As the literature on how teacher beliefs affect teacher practices multiplies (Hollingsworth, 1989; Holt-Reynolds, 1992; Powell, 1992; Sleeter, 1994), research on teacher reflection has shown that we are no more predetermined as educators than we are as individuals (Wildman & Niles, 1987; Zulich, Beam, & Henick, 1992). If the roots of our cherished beliefs reside in our private thoughts and impressions, and the basis of our future acts abides in our beliefs, then our motivations can be examined and redirected. The growing disparity between student and teacher demographics (National Center for Education Statistics, 1995) can begin to be addressed through the cultivated habit of reflective teaching.

We must continually ask ourselves, "Who am I in relation to my students, and what do I have to offer them that is of real value to their present as well as to their future?" Finally, we must explore what we each believe holds intrinsic "value." I value independent thought over social status, ideas over things, my students over policies. Thus, I can summarize myself and my teaching by saying, I am a Chicana educator who teaches not to any test or standard, but to a belief that achieving high levels of literacy is important for more than getting a job. Being critically literate will help my students understand their historical place in the balance of power.

References

Bernstein, B. (1990). *The structuring of pedagogic discourse.* London: Routledge.

Chamot, A. U., & O'Malley, M. J. (1994). *The CALLA handbook: Implementing the cognitive academic language learning approach.* Reading, MA: Addison-Wesley.

Coles, R. (1989). *The call of stories.* Boston: Houghton Mifflin.

Delpit, L. D. (1988). The silenced dialogue: Power and pedagogy in educating other people's children. *Harvard Educational Review, 58*(3), 280–298.

Dorris, M. (1994). *Guests.* New York: Hyperion Books.

Flores, B., Cousin, P. T., & Díaz, E. (1991). Critiquing and transforming the deficit myths about learning, language, and culture. *Language Arts, 68*(5), 369–379.

Freire, P., & Macedo, D. (1987). *Literacy: Reading the word and the world.* South Hadley, MA: Bergin & Garvey.

Giroux, H. (1987). Critical literacy and student experience. *Language Arts, 64*(2), 175–181.

Giroux, H., & Simon, R. (1988). Schooling, popular culture and a pedagogy of possibility. *Journal of Education, 170*(1), 9–25.

Goodman, K. S. (1992). Why whole language is today's agenda in education. *Language Arts, 69*(5) 354–362.

Hansberry, L. (1958). *A raisin in the sun.* In L. A. Jacobus (Ed.), *The Longman anthology of American drama.* (pp. 447–489). New York: Longman English and Humanities Series.

Hirsch, E. D. (1987). *Cultural literacy: What every American needs to know.* Boston: Houghton Mifflin.

Hollingsworth, S. (1989). Prior beliefs and cognitive change in learning to teach. *American Educational Research Journal, 26*(2), 160–189.

Holt-Reynolds, D. (1992). Personal history based beliefs as relevant prior knowledge in course work. *American Educational Research Journal, 29*(2), 325–349.

Hugo, V. (1989). *Les misérables* (C. E. Wilbour, Trans.). New York: Fawcett Premier. (Original work published 1862)

Martinez, V. (1996). *Parrot in the oven: Mi vida.* New York: Harper Trophy.

McGinley, W., Kamberelis, G., Mahoney, T., Madigan, D., Rybicki, V., & Oliver, J. (1997). Re-visioning reading and teaching literature through the lens of narrative theory. In T. Rogers & A. O. Soter (Eds.), *Reading across cultures: Teaching literature in a diverse society* (pp. 42–68). New York: Teachers College Press.

National Center for Education Statistics. (1995). *High school students ten years after a nation at risk.* Washington, DC: U.S. Department of Education, Office of Education Research and Improvement.

Nussbaum, M. C. (1991). The literary imagination. *New Literary History, 22*(4), 877–910.

Paulsen, G. (1995). *Rifle.* New York: Bantam Doubleday.

Powell, R. R. (1992). The influence of prior experiences on pedagogical constructs of traditional and non-traditional preservice teachers. *Teaching and Teacher Education, 8*(3), 225–238.

Reyes, M. de la Luz. (1992). Challenging venerable assumptions: Literacy instruction for linguistically different students. *Harvard Educational Review, 62*(4), 427-446.

Sleeter, C. E. (1994). Resisting racial awareness: How teachers understand the social order from their racial, gender, and social class locations. In F. Schultz (Ed.), *Multicultural education* (pp. 42–53). Guilford, MA: Duskin.

Vygotsky, L. S. (1978). *Mind and society: The development of higher psychological processes* (M. Cole, V. John-Steiner, S. Scribner, & E. Souberman, Trans. & Eds.). Cambridge, MA: Harvard University Press.

Wildman, T. M., & Niles, J. (1987, July–August). Reflective teachers: Tensions between abstractions and realities. *Journal of Teacher Education, 38*(4), 25–31.

Zulich, J., Beam, T. W., & Herrick, J. (1992). Charting stages of preservice teacher development and reflection in a multicultural community through dialogue journal analysis. *Teaching and Teacher Education, 8*(4), 345–360.

CHAPTER 12

Literacy Development of Latino Students

Using Our Present Realities to Shape Our Futures

BOBBI CIRIZA HOUTCHENS

I knew them the minute they swaggered into my room, Frankie, Joe, Ruby, Miguel, Myra, Hector, and the others (names are pseudonyms). Their stance and flat affect challenged other students, the system, and, most of all, me to try to teach them. These were the survivors, the ones the system had not yet devalued or destroyed. They either had someone at home who would kick their ass if they didn't come to school, or attendance was a term of their probation, or school was the safest place to go. They had outsmarted the system and were still here, these clever ones. They could all read, but were not readers. School had done a good job of teaching them to decode and bark words, but school had not shown them literature that reflected their lives, that touched their hearts. They wanted to know if I was going to force them to read more of that "boring stuff." Some had not even had enough time with that "boring stuff" to find the magic of literature that could transport them away from their lives and their troubles to a place of hope and peace.

Frankie was one of those extraordinary students. He showed up about once a week in my alternative English class, held after the regular school day for kids who couldn't quite make it in the "normal" school population. I can still see him hunched over a *Low Rider Magazine* at the back table, head shaved, carefully starched and pressed J. C. Penney T-shirt revealing "Lola" tattooed on his arm. Unacknowledged, I sat next to him, touched one arm, and asked "Who's Lola?" "My mom," he replied in his usual monotone, firmly focusing on the magazine in front of him, making it clear I was not welcome at his table.

This class was small, but the girls in all three classes were in dispute over who got to read the new book I had just bought, *Two Badges: The Lives of Mona Ruiz* (Ruiz & Bucher, 1997). I resolved the conflict by allowing one girl in each class to claim the book for herself by placing a bookmark in the place where she had left off. At the end of class, she was to leave the book on my desk, forbidden territory for all students except the girls with bookmarks. No one could take *Mona* home. This system worked until I was absent for 3 days and came back to find the book was gone. Needless to say, the privileged readers were angry and so was I. Then Frankie, late as usual, sauntered in. "Hey, Mrs. H., I like that book." "What book, Frankie?" "You know." And he pointed to the empty corner of my desk. "You lifted my book!" I nearly grabbed him. "Ah, don't be like that. I like it. Ya know, her life's like mine." Something at school finally had connected with Frankie. I had to negotiate with him to bring back the book. We agreed he could take *Mona* home daily after the dismissal bell, and return it before classes the following day to the corner of my desk if he wanted to keep reading it. He couldn't read it during class because the girls had it reserved. He agreed, and, for a change, Frankie started coming to school every day. I felt as if I'd won a small victory. He was, after all, a man of his word. And then, no more book; Frankie stopped coming. I made repeated trips to his house in a menacing neighborhood with threatening young men glaring at me as I got out of the car, until they found out I was Frankie's teacher. I discovered he had stayed home to protect his mother from an abusive old boyfriend, but promised to send the book daily when he couldn't come to school. That worked for a month or two and then he stopped coming altogether. I returned to the house and found he had been picked up for carrying a gun. Four months later, a letter arrived from Frankie (this and all student writing is presented in its original, unedited version).

> How are you doing Mrs. Houtchens? I'm just writing to let you know how I'm doing because I was thinking about when I was in your class. I know your class especially helped me. You helped me start to change alot but I kept myself down. I still got that book "Two Badges." When I got locked up in the hall, I started to think alot. I thought about the book and how Mona Ruiz didn't give up. So I didn't give up. I'm in School right now and I got to stay here for 14 months . . . I'm doing good, I keep my mind focus. I should take my GED test in 3 months

than after that I'll be working on my high school credits. I'm going to get my diploma so I could keep the book. I have not forgot our deal.

I know he will graduate. Frankie is, after all, a man of his word.

Background

Jail is certainly not the destination for all of my students, but life for most is a constant struggle. My urban high school is in a progressively deteriorating neighborhood in the center of San Bernardino, California. More than 60% of the students qualify for free lunch, meaning that their families live at or below the federal poverty level. The student population is fairly diverse: 57% Latino, 15% Black, 20% White, and 8% Asian, American Indian, South Pacific Islander, and Middle Eastern. The Mexicano/Latino population consists of students whose families have lived here for generations, many arriving to work on the Santa Fe Railroad in the 1930s, as well as those who have arrived since, including 500 very recent immigrants who speak little or no English. Our school motto, "The Very Best," speaks strongly of our high expectations for all students, regardless of their backgrounds.

Dropout statistics clearly reflect the lack of relevancy that schools have had for most Latinos. Schools do a good job of teaching Latino students to decode written text, but fail in the areas of developing comprehensive literacy and an academic consciousness. Reading and reflecting on that reading is one way to help shape the critical consciousness of adolescents, but only if the reading grabs the students' interests by reflecting their realities (Freire, 1970). When a culture becomes too large and too decentralized for oral tradition to transmit cultural values, the culture breaks down and its children become lost. This is happening in the neighborhoods where my students live. Through literacy, cultures become more cohesive because reading disseminates values and connectedness to its members, providing youth with direction and hope. By developing literacy in my students and helping them to find connections to literature that inspire them and give them direction, I hope to prevent losing some of them to the streets.

The staff at San Bernardino High School is very concerned about the high dropout rate and the general perception of ineligibility of Mexicano/Latino students to even qualify to apply to the 4-year college system, and then to succeed in the university if they are accepted. As part of our remedy, we eliminated all remedial and average classes. Our courses are now mostly college preparatory and honors, raising the stakes for both the school and the students. But major problems remain.

Most of the students entering my ninth-grade, college-prep English classes hate reading, have never owned a book of their own, have no books other than the Bible at home, and read at around the fifth- or sixth-grade level. Most believe that a good reader is someone who knows how to pronounce all the words on a page correctly. They are still stuck at the word level, seldom seeing "mental movies" when they forget the words on the page and visualize the story in their heads, losing track of time. I know that if they are going to make it beyond ninth grade, their reading levels and attitudes toward literacy must change. Based on current sociopsycholinguistic reading theory (Goodman, 1982) and the sociocultural theory of teaching/learning (Vygotsky, 1978), I started the Cardinal Reading Program. The entire English department currently is implementing some form of it.

Organizing for Success

At the beginning of the year, I administer a reading survey to all my ninth graders. The survey confirms what I already know about them: They have never read enough to fall in love with literature. After brainstorming about why reading is important in our lives, I break the news: They must all read for 30 minutes a night, every night of the school year. They may read novels, biographies, autobiographies, or other extended stories. I want them to become involved over time with stories and characters. There is no time off for holidays, birthdays, funerals, or illnesses. If they miss reading one night, they must make it up the next night. If they miss half an hour of reading in the semester, they will fail English. If they read 30 minutes every night during the semester, the worst grade they will receive in my class is a D. I tell them I'm so serious, that if, God forbid, they should get into a horrible motorcycle accident and end up in a coma in the hospital, they can still pass my English class if their parents will read to them daily and let me know about it. I tell them that even the doctors will recommend reading to stimulate their brain, that reading is so powerful that it can save their lives. None of my students are initially as excited about this program as I am. To reach the levels I expect from them, I know I must organize their learning so that they all meet success.

Because most of my students are inexperienced readers, they must learn and practice most skills that accomplished readers have. A critical first skill is where to locate good books, so we brainstorm about possibilities. The students always mention neighborhood stores, the mall, libraries, friends, family, and my classroom. A few years ago at one of many conferences I attend, Stephen Krashen told me that if adolescents have books within arm's reach, they will read, so I found a discarded paperback book carousel for my room and filled it with at least 300 donated paperback books. Students can take and return any of these paperbacks as they like. In addition, I spend $1,000 each year buying books by and about Latinos, immigrants, sports, and other topics that might be of interest to my students. Some are popular adult books, some are young adult books, and some are wonderful children's books. These books are on separate shelves in my room and students are free to check them out in an honor library system.

After we have exhausted our list of places to find books, we discuss how to discover if a book is worth reading. They all know to look at the cover and to read the title. Most don't know to read the back cover, the inside book flaps, and the first two or three pages before deciding. After discussing these simple previewing techniques, I put a stack of books on each table, pulling heavily from my special books, at a variety of reading levels, and ask my students to preview them. This takes half of the period. At the end of the period, they share their discoveries with the class. Not so incredibly, many find a book they might like to read. Then I let them in on an amazing secret—good readers don't always finish every book they start. I give them permission to abandon a book if they find one that is inappropriate, too hard, uninteresting, or offensive, or if their parents would find it objectionable. From now on, the books they choose to read for this program are up to them.

Their first question is, "How many pages do we have to read every night?" This, of course, varies with each book and each student's reading ability. That's why I prefer to have them read for 30 minutes. To give them an idea of the intensity with which I expect them to read, however, I have them read for 10 minutes in a book of their choice. This number is noted in their journals. We then count pages and multiply the number by three. This gives us both an idea of their capabilities and my expectations for their nightly homework.

In order to keep track of their reading, the students keep a reflective journal while they read. They keep a log in the back of their journals of the books they have read and abandoned. At the top of each page in the journal, they note the date, the times they start and stop reading, as well as the page numbers where they start and stop. In about 5 or 6 lines, I ask them to summarize what they have read. Before they can do this, we practice summarizing in class, because many of them think that summarizing means copying directly from their books. After the summary, I ask that they reflect on their reading. Of course, we also must practice this, and I use the five strategies for active reading defined in our literature text: predicting, connecting, questioning, clarifying, and evaluating. To provide a scaffold or a structure for their reflections, I provide sentence starters for the type of reflections I would like to see in their journals. Some of these include "I think that _____ is going to happen because . . ."; "This character re-minds me of myself because . . ."; "I wonder what _____ meant when he said _____. Maybe he thought _____." Stu-dents are expected to write in their journals every day while they read or immediately afterward. Journal writing should take them no more than 10 or 15 minutes.

Every Friday, the students bring their novels and completed journals to class. They read silently all period. Of course, few students in class are able to sustain their reading more than 10 minutes when we first start the program, so we discuss avoidance behaviors, such as falling asleep, needing to go to the bathroom or to get a drink of water, making noise, writing notes, daydreaming, and so forth. We also compare reading with athletics, how when training to run a mile for the first time, we often want to stop; we get pains in our sides or are too out of breath to continue. If we give up, we never get into shape. We know that to get into shape, we should not stop, but should slow down, walk for a while, and then continue running. If we do this every day, we will get a little better. We discuss how developing physi-cally is just like developing habits of the mind. They both take practice and self-discipline. I tell them that if they find themselves engaging in avoidance behaviors, to recognize them for what they are, look away from the book for a few minutes, and then continue reading. It's the best way to get their flabby brains in shape and to improve their reading.

To motivate them even more, I share their previous year's standardized test scores in reading and language and discuss with them what the scores mean. Most are discouraged, but I promise them a marked improvement if they will follow the program for just this school year. Those who do follow the program for the entire year have always shown great improvement.

While the students read silently on Fridays, I read and grade their jour-nals. I usually have time to conference with them about their books and journal entries. In addition, I can spend time with the most reluctant read-ers, discussing their interests and their past histories with reading, and rec-ommending books they might enjoy.

At the beginning of the year, I ask the students to estimate how many books they think they can read during the school year if they read 30 min-utes every night. Their estimates range between one and ten. By the end of the first semester they have all surpassed their estimates, reading between 15 and 36 books by June.

This reading program is merely a supplement to the regular curricu-lum. We still read stories from our anthology and novels on the recom-mended core, as well as *Romeo and Juliet.* The students are still responsible for other homework in my class, mostly writing, comprehension, and re-search assignments.

The types of literature from which my students can select is important to their success. I make a concerted effort to buy as many novels and biographies by and about Latinos as I can find. These, for my students, are not more "boring stuff." If I can hook reluctant readers with these books and they can read enough to become fluent readers, then they usually expand their selections beyond books that reflect their own lives. Most of my students have seldom encountered Latinos with lives similar to theirs in the literature that they read at school. Latino students are not invisible in school; they should not be invisible in the literature to which we expose them. When students find themselves and their lives reflected in the books they are reading, their own lives become validated. What follows are excerpts from my students' journals as they discuss their reading choices. I have chosen *not* to edit their writing, in order to demonstrate the difference between their level of writing and their choices in reading, and also to retain the original flavor. These students' families are all of Mexican origin.

Student Voices

Ruby's grandparents immigrated to San Bernardino when they were young. Ruby, who began her academic career in San Bernardino in kindergarten, was the youngest of five children, and the only girl. I had taught several of her brothers and knew they were in a gang. Ruby's responses to Luis Rodriguez's *Always Running* (1994) included, "This guys life is too hard. My mom threw my brother out to live in the garage just like him cuz she didn't want his friends in her house. He was real stubborn too just like this guy in the book. My brother didn't learn nothing from that and now he's in prison." In another reflection she added, "I cant believe how good this guy writes about his barrio. You can realy tell how life is there and it sounds like where I live. I even know guys just like the guys he hangs with. They sound just like my brother's friends. I wish somebody would write about my barrio like this cuz I think there are interesting kinds of people there too." Ruby did start to write poetry and short stories about her barrio, but I don't know how her year turned out. A dangerous set of drive-by shootings on her house forced her father to move them in the middle of the night to a nearby community. I am sure, however, that Ruby's life will not go on as it did before *Always Running.* Rodriguez showed her that Latinos have powerful voices and helped her to find her own.

Salvador had been in the United States for only a couple of years, and I didn't believe that his English was advanced enough to read *Always Running* easily, but he prevailed. His life and response were much different from Ruby's. He wrote, "I was thinking that night about my life and Ramiro's life and I saw a very big difference for example: I like the school, sports. I like to work and I like my safe life . . . , I would like to study at the college or the University, and this book has helped me to give value to my life, my school, and my family." Books about real life can reaffirm even the lives of students who are not attracted to gangs. Salvador graduated this year and is heading to college to become a teacher.

Not all my students read about gangs. Myra, who recently immigrated alone to live with her father, was reading *Lupita Mañana* (Beatty, 1992). This young adult novel is about a young Mexican girl forced to look for work in the United States to help support her widowed mother. Since many of my students cross the border without documentation, they easily sympathize with Lupita. Myra wrote:

> Lupe is very upset in a problem she had to face. It was men being treated more highly than woman, and not them being treated equally. But life goes on and stuff happens! Lupe is very strong and stands up for what she believes in. She is very determined to achieve what men can, to let people see that women and men are equal. Sometimes this book makes me fill like crying. I get jealous when I read about Lupe and her mother when they talk because it looks so special. I would want to have that relationship with my mother that Lupe has with hers.

Myra connected with the dichotomies my immigrant students are forced to live: the cultural boundaries they must negotiate, as well as their longing for distant relatives and a desire for an education.

Hector, who had been in the United States for 7 years, is the type of student who is easily overlooked in most classrooms. He never called attention to himself, and his work first semester of his freshman year was, at best, mediocre. I felt he could do much better. After a long conversation with his mother, she agreed to have him complete his reading at the kitchen table while she prepared dinner. She speaks no English, so could not read over his work, but agreed to sign his journal every day after he had read his 30 minutes and written his reflections. Hector's grade and classroom participation improved throughout the second semester. Between March and June, he completed 15 novels. He abandoned *The Wedding* (West, 1995), finding it too difficult. Hector filled a spiral-bound notebook with his reflections, certainly more work than he had ever completed in one semester in his academic career. *Dogs of Illusion* (Alvarez, 1994) was the first book he read. He was so enthralled by this book that he could not keep it to himself. He and another equally reluctant reader spent their Friday silent reading periods outside my room in the hallway, reading the book aloud to each other.

As a result, they both started reading more. *Dogs of Illusion* is a graphic novel about two young Chicanos serving in Vietnam. This book was difficult for Hector, but he persevered because he found it engaging. When he finished this book, he selected other books about Latinos. While reading *The Secret of Two Brothers* (Beltrán Hernandez, 1995), Hector wrote, "I think that it is good to learn something about places like Mexico City like me I like to learn about the revolution & independence and I guant to learn about Hidalgo, Villa and Zapata." Of *The Old Man Who Read Love Stories* (Sepulveda, 1994), Hector wrote, "I think that it is good to have a dentist on the town because it helps like in the town of my that theres no dentist." From *Journey of the Sparrows* (Leeper Buss, 1993), Hector reflected, "I think that it is dangerous to be imigrating in a little truck you can die. Sometimes my dad pass in a car and in Tijuana they put persons in "La Cajuela." He also wrote:

> I think that Alicia must be sad of being in the migration. I know that because I have been their two times. The first one was with my mother and brother for five hrs. and the second one they caught me and my brother for 12 hrs. I was sad but happy too because my mom scape.

Hector often discusses what he finds different in the United States from his experiences in Mexico. About *Soccer Sam* (Marzollo & Sims, 1987), he wrote:

> I think that when you are in a knew contry you see games that you don't know and then you play and if you do something wrong they started to laft. I didn't know how to play handball but I wanted to play and sometimes I made some mistaiks and Olivar started to laft.

Hector chose young adult books before tackling a more challenging book, *Sacred Hoops* (Jackson, Delahanty, & Bradley, 1996). From this metaphorical book comparing basketball to life, he wrote, "I think that this book use good words that are like a poem and this is great so you can learn both." Hector continued to read a variety of books and even his attitude in class changed as his grade improved. His pride in becoming one of the most prolific readers in class carried over to his other academic subjects as well, and his mother noticed a less sullen attitude at home.

Not all the reading the students completed had positive effects. Sometimes feelings brought forth through the literature were uncomfortable reminders of the students' own past. Joe, a junior, was very quiet, a loner. He had low academic skills and poor self-esteem. When forced to read, he chose a young adult book about two Asian siblings trying to survive alone during a war. In his journal, he would quote a passage from the book and then respond. The burden of sorrows that life had given him became apparent in his responses, and in this book he found powerful reminders of his past. From the book: "I went back to work the following day. We had to methodically clear out the dense weeds that sprang up between the newly sown rice seedlings." His response: "When I had my last vacation I went to work with my brother-in-law. It was a hard job but I have to work hard so that my body can get used to it." The next day, he quoted: "My sister Naroven picked that moment to have an attack of malaria. Her teeth chattered and her whole body was shaking." He responded:

> I don't like to remember this things but I got to do it. I only want you to know this. . . . When I lived in Mexico I got sick of something that is similar to the malaria. I lost weight and I almost died. I remember that my mom took me to the doctor with just one vaccination I got cured. Since then I feel that my life changed. I hate to remember things from the past. Only bad and sad things happen to me.

From the book: "The day passed and then the next. Navreoun was still feverish and exhausted." Joe's response:

> I just feel that life hasn't been fair with me. Sometimes when I listen to music in Spanish, I remember the past and think of the present and the future. And the tears start coming from my eyes slowly. Especially when I think of my past.

The next day, he quoted: "He walked twenty-five kilometers on that road, a nightmare. One foot in front of the other." His response:

> This reminds me of the things my mom tells me and my brothers. That when she was little she suffered a lot. She didn't go to school cause her mom died when she was little. There wasn't enough food. And they didn't have clothes. I'm sorry just to write sad things but that's my life.

In his final entry, he quoted: "The harvest was almost over. What would they do with us?" His response: "Today I don't feel like writing. This book makes me remember things I don't want to remember." Tellingly, on the front cover of his journal, Joe had expertly drawn the smiling face of a court jester, superimposed over his first name, with a sparkling smile and a large tear coursing down his cheek.

Chuy, a freshman class clown who connected with *Bless Me Ultima* (Anaya, 1995), wrote:

> This story is like my life there parents worked hard in the fild and
> tring to make a living they moved over here for me to have a better
> to go to school and have a better education to have a better job. But
> where they live there is not that many people many schools for the
> children but they still work in the ranchos with the animals. I like
> this story. I like to work in the rancho and in the fild. I realy don't
> now why but I do. I like to work hard.

In discussing his reflection with him, I was able to help him see the connection between hard physical work and working hard in school.

Aída's appearance is deceiving. She wears the pencil-thin eyebrows and black outlined lips of a *chola* (Chicana gang member), and her father is said to demand respect by his tough appearance alone. She is a student who has a tough exterior but excellent academic capabilities. Aída devoured books about Chicanos and pestered me incessantly whenever she had exhausted my supply. While reading *Locas* (Murray, 1998), she commented:

> I would never gang bang like Cecilia, I'm not into that. I like the
> dress code that now the little cholos and little cholas wear but more
> than that I don't think so I don't do the drugs and throw barrios
> that's not me. I'm not a chola.

She discusses Manny, one of the protagonists, and how he dropped out of school to gang bang. She reflects: "I think that Manny is not getting anywhere he has ruined his life for good, If he keeps on going the way he is probably he is going to regret everything and you can't change the past. Even if you wanted to badly you just can't."

Other teachers have argued that letting students read novels about gangsters only lends credibility to the gang life and encourages students to join, but Aída's comments from this book include:

> I think that as for me I would like to be a gangster but now I under-
> stood that it doesn't bring you any good at all. A gang doesn't bring
> you an education, a good job. All it brings you is illegal things like
> selling drugs and all that and I understand that this ain't good.

Aída's reading choices continue to affirm that the gang life is not for her. *Homesick: My Own Story* (Fritz, 1982) is about a 10-year-old girl in China who is going to visit her grandmother in the United States. The ethnic hatred this young girl feels from her peers in China resonates in Aída's journal.

> And about that Bund. I think its mean, Not letting people come to that place. Well actually chinese and dogs. I guess what do they hear against Chinese. People call me chinese because I look like. And thats mean I think. . . . Jean is scare like me. I guess she is not that kind of girl who likes to fight. And this part its like me. But I don't skip school I just avoid them. I hope her problems go away.

Without this reflection, I would not have realized that Aída felt threatened by a group of girls at school; together we worked on solutions.

When he entered my class in February, Miguel had never read an entire book on his own. He lacked both skill and confidence. His first choice was an author's biography. He wrote:

> I started reading the book. I don't understand nothing of the first 8 pages that I read. The story simed lacke a autobiography about this guy named Robert Ervin Howard. It has big words that I cant understand lake cordiality, viviality, and sterile. Im going to start to read another book that I can understand.

The next day he continued:

> I curent find another book yet so I read another 5 pages. Im not shure, but its turning into a scary story. I still cant understand some words. I dout that it was going to be a story about a werewolf. Im going to start riding a eseer book.

Two months later, while reading a young adult book he never named, he wrote:

> Ive seen Death Ive been more closer to death than doctor and trust me you want to kill death when he takes one of your own lacke death touk David's little broder shust seeing hes mom cry he found out right afther he came from dance lessens he new something was up but he dirent pay much atenchun.

Miguel tried several additional "boring" books, until he found one that connected. He powered through this book, sometimes reading for 2 hours at a time. He identified with Linc, the protagonist, who was "Mexican so he is tuff." By June, Miguel had discovered that he enjoyed reading.

Not all of my Mexicano/Latino students chose books by or about Latinos, but the power of choice still influenced their reading. For example, Jorge, a shy but studious freshman, surprised me when I started reading his journal about a vaguely familiar, but unexpected, novel.

> Hindley is a jacked up man because he left his son, Hareton, a begger with no money or house. If I were Hareton I wouldn't slave for Heathcliff. . . . Heathcliff is nothing but a user and abuser because he don't even like Linton, he is just using Linton to get his revenge on Edgar and Isabela . . . I don't think its right for Cathy and Linton to marry because they are cousins. I wouldn't marry or date any of my cousins . . . . Cathy should listen to Edgar about the Wuthering Heights because she's just going to get herself in trouble.

I would never have chosen this novel for Jorge. I thought it too complex and above his reading level, but when he had the power to choose his own literature, he, like many others, went far beyond my expectations. Jorge was not alone.

Anita, another freshman, chose a non-Latino book and wrote about it in dialectical journal format. Her reflections include:

> I think she is compare herself to someone and she envy Amy. She thinks she's got the bad part other people get good part . . . I think her mother thinking what Jo is thinking, that is why she could understand Jo and rob her heart with her tenderest heart. . . . I think Meg is having fun life with her husband and children.

Anita used Alcott's *Little Women* (1868–69/1983) to inform her own knowledge about writing when she noted:

> Also I found out something in this sentences is that HE doesn't have to be capitalized but it is. I think the author wanted to make that word stand out strong. I've noticed she did couple more words in same way. . . . I think the author didn't like to say Beth is dead because I've noticed that says "Beth left the old home for the new" couple times in this chapter.

Even though Anita had been in the United States for 2½ years, reading *Little Women* was more than I would have recommended. Not only did her reading improve, but she used the author's style to inform her own writing. Once more, a student surpassed my expectations.

Conclusion

These few student samples demonstrate that students who previously may have been regarded as unproductive, unmotivated, and resistant to succeeding in school are capable of becoming active, engaged readers. The road to success is not easy, and I am very insistent that they participate, often forming alliances with parents to encourage the most reluctant. The rewards are apparent, however, as students analyze their changing reading habits, view the unpredicted list of novels they read, and review the amount of writing they have completed in their journals, often filling two spiral-bound notebooks.

Although becoming a good reader is not a life goal that many of my students cite in their first essay for my class, their excitement shouts from the pages of their journals when they finally see "mental movies." They know that this is a sign that they have crossed the threshold to becoming literate. As their teacher, I have refused to organize their academic studies at a low level. On the contrary, I believe that my role is to *expect more*, to organize for their potential, and to deliberately mediate their learning by providing them with structure to guide them. In doing so, I believe that they learn to respect and value themselves and their education. When given the power of choice over their reading selections, along with rich literature that reflects their own experiences, and support in achieving success, these students continue to surpass everyone's expectations of them.

Students like Frankie, Joe, Ruby, Miguel, Myra, and Hector will continue to swagger into classrooms, but beneath their swagger will lie the realization that literature is about them. I know I cannot prevent all of them from becoming lost to the streets, but their awakening literacy will prevail. The magic of literature will continue to reflect their lives, will help them escape their troubles and perhaps reveal solutions to their problems or the problems of their children.

References

Alcott, L. M. (1983). *Little women.* New York: Price Stern Sloan. (Original work published 1868–69)

Alvarez, H. (1994). *Dogs of illusion.* San Jose: Chusma House.

Anaya, R. (1995). *Bless me, última.* New York: Warner Books.

Beatty, P. (1992). *Lupita mañana.* New York: Morrow.

Beltrán Hernandez, I. (1995). *The secret of two brothers.* Houston: Arte Público Press.

Brontë, E. (1983). *Wuthering heights.* New York: Bantam Classics. (Original work published 1942)

Freire, P. (1970). *Pedagogy of the oppressed.* New York: Continuum.

Fritz, J. (1982). *Homesick: My own story*. New York: Putnam.

Goodman, K. (1982). *Language and literacy: The selected writings of Kenneth S. Goodman*. (F. Gollasch, Ed.; 2 vols.) London: Routledge.

Jackson, P., Delahanty, H., & Bradley, B. (1996). *Sacred hoops: Spiritual lessons of a hardwood warrior*. New York: Hyperion Books.

Leeper Buss, F. (1993). *Journey of the sparrows*. New York: Lodestar Books/Dutton.

Marzollo, J., & Sims, B. (1987). *Soccer Sam*. New York: Random House.

Murray, Y. M. (1998). *Locas*. Grove Press.

Rodriguez, L. (1994). *Always running: La vida loca: Gang days in L.A*. New York: Simon & Schuster.

Ruiz, M., & Bucher, B. (1997). *Two badges: The lives of Mona Ruiz*. Houston: Arte Público Press.

Sepulveda, L. (1994). *The old man who read love stories* (P. Bush, Trans.). New York: Harcourt Brace.

Vygotsky, L. S. (1978). *Mind in society: The development of higher psychological process* (M. Cole, V. John-Steiner, S. Scribner, & E. Souberman, Trans. & Eds.). Cambridge, MA: Harvard University Press.

West, D. (1995). *The wedding*. New York: Doubleday.

CHAPTER 13

It's About YOUth!

Chicano High School Students Revisioning Their Academic Identity

MARÍA E. FRÁNQUIZ

In a political environment hostile toward meeting the needs of linguistically and culturally diverse students, it is important to locate caring adults and students who are embracing the principles of a culturally relevant and socially responsible literacy approach to examining and transforming unjust learning conditions. From 1995 to 1999 I was involved with a particular community organization, It's About YOUth! (IAY)[1] My interest in the group was precisely because adults and youth together sought nonviolent ways to engage in actions that effectively linked knowledge from home, peer culture, and school. Making visible how literacy can be used to create possibilities for personal liberation (Freire, 1973; Shor & Freire, 1987), rather than domestication (Freire, 1973) or stupidification (Macedo, 1993), was the alternative vision that IAY offered to address the pervasive pushout rate of Chicano/Mexicano/Latino youth from high school.

The youth with whom I worked lived along the Front Range of the Rocky Mountains. They are all descendants of "*la gente*—literally, the people: i.e., *la raza*, Americans of Mexican descent, *Hispanos*, Spaniards, Mexicans, Mexican Americans, Latinos, Chicanos" (Longmont Hispanic Study, 1988, pp. 1–2). Their legacy has been tainted by many discriminatory acts against their families. These acts have been recorded in a collection of oral histories, *We, Too, Came to Stay* (Longmont Hispanic Study, 1988) by and for members of their local community. The realities of past racism toward relatives included the erection of an 8-foot cross by the Ku Klux Klan to remind Mexicans to be off the street by sundown, refusal to serve Mexican American World War II veterans in local bars, posting of "White Trade Only" signs on restaurant and shop windows, and the murder of two unarmed brothers-in-law by rookie police officers in 1980.

Grandparents and parents of the youth provide living testimonials of these events. One parent wrote down her recollections for an It's About YOUth! meeting. She wrote about the 1980 shootings:

> The two officers involved were sent home on paid leave until an investigation was done. The findings were that the officers were innocent. The U.S. Justice Department was called in because Louie and Beaver's civil rights had been violated. The two officers were put on desk jobs. They later left the police force. The families of Louie and Beaver filed a civil lawsuit against these officers and were awarded an out of court settlement for the deaths. It took about three years to find that a wrongful death had been committed. Through all this the Hispanic community united to bring changes to our town to get minority officers on the force and to have a person added to act as a go between for the citizens and police. It helped us to realize that by coming together changes can be made and people listen. (personal communication, October 1996)

A group of concerned Latinas/os formed in 1980 to address the concerns outlined by the parent above. *El Comité* helped the city avoid crisis due to heightened racial tension from the shooting incident. Since then the local newspaper keeps the memories of Beaver's and Louie's shootings alive by interviewing on a yearly basis members of *El Comité*, "the County's only Latino-run grassroots organization" (Glairon, 1999, p. 5B). Concerns of racism peaked when one of the police officers involved in the shootings joked to fellow officers, "Now I'm going to have to carve two notches in my gun" (p. 5B). Although *El Comité* asked for and received an outside evaluation of the police department that resulted in improvements, a former member reports: "It's probably the most courageous and most unappreciated group in the city" (Glairon, 1999, p. 5B).

Students in It's About YOUth!, and after-school program, were provided with effective literacy models that helped them develop a sociopolitical or critical consciousness. This was accomplished by access to the oral histories of *la gente*, access to an IAY parent's firsthand account of the murder of Beaver and Louie in 1980, and access to newspaper articles regarding *El Comité's* ongoing exposure of inadequate city-funded services to address the 7,800 Latina/o people it represents. Such a culturally relevant approach helped students understand, critique, and take a position regarding the inequities that local institutions perpetuated from one generation to the next (Ladson-Billings, 1995).

In this chapter, I examine how three culturally relevant projects under-taken by members of the after-school group helped the students re-vision the purpose of literacy in their lives. One was the construction of a film for public access television, the second was the construction of a mobile mural sculpture, and the final, the presentation of the mural to local, national, and international audiences.

Establishing a Relationship

As a teacher and researcher I was interested in learning about the con-ditions for Chicano youth and their families within the county where I was employed as a university professor. The director of teacher education sug-gested I meet the Chicana co-directors of It's About YOUth! In the fall of 1995, following our initial introductions, I was invited to attend youth meet-ings. With the consent of the directors and middle and high school students, I became a member of the advisory board for the group and began main-taining documentation of discussions and events. Soon I also began arrang-ing dialogues between the youth and my graduate students at the university on ways to effectively transform negative cultural stereotypes that outsiders and insiders of the Mexican community may hold.

My specific roles with It's About YOUth! varied. As a member of the board I participated in ongoing biweekly meetings to set agendas for weekly youth meetings. I also planned future social and educational activities for youth; assessed the need for future funding of group activities; arranged for facilitators, speakers, and trainers to participate in youth meetings; and wrote proposals to be presented at local and national conferences. As a researcher, I wanted to learn from "marginalized" students and their allies how cultur-ally relevant literacy projects influence or constrain the emergence, construc-tion, and reconstruction of students' social and academic identities.

Social identity includes social statuses, roles, positions, relationships and institutional and other relevant community identities an individual may claim or assign in the continuum of social life. Academic identity, or scholar ethos, refers to the definitions of scholar and scholarship that students develop to permit them to achieve academically. This requires that they learn how to interpret and attribute meaning to their schooling experiences. (Welch & Hodges, 1997).

In an attempt to be sensitive to the confidential nature of group meet-ings, I was careful not to introduce traditional research tools prematurely, so I wrote my notes after the meetings. Later, one of the students revealed: "I think it's awesome that you think what we say is important enough to write down." Besides field notes, I collected ethnographic data via video and audio recordings, photos, slides, student evaluations of projects, and semistructured interviews. I also involved some of my doctoral students to assist with observations of students' classes and other important events. Records of advisory board meetings and structured meetings between youth mentors and adult facilitators were also collected. Mentors were Latina/o youth who had graduated from high school and were available at any time to a smaller set of students in IAY. Adults on the advisory board included school therapists, school interventionists, parents, police officers, life skills teachers, fire fighters, community college students, and a university professor.

The majority of the students in It's About YOUth! were born in the United States. Among the 20 youth, 18 reported the United States as their birthplace, including one born of Native American and Mexican parents. Two youth reported births in Mexico. The youth identified themselves as Mexican, Mexican American, or Chicana/o. No youth member self-identified as Hispanic. Some of the students had received bilingual or English-as-a-second-language services in their elementary grades. Many were officially enrolled in the Access to Learning Classroom (a pseudonym for the alternative high school program) at the high school nearest to the youth center where weekly IAY meetings were held.

The Access to Learning Classroom (ALC) is a special "school-within-a-school" alternative program for youth in grades 10 through 12 who do not experience success with the regular high school curriculum and schedule of classes. In the 1998–99 academic school year all 19 students enrolled in ALC were of Mexicano/Latino background. An Anglo-American female teacher provided instruction exclusively in English. According to her, referrals for Anglo students are made, but most Anglo students do not feel comfortable in the class and choose not to become a part of it. In contrast, the Mexican-origin students in her class report during ethnographic interviews: "People get along here. Everybody talks to one another, so it's not like being in other classes where some people are quiet and others do all the talking. . . . In here it's not like that. We're all part of something. . . . We're a family." (See Fránquiz, in press, for an extended discussion of life in ALC.)

The positive relational nature of students and teacher in ALC was the same type of relationship that students and adults shared in the It's About YOUth! after-school program. The goals of IAY were to promote educational success, cultural enrichment, and healthy recreation for Chicano/Mexicano/Latino youth who were experiencing personal, familial, or institutional problems. Students referred themselves or were referred to the program by parents, teachers, counselors, probation officers, or priests. Weekly meetings provided a safe space for exploring program goals. In this safe space the struggle among what Spindler and Spindler (1990, 1993) call the three notions of self are embraced and transformation of negative patterns within the struggle are encouraged. As described by the Spindlers, the struggle is manifested in tension between students' enduring self (past and continuity of experiences), their situated self (coping with a situation in the present), and their endangered self (the situational and present threatening and undermining one's enduring self).

Creating Respect Through Public Access Television

During the spring of 1996, a volunteer from the local access television program was invited to speak at one of the regular IAY youth meetings. He explained that the purpose of Public Access Television is "for a normal everyday person to express an opinion." He prompted the students to think about making a video and asked them to share their thinking: "If I had a camera right here, what would you say to the television audience?" One student said, "Chicanos are not ashamed of who they are." Another student added, "I would tell them about our group." The group decided together that getting the word out about the group was a positive thing for the community to know and that Public Access was an effective way to communicate their message.

As students brainstormed on what to say on their video clip and how to say it, one student reported that a discriminatory statement had been made about him because he was seen riding his lowrider bike to the store. Students were upset about the negative stereotypes and derogatory views held by the dominant group of Anglos in the community regarding Mexican youth who hung out together to work on their bikes or cars. In a way, one could say that they were expressing concern about their individual and collective "enduring selves" and decided to make a video on lowrider bikes in order to "create respect under conditions of little or no respect" (Cintrón, 1993).

As teens, many of the students in IAY spent time together building and improving their bikes, and like many Mexican American youth across the country, they considered this influence as a positive alternative to gang activities. Subsequent IAY group meetings were spent discussing the appropriate script for a video on lowrider bikes for Public Access Television. Students taught the adults in our IAY group about "bondo," a material applied to the frame of an older Schwinn bike in order to create a canvas for color, patina, and visual art. The *bajita* wheels, crushed velvet seats, brass spokes, and shocks were all part of the detailing of the bikes. One bike even had a sound system attached. Just as Cintrón (1993) found among Mexican American young men who owned "thumpers," the stereo served as a brilliant extension of the self's ability to occupy space beyond the visual, that of sound space (p. 115). Boys who owned bikes showed and described them on the film. One 17-year-old student interviewed the bike owners with a great deal of respect and professionalism. The girls wrote a script about how pride in bikes was showing pride in Chicana/o culture. The volunteer from the radio station donated taping time and editing expertise. A relevant literacy event was fully constructed by the students and there was an evolving sense of pride as *Personas Mexicanas* planned to show society what they could do with culturally relevant materials. (See Vigil, 1997, for case studies of Mexican American high school students in urban and suburban settings and their struggles with ethnicity, Americanization, prejudice, and schools.) During the week of October 20–26, 1997 the lowrider video appeared six times on Public Access TV.

From a literacy perspective I wondered how many teachers listened to and explored with their students interests such as lowrider bikes and lowrider cars. In major urban cities there are lowrider shows every year. These make excellent subjects for discussions on social responsibility. For example, the visual art on bikes and cars carries strong statements about religious icons, historical figures, and memories of recent loved ones. It also portrays images of women as sexual objects, alcohol and drugs, or gang affiliations. The latter requires critical discussion; otherwise, ideas generated from these visual images can contribute to negative stereotypes. Through critical discussion students are more apt "to build culturally grounded self respect" (Heath & McLaughlin, 1993, p. 13) and to make informed choices for the visual art represented on their bikes and cars.

Representing *Conocimiento* in a Mobile Mural Sculpture

One strategy valued by members of the advisory board of It's About YOUth! was to provide Latina/o role models as facilitators for some group meetings. After the making, airing, and reflecting on the video made for Public Access Television, students chose to spend time inquiring about their historical and cultural backgrounds. They reported that this opportunity was not provided in their regular curricula at school. One student clearly stated: "With my civics teacher, we study American history. I have requested that I want to learn Chicano history but they don't really want to listen." This student named a specific omission, the Mexican American War which she considered relevant to her engagement and acquisition of knowledge (i.e., *conocimiento*) in civics.

Adults in IAY agreed with students that in order to address negative stereotypes and inspire civic participation, students needed to know their history. So we began learning about the struggles, past and present, of the United Farm Workers. Initially, students reported knowledge of Julio César Chávez, a Mexican boxer, but did not share their *conocimiento* of the founders of the farmworker movement, César Chávez and Dolores Huerta. Their interest in art prompted me to introduce them to artists such as Antonio Burciaga and his famous mural, "Last Supper of Chicano Heroes." We also read the poetry of Jimmy Santiago Baca and made note of Chicano authors of children's literature such as Gary Soto and children's book illustrators such as David Díaz. Then, in September 1996, we met Chicano artist and playwright Leo Tanguma.

For over 30 years, Leo has made murals to educate the public. His art has the three guiding characteristics of activist art: It has political content, is created or displayed in public places instead of museums or galleries, and creates interactions with the viewing public (Felshin, 1995). The social consciousness he evokes has the capacity to both indict society and offer possibilities for change. In 1993 he was commissioned to create four murals dealing with our endangered environment and our endangered humanity. These murals can be viewed at the Denver International Airport. Between September 1996 and January 1997, this grandparent and *veterano* of the Chicano movement was the primary Latino role model for IAY youth. He generously donated his time to introduce the students to the Chicano history integrated in his art, to the tools located in his studio, to his home cooking of rice and beans, and to his expertise for the construction of an IAY mobile mural sculpture.

One of the first assignments Leo Tanguma recommended to IAY was for the students to collect stories from their families regarding the history of Chicanas/os in their local community. This assignment prompted a parent to write to her daughters the four-page account mentioned earlier about Beaver and Louie and their wrongful deaths at the hands of rookie police officers in 1980. The students decided to construct the mural in memory of the two slain youth.

An interesting aside to my ethnographic record of this evolving project was the regular participation at meetings of an Irish American police officer who had witnessed firsthand the deaths of Beaver and Louie on Main Street in 1980. This man had dedicated his efforts since 1980 to the training of rookie police officers regarding the culture of Mexicano/Chicano/Latino youth and their families. The students respected his presence in the group (and at their school), and he agreed to take two of the young teens in IAY to police archives so they could understand better the official and unofficial stories surrounding the deaths of Beaver and Louie. This was a particularly meaningful gesture since two siblings in IAY were children of the driver of the car when Beaver and Louie were killed. Thus, in the planning of the mural many personal stories were intertwined with official stories and decisions were made as to how these stories would be represented visually for others to "read."

From a Freirian perspective (Freire & Macedo, 1987), individual students were encouraged to "read their world" from various perspectives. These diverse readings were then used to represent a particular "reading of the world and the word." What this means is that the visual arts were the medium for *la palabra*, the word, as understood and accepted by the youth. The visual images, like the written word, expressed the struggles of individual IAY members and had the power to influence everyone participating in the making of the mural. According to Anzaldúa (1987), persons and society are inextricably linked such that insight and transformation on a personal level alters the larger context. She believes that the arts have the power to transform the artist as well as the larger social context within which the art exists. If Anzaldúa's theory is viable, then Flood, Heath, and Lapp (1997) make a powerful argument when they recommend that the visual arts should be located in a central place in literacy, language, and cultural education.

As is common for work influenced by Leo Tanguma, the IAY mural depicted contrasting themes—negative and positive influences in the Chicana/o community. In the center is a mirror where the "reader" of the art piece reflects on whether his or her relationship with the Chicana/o community will be built on the negative or positive cultural elements identified by the IAY youth. The negative elements are located at the bottom of the mural sculpture. They include peer pressure and internalized racism, the two elements that promote the performance of violence between brothers and sisters of *la gente,* between homeboys of *la Raza.* Negative elements also include violence inflicted on others or ourselves due to influences of drugs, alcohol, and negative media messages. *Mi Vida Loca* [my crazy life], are the words used to represent all the negative influences that often come together when students drop out of school, break the law, or have unplanned pregnancies.

Positive cultural elements were represented inside an eagle located on the upper part of the mobile mural sculpture. These include figures who struggled for peace such as Jesus Christ, *La Virgen de Guadalupe,* Juan Diego (Indian to whom the Virgin of Guadalupe appeared), César Chávez and Dolores Huerta (founders of United Farmworkers). They also include Jeff (Beaver) Cordova, Juan Louis (Louie) Garcia, Jesse Maldonado (murdered homeboy), and Carmen Sierra (mother of IAY member who lost her life to cancer). *La familia,* as the heart of the Chicano community, also commands a space on one of the wings of the eagle. The eagle tail feathers are where students write their names and year of high school graduation. In this way, the mural is a public and visual space for maintaining a living record of the names of youth from *la gente* who beat the odds of being pushed out of high school.

The mural is made of wood panels that are connected with hinges. It stands 10 feet by 20 feet (see Figure 13.1). During the construction of the mural, Leo shared a statement with the students, which he attributes to the psychologist Carl Jung: "Art is to the community, what dreams are for the individual." Leo believes that the centrality of art is critical for connecting and integrating the images in our heads with images representing a strong Chicana/o community. Therefore, he suggested placing the eagle (positive influences) flying away from its perch (negative influences). He also suggested the mirror at the center to represent the place where any community member can see her or himself in relation to the positive paths embedded in the eagle or the negative paths represented by the shape where the eagle is perched.

During the process of making the mural, some disagreements arose. For example, on the wooden canvas where negative influences were drawn, one student drew a gang abbreviation. He drew the gang "tag" as a tattoo on the upper arm of a man walking away from school with alcohol in his hand. Although this was an authentic representation of someone following a negative path, adults insisted on the erasure of the tattoo. Students critiqued the adults for condoning artistic censure, and the adults insisted the gang abbreviation could be interpreted as IAY condoning gang behaviors. Since the aim of social responsibility education is to help young people develop a personal investment in the well-being of other people (Berman, 1990) and since misinformation could be inferred from the symbol, consensus regarding the removal of the tattoo was eventually reached. There were many other "literary" discussions regarding the appropriate semiotic symbol to represent cultural elements of the local Chicana/o community. Final agreements regarding what the images represented on the "final draft" of the mural were recorded. These explanations were incorporated into the handouts used for future local, national, and international presentations.

The Role of an Audience for Emerging Social Responsibility

Social responsibility education is a new field of study that has emerged over the past decade. It "encompasses both developing students' social skills and enabling students to be active and responsible members of the larger social and political community" (Berman, 1997, p. 11). This is precisely what

FIGURE 13.1: The Students' Mural

Photo by María E. Fránquiz

It's About YOUth! was—an after-school learning environment where young people had the opportunity to work together in positive ways to develop skills (e.g., artistic, literary, communicative, and leadership skills) that would support their active engagement and participation with their schooling and the wider civic community. In this endeavor, students benefitted from Latina/o role models such as Leo Tanguma, and in some cases from Anglo role models, such as my doctoral students who volunteered their services to the youth group.

An audience is an important element for these emerging skills. To provide a real audience, I submitted a proposal to have the students attend the annual conference of the National Association of Bilingual Educators (NABE) in Albuquerque in 1997. Fourteen students received permission from their families to attend. They planned to present the history of the youth group, the lowrider video, the meanings behind the images on the mural, and their reasons for being and staying in IAY. The students also wanted time to dialogue with the participants at the session regarding reasons children develop an oppositional stance toward school-based literacy.

On January 15, 1997, one of the mentors of IAY escorted the principal of the high school nearest the youth center to an IAY meeting. The principal committed $200 to help IAY students with finances for the trip to the conference in Albuquerque. He also agreed to have a formal unveiling of the IAY mural for teachers, parents, and community members at the high school commons area upon students' return from NABE. (The photo represented in Figure 13.1 was taken during the evening of the unveiling.) The agreement to unveil the mural at the high school was a first step toward recognizing and legitimizing the positive influence of Mexican cultural presence within the academic domain. It also served as a catalyst for students to feel confident about addressing "opposition" as not necessarily synonymous with academic failure. They saw how opposition to cultural stereotypes could be effectively communicated to a predominantly Anglo audience in various and multiple ways, including the visual arts (see Davidson, 1996, for similar conclusions among 55 high school adolescents of color).

At the NABE presentation, students spoke openly about the support IAY provided for their continued participation in high school activities. One 17-year-old male who graduated in spring of 1998 said:

> My sophomore year I got scared because I was the only Hispanic person on our wrestling team and when I came to the group, you know, I would go to 'em about the wrestling team . . . and so I went out this year. And every time I had a match I would see a familiar face, a lot of support. And it's hard, you know. There's a lot of jokes that pop up. . . . And I couldn't have joined wrestling and a lot of things I do for the community. I do speeches. I just do a lot of stuff to try to help young kids but I wouldn't be able to do these things without all these people trying to support me.

When asked by an administrator how the group helped him with academics, the same youth responded:

> I didn't go to school for awhile and I came to group and I talked to them. They wanted to know why I wasn't going and I told them. And they just said go to school and try to figure out a way to beat the system. If you don't, nothing changes. And then I go tell the teacher, well, you know, instead of doing my report on your guy's history, can I do it on my own history?

Preliminary results from a survey conducted by an outside agency indicated that students who participated regularly in the IAY program reduced their drug and alcohol consumption. Although the survey did not address tobacco use, many students reported that reduced use of drugs, alcohol, and tobacco was due to participation in spaces where adults listened, took their struggles seriously, and aided them in finding positive solutions to problems such as arrests, fights, homelessness, probation, pregnancy, or unemployment. Preliminary results also showed behavior problems at school decreased and high school graduation rates improved when students were enrolled both in the Access to Learning Classroom and IAY meetings regularly. In 1999, two youths graduated and in 2000, four of the youths who participated in making the mural sculpture graduated from high school.

Becoming Emissaries: Should We Always Feel Like a 10?

Many IAY group meetings began with "checking in." This meant individuals rated their feelings from one to ten and explained why. For example, a student might say: "I feel like a three today because I got into a fight and had to call my parents," or "I feel like a ten today, 'cause the kids at the elementary school really liked our presentation."

Checking in was a very important practice for a variety of reasons. First, students who did not speak up at any other time had an opportunity to be heard by the group. Although an individual was allowed to "pass" on his or her turn, this was a rare occurrence. Second, checking in helped students diffuse pent up anger and solicited support from the group. Unlike 12-step meetings such as Alcoholics Anonymous, Narcotics Anonymous, or Alanon, there was plenty of cross talk during checking in. Third, if there was something pressing in the life of any one member, the group engaged in whatever challenging idea emerged in that life context. For example, a parent committed suicide during the winter break and the act had an impact on the life of his child as well as other students who had lost loved ones. While the grieving daughter could not say much to the group, IAY members shared many stories that connected her experience with theirs.

Sometimes students were given a sentence stem to help them deal with problems that arose during checking in. For example, "If I were in charge at school, I would (student fills in the sentence)." In this particular case, students finished the sentence stem with, "hire teachers who will tell us more about our culture and history, hire teachers who aren't prejudiced, hire teachers who are more sensitive and don't make fun of you or won't put you down in front of the rest of the class, and hire teachers who give kids more support."

Some of the practices used in IAY were shared with teachers, researchers, students, parents, and administrators who attended the conferences where IAY presented. I submitted another proposal for the twenty-fifth annual meeting of the National Association of Chicana and Chicano Studies (NACCS) in Mexico City in June 1998. Ten students successfully solicited financial support for the trip from many organizations, including the City Council, the university, a senator from out of the state, local radio stations, and numerous private donors. Doctoral students from the university and parents also helped IAY raise money by selling burritos at a lowrider car show and holding dances at the youth center.

The trip to Mexico provided students an opportunity to reflect on the meaning each of us had constructed or was constructing about what it means to be Mexican or Mexican American or Chicana/o in race-conscious societies. Instead of seeing themselves as raceless, the youth at the conference saw themselves as emissaries. Fordham (1988) describes racelessness as a strategy whereby individuals assimilate into the dominant group by de-emphasizing characteristics. In contrast, Tatum (1997) describes an emissary as "someone who sees his or her own achievements as advancing the cause of the racial group" (p. 64). At the presentation in Mexico City there were high school students (from Mexico) in the audience who complimented the IAY youth group for sharing socially responsible ideas with the diverse international audience.

A Work in Progress: John as a Telling Case

For presentations, the youth were encouraged to write a statement as to why they participated in It's About YOUth! For the NABE meeting where IAY youth presented in January 1999, one Chicano male, John, wrote: "I joined It's About YOUth! because I felt that it would help me stay in school. Being in the program gives me the opportunity to learn about my culture and about who I am. It's About YOUth! helps me be motivated to go to school and the youth encourage me to keep focused on graduating in the year 2000. My plans after I graduate are to become a mentor myself and to go to college and become a photographer."

John learned to overcome adult challenges as a teen. He lived on his own since his family moved out of state. Although it is not typical that a young teen choose to be solely responsible for his well-being, John became "one of about 400 students in St. Vrain who are considered homeless. The district defines homeless students as those who no longer live at home for a variety of reasons" (Bounds, 1999, p. 4B–5B). John valued his education and was determined to stay in school and reach adulthood on his own. He joined the IAY group in 1996 when he was suspended and expelled during the middle of his freshman year in school. "Instead of giving up, he enrolled at Clearview—an alternative school for St. Vrain's suspended and expelled students" (Bounds, 1999, p. 4B–5B) and worked his way back to his regular high school.

John was one of the students working with Leo Tanguma on the IAY mural. Although John was unable to attend the NABE conference in Albuquerque, he did present the history of his affiliation with the group at NACCS in Mexico City. During 1998 and 1999 he served as a facilitator in an after-school leadership program for middle school Latinas/os. He attended the Learning for Access Class and used his senior year as preparation for college. This was no easy task, as he also worked 50–60 hours a week for $5.95 an hour as a shift manager at Taco Bell in order to pay for his health insurance, phone bill, rent, food, clothes, and books. In 1999 John was awarded the state's Metropolitan Mayors and Commissioners Youth Award for his perseverance in overcoming adversity. The award included a one-year scholarship to a community college.

Like John, the other students in It's About YOUth! are succeeding "without selling out." They are hungering to understand the structural factors that constrain the dreams of "marginalized" youth. In the company of respectful and caring adults, they are willing to learn and transform themselves in order to become legitimate actors in the academic and civic domains. They are profoundly invested in investigating the multidimensional aspects of ethnic identity. They are willing to reflect on aspects of their thinking, feelings, perceptions, and actions that are due to ethnic group membership and to the sense of belonging to an ethnic group (Rotheram & Phinney, 1987). Most specifically, they are considering one big decision: whether to be closely identified with mainstream culture, to strongly identify with their own ethnic group, or to develop a bicultural orientation (Rotheram-Borus, 1993). In It's About YOUth! most students are there to develop a bicultural social and academic identity.

Conclusion

El Comité was created in 1980 as a response to anger regarding the extreme violence of police officers against Mexican adolescents. It's About YOUth! was created in 1995 as a response to the violent murder of a young homeboy by another homeboy. The original charges of *El Comité* and IAY, then, were the same—to prevent violence between and within members of ethnic groups. The community, in which Chicano youth struggle to survive financially, does not desire violence, whether blatant or internalized, as the solution to racism. The youth take this charge seriously and have found a viable solution to address racism in the community—caring adult volunteers who are willing to listen, willing to teach, and willing to learn.

In the case of IAY, the youth want adults in their lives who are willing to take their concerns seriously and willing to teach them to aspire to academic excellence. They have demonstrated that youth of Mexican origin want to become biculturally competent and socially responsible through meaningful learning—learning that is less "abstract" and more "hands on," such as participating in the construction of activist art. Above all, they want to be respected. They report needing affirmations on a daily basis because racism, stereotyping, prejudice, and their manifestations in bullying behaviors do exist and are too often tolerated in the social and academic worlds in which they live.

What I've learned from working with members of It's About YOUth! is that adolescents want familiar ways of knowing to be the foundation for learning unfamiliar content. They want to be partners in making the process of acquiring literacy less "linguicist," less racist, less sexist, less classist, less ableist. They want to be included in decisions for making positive change— change that will transform their schools into more caring, more relevant, more creative, and more just places.

Note

1. The research for this study was partially funded by the National Academy of Education Spencer Postdoctoral Fellowship Program. I wish to express my gratitude to research assistant Sandra Wolf and Title VII fellow Claudia Peralta Nash for their assistance in collection and discussion of the data.

References

Anzaldúa, G. (1987). *Borderlands/La frontera: The new mestiza.* San Francisco: Aunt Lute Books.

Berman, J. S. (1990). The real ropes course: The development of social consciousness. *ESR Journal, 1,* 1–18.

Berman, J. S. (1997). *Children's social consciousness and the development of social responsibility.* Albany: State University of New York Press.

Bounds, A. (1999, May 24). He's got that teen spirit. *Daily Times–Call,* pp. 4B–5B.

Cintrón, R. (1993). *Angels' town:* Chero *ways, gang life, and rhetorics of the everyday.* Boston: Beacon Press.

Davidson, A. L. (1996). *Making and molding identity in schools: Student narratives on race, gender, and academic engagement.* Albany: State University of New York Press.

Felshin, N. (Ed.). (1995). *But is it art? The spirit of art as activism.* Seattle: Bay Press.

Flood, J., Heath, S. B., & Lapp, D. (Eds.). (1997). *Handbook of research on teaching literacy through the communicative and visual arts.* New York: International Reading Association.

Fordham, S. (1988). Racelessness as a factor in black students' school success: Pragmatic strategy or Pyrrhic victory? *Harvard Educational Review, 58*(1), 54–84.

Fránquiz, M. (in press). Caring literacy and identity struggles: The transformation of a Chicano student. In L. Soto (Ed.), *Making a difference in the lives of bilingual/bicultural children*. New York: Peter Lang Publishers.

Freire, P. (1973). *Education for critical consciousness*. New York: Seabury.

Freire, P., & Macedo, D. (1987). *Literacy: Reading the word and the world*. South Hadley, MA: Bergin & Garvey.

Glairon, S. (1999, June 13). Group formed to defuse tension. *Daily Camera*, pp. 4B–6B.

Heath, S. B., & McLaughlin, M. W. (1993). Building identities for inner-city youth. In S. B. Heath & M. W. McLaughlin (Eds.), *Identity and inner-city youth* (pp. 1–12). New York: Teachers College Press.

Ladson-Billings, G. (1995). Toward a theory of culturally relevant pedagogy. *American Education Research Journal, 32*(3), 465–491.

Longmont Hispanic Study. (1988). *We, too, came to stay: A history of the Longmont Hispanic community*. Longmont, CO: Longmont Hispanic Study and El Comité.

Macedo, D. (1993). Literacy for stupidification: The pedagogy of the big lies. In C. E. Sleeter & P. L. McLaren (Eds.), *Multicultural education, critical pedagogy, and the politics of difference* (pp. 71-104). Albany: State University of New York Press.

Rotheram-Borus, M. (1993). Biculturalism among adolescents. In M. E. Bernal & G. P. Knight (Eds.), *Ethnic identity: Formation and transmission among Hispanics and other minorities* (pp. 81–102). Albany: State University of New York Press.

Rotheram, M. J., & Phinney, J. S. (1987). Introduction: Definitions and perspectives in the study of children's ethnic socialization. In J. S. Phinney & M. J. Rotheram (Eds.), *Children's ethnic socialization* (pp. 10–28). Newbury Park, CA: Sage.

Shor, I., & Freire, P. (1987). *A pedagogy for liberation: Dialogues for transforming education*. South Hadley, MA: Bergin and Garvey.

Spindler, G., & Spindler, L. (1990). *The American cultural dialogue and its transmission*. London: Falmer Press.

Spindler, G., & Spindler, L. (1993). The processes of culture and person: Cultural therapy and culturally diverse schools. In P. Phelan & A. L. Davidson (Eds.), *Renegotiating cultural diversity in American schools* (pp. 21–51). New York: Teachers College Press.

Tatum, B. D. (1997). *Why are all the black kids sitting together in the cafeteria?* New York: HarperCollins.

Vigil, J. D. (1997). *Personas Mexicanas: Chicano high schoolers in a changing Los Angeles*. Orlando, FL: Harcourt Brace & Co.

Welch, O. M., & Hodges, C. R. (1997). *Standing outside on the inside: Black adolescents and the construction of academic identity*. Albany: State University of New York Press.

Chapter 14

Parent Narratives

The Cultural Bridge Between Latino Parents and Their Children

ALMA FLOR ADA
AND ROSA ZUBIZARRETA

One of the best ways to help students learn is to help them develop a deep cultural understanding and respect for who they are. This type of understanding and respect generally requires a strong connection between children and their families. Helping parents connect with their children through literacy activities; in particular, parent narratives that affirm their knowledge, ideas, and experiences are some ways that have proven successful for us in our work with Latino parents. Given the marginalization and oppression of culturally different members of our society, this type of understanding and respect is not something that Latinos can take for granted—rather, it is something we need to promote and a goal we need to work toward.

The purpose of this chapter is threefold: (1) to explore how Latino parents view their children's education and their own role in it, (2) to explore, through the lens of social capital theory, schools' influence on and responsibility toward families and communities, and (3) to offer two models for literacy practice. These two models are a classroom-based approach that invites family and community into the curriculum, and a family literacy program inspired by the work of Paulo Freire (1970) that works directly with parents.

The Voices of Latino Parents

The content of this chapter draws primarily from Alma Flor Ada's work with parents conducted over the past 28 years. This fieldwork involved a large number of parents, principally from California and Texas but also from Florida, New Mexico, Colorado, New York, and Oregon. Alma Flor Ada's meeting with Latino parents began in 1973, taking place monthly, often weekly, and sometimes three or four times a week, with the number of participants ranging from 20 to 200. The nature of the sessions was interactive, encouraging parents to share their thoughts on various topics. In spite of the wide range of differences among these parents, including their backgrounds (Mexican, Central American, Puerto Rican, and Cuban), their length of time in this country (first, second, third generation), and their economic circumstances (both migrant and nonmigrant families), common themes have consistently emerged. These themes include parents' high hopes for their children, parents' role in their children's education and moral development, a desire for the development of cooperative social values, and the desire to maintain the home language and culture as a way of supporting strong family ties. The most frequently cited themes are discussed below.

Parents' Hopes for Their Children's Future

When asked, Latino parents overwhelmingly and consistently express the highest hope for their children's future. In fact, they often look bewildered when someone poses such an obvious question. For them, it is a given that they want their children to continue their schooling and attain a professional career; otherwise, why would they be sending them to school? This is especially true in the case of parents who themselves were not able to attend school and who have limited financial resources. To them, the very fact that they are encouraging their children to attend school is a major statement of their hopes for their children's future. When asked what they want for their children, we often hear the following:

> Quiero ayudarles a mis hijos para que en el mañana sean unos doctores o abogados y no tengan que pasar por tanto problema como uno, que siempre lo miran inferior.
>
> [I want to help my children so that in the future, they will be doctors or lawyers and not have to face as many obstacles as we have, being always looked down upon as inferior.]
>
> Sra. Mendoza, Santa Ana, CA (1995)

Una buena preparación universitaria y que se puedan defender por
sí mismos. Enseñarles valor.

[A good university education, so that they can make their own
way in life. To teach them courage.]

Sra. Gómez, Salinas, CA (1992)

Unfortunately, the typical educator rarely understands the high expectations parents have for their children. In fact, we often have encountered
well-meaning teachers who hold the assumption that Latino parents do not
place a high value on their children's education. These teachers believe that
if parents had high hopes for their children, they would express them in a
manner similar to European American parents. This translates into actively
requesting information, participating in the PTA, and making overt references
to their plans for their children's academic futures. Many Latino parents,
however, have not had the opportunity for much schooling and see themselves
as having a limited contribution to their children's education. Many of them
believe that their role is to lay the foundation at home, and trust that the school
will take care of the rest (Delgado-Gaitán, 1994; Valdés, 1996).

Parents' Contributions

According to most parents, the home plays an important role in shaping children's moral development. When parents are asked about the most
significant lessons they teach their children, the majority of them cite
respeto—a profound sense of respect for self and others. This *respeto* mani-
fests itself as a quiet, internal dignity that includes a commitment to hon-
esty, to cooperation, and to protecting others, as well as a deep sense of
respect for elders, youth, and one's family. Some have expressed the importance of *respeto* in the following manner:

Que sean honestos, porque así tendrán siempre las puertas abiertas,
y que sepan respetar y amar a los demás.

[To be honest, as that way they will always find an open door,
and to know how to respect and love others.]

Sra. Pérez, Laredo, TX (1994)

Que respeten, para que ellos también sean respetados.

[That they respect others, so that they in turn shall be
respected.]

Sra. Botero, Fresno, CA (1995)

Parents are clear that *respeto* is a primary cultural value they are transmitting to their children. Thus, it is deeply painful when educators view Latino children as "lacking in self-esteem," or self-respect, and do not recognize the strong ethical base Latino children bring to school.

Another topic that parents often bring up is the value of persistence; that is, the importance of not giving up, "de no darse por vencido."

Que no se desalienten en los fracasos, porque de ellos van a aprender para triunfar.

[That they not become discouraged by failure, because from those experiences, they can learn how to succeed.]

Sra. Baca, San Antonio, TX (1993)

No importa ser hijos de migrantes. El alcanzar las estrellas es para todos.

[It does not matter that you are the child of migrant parents. Reaching the stars is for everyone.]

Sra. Obregón, Laredo, TX (1995)

Given these parental aspirations, it is an especially painful contradiction to learn that low graduation rates among Latino students are attributed to "lack of persistence." Other values often mentioned by parents include generosity, friendship, and solidarity: Be there for others, do good to others, find joy in helping others.

Que sean buenos estudiantes, y buenos consejeros para sus compañeros.

[To be good students, and to offer good counsel to their friends.]

Sra. Castillo, Pájaro, CA (1992)

Que alcanzen todo lo que desean, pero no a costa de quitárselo a nadie. Sino más bien para ayudarlos.

[That they accomplish everything that they desire, but not at the cost of taking anything away from anyone else. Rather, in order to help others.]

Sra. Morales, Salem, OR (1998)

Maintaining One's Native Language and Culture

It is overwhelmingly the case that Latino parents want their children to retain their language and culture so they will be able to communicate with grandparents, the parents themselves, and other relatives. Regarding the maintenance of language and culture, parents report:

Yo aspiro a que mis hijos lleguen a enriquecer sus dos idiomas y que nunca olviden sus raíces y de dónde vienen.

[I wish for my children to develop the richness of their two languages, and that they never forget their roots and where they came from.]

Sra. García, Pájaro, CA (1994)

Debemos enseñarles a los hijos que es importante hablar en español y no perder el habla ni la cultura hispana.

[We should teach our children that it is important to speak Spanish, and to not lose our language nor our culture.]

Sra. Herrera, Salinas, CA (1992)

Unfortunately, most Latino parents do not understand how easy it is to lose a language. Since many learn their second language as adults when they are not at risk of losing their first language, and the second language is difficult to learn, it is not readily apparent that the situation for their children is quite the opposite. In fact, the preeminent status of English in schools and in the larger society, together with the social pressure to become "American" (i.e., speak English), is a tremendous pressure facing Latino children that makes it very difficult for them to maintain their native language (see Chapter 4).

A Critical Understanding of Social Capital

Having heard some voices of Latino parents, let us now examine critically the mainstream theory that underlies the general field of parent involvement. One of the most comprehensive theoretical frameworks is Coleman's (1991) elaboration of the notion of "social capital" in the historically changing roles of home and school. While this theory offers valuable insights, ethnocentric attitudes often have accompanied it, leading to erroneous and harmful conclusions.

The term *social capital* per se is used to denote the idea that human relationships are a significant factor in attaining desired outcomes, and serves to highlight the role and importance of these relationships. When applied to the study of schooling, it can serve to emphasize the interdependence between academic learning and social learning. Yet, too often, mainstream exponents of social capital theory have begun with the unstated assumption that "differences" in social or cultural expression equal "deficits." This has, in turn, led to the false conclusion that schools' limited effectiveness with certain populations can be blamed on the supposedly weak social capital of those communities. Unfortunately, blaming families for schools' lack of success with non-mainstream children is still widespread in the field of education. As Kerbow and Bernhardt (1993) point out, many parent involvement initiatives operate on the false assumption that "levels of parental involvement for these parents are inadequate or at least below expected levels" (p. 115).

Research evidence, however, contradicts these prejudicial beliefs, confirming instead that parents from marginalized groups are highly interested in collaborating with schools to help their children succeed (Moles, 1993). Exhaustive studies now confirm what Latino educators (e.g., Delgado-Gaitán, 1994; Nieto, 1992; Trueba, 1988; Valdés, 1996) have been saying all along: Parents of all ethnic backgrounds have high educational expectations for their children and invest the resources at their disposal in their children's education (Muller & Kerbow, 1993). As Kerbow and Bernhart (1993) conclude: "To claim that these parents are inadequate in their attention to their children's education is straightforwardly mistaken" (p. 134).

While the original application of social capital theory to parent involvement included unfounded and harmful biases, the concept of social capital can lead us to ask some very useful questions. For example, How is social capital of families affected when children witness that parents are not treated with respect at school? What happens to students' relationships with their families and communities when these are made invisible rather than being honored in the school's curriculum and practices?

Of course, these difficulties are not experienced just by Latino students. As stated so eloquently by African American psychiatrist and educator James Comer (1988): "When we ask low-income, minority-group children to achieve well in school—an instrument of mainstream society— we are often asking them to be different than their parents. With parents involved there is no conflict" (p. 219). Our experience is that children's sense of conflict is reduced when parents' knowledge, experience, and wisdom are included in the curriculum.

The effect of the curriculum on family social capital has yet to be studied by mainstream researchers. Nonetheless, in discussing a research finding that minority parents seem to have a somewhat lower incidence of communication about school-related activities with their children than mainstream parents, Muller and Kerbow (1993) present the following hypothesis:

> Discussion of current aspects of the educational experience may be more likely to come about in families in which parents are able to in some sense "put themselves in the context of the school", figuratively speaking, so that the student and parent have enough commonality of understanding to be able to talk about what happens to the student. (p. 18)

In other words, one of the effects of the difference between the respective cultures of school and home might be reduced communication between parents and children about school matters. From a sociocultural perspective (Vygotsky, 1978), the "context of the school" includes classroom culture, where teachers can influence the role played by children's families and communities. How teachers organize instruction, and their decisions to include culturally relevant curriculum, can support a commonality of understanding between students and parents.

Ada (1993b), Huerta-Macías and Quintero (1993), and McCaleb (1994) explore what schools can do, beginning with promoting at-home parent–child conversations that draw on parents' life experiences, family histories, and cultural knowledge. Teachers can then use these home conversations as a springboard for conversations in the classroom. "Homework," no longer "schoolwork done at home," becomes, instead, a meaningful collaboration between parents and children designed to access parent strengths (see Chapter 5). Inviting the result of that home learning back into the classroom, incorporating parents' "funds of knowledge" into classroom curriculum and practice, helps the "context of the school" become more reflective of children's families and communities (Moll, 1990; see also Chapter 1). This, in turn, facilitates further parent–child communication.

Other crucial questions we can ask using the language of social capital include: How is family social capital affected when students and parents no longer speak the same language? What is the school's responsibility in this regard? Aside from the issue of whether a school has bilingual education programs, we are raising an even more fundamental issue: What is the school doing to promote continued communication at home between parents and children in their native language? It is sadly ironic that, while the rationale for bilingual education programs is based on worldwide research showing the academic advantage of sustained home-language use in the home (e.g., Cummins, 1981; Dolson, 1985), most "parent involvement" literature is silent on the value of promoting home-language use (noteworthy exceptions include Montecel et al., 1993, and Ramírez & Douglas, 1989). If we truly wish to support social capital, we need to support children's ability to continue speaking the language of their parents and their extended family, whether we ourselves speak that language or not. When the intention to promote native-language use at home is present, much can be accomplished by educators who may not themselves speak the home language or languages. Supporting home-language use needs to become the responsibility of *all* educators toward *all* students, not just of teachers and students in bilingual classrooms.

In concluding this section, we note that mainstream parent involvement programs have tended to focus almost exclusively on what parents can do to prepare their children for school. To address this imbalance, we need to widen our focus to include what schools can do to nurture children's pride in their own families and communities, as well as how schools can work with parents in ways that are both respectful and rewarding. (For a model approach to designing ESL programs for parents, see the work of Auerbach, 1990, and for a model for helping parents become advocates for their children's learning, see Rodríguez, Rothstein, & Santana, 1994. Both of these programs also are informed by the work of Paulo Freire.)

Suggestions for Practice

A recurring thread woven throughout this chapter is that, by definition, authentically child-centered education needs to make a child's home, family, and community a central part of the curriculum. The presence of family and community in the curriculum does not necessarily require their physical presence in the school (although it certainly can be a good idea whenever feasible). It does require, however, the presence of parents' perspectives, their experience, their history, and their words. The practical approach for doing so that we are presenting here has been described previously by Ada (1993b) and Ada and Campoy (1997b).

Honoring Family in the Classroom

Whether or not we speak students' home languages, we can send home on a regular basis oral or written questions and dialogue prompts to encourage conversations in the home language. These invitations are designed by the teacher to elicit and welcome parents' experience, wisdom, and cultural knowledge.

In many cases, there may be initial barriers to overcome as we begin this deeper dialogue between home and school. We have found that an excellent way for teachers to "break the ice" is to author a personal book to be sent home and shared with families. By taking the initiative of self-disclosure, teachers make it easier for parents to share their own life experiences.

Books based on the teacher's own life or family can provide a fruitful starting point for dialogue (see Chapter 8). When teachers share their own personal stories, they begin to bridge the formidable barriers of social class and educational status that can exist between them and the parents of their students. For example, a teacher who wrote a book about her mother and sent it to all the mothers of her students, received a strong positive response from the parents to her message of equality and respect conveyed by her offering. As we have shown (Ada & Campoy, 1997b), these books written by teachers for other teachers in subsequent workshops have been a source of inspiration to their colleagues.

Many different factors may account for the positive responses received by teachers using this approach. When parents receive the teacher-authored book, they are able to read it at home at their own pace, or have it read to them by their children. This generally inspires them to remember their own stories, to honor their own memories, and to bring to light the experiences of their own lives and the lives of their loved ones.

Teachers often begin by writing a book on the story of their name. Other teacher-authored books include *I Was Not Always a Teacher*, *My Bed Is Not at School*, and *The Foolish Teacher*, all aimed at helping parents and children understand that teachers are human. Teachers also have chosen to write books about their parents, grandparents, spouses, children, nephews, nieces, and others as a means of sharing cherished stories with parents.

Once initial trust has been established, teachers continue the process by inviting students to initiate conversations with their parents, in their own home language, on a variety of possible topics. For example, if the class is studying the theme of friendship, students can be encouraged to ask their parents for their own memories on the subject: Who were their parents' friends when they were young? Did they ever have differences of opinion with a friend? How did they negotiate the situation? Did they ever need to resolve a conflict with their friend? What do parents seek in a friend today? What would they be willing to do for a friend? Parents also can be invited to share, via their children, their thoughts about universal values: What would they like to do to create a more just society? What would they like to change? What would they preserve? As we design our questions, we ensure inclusiveness by focusing on general, shared human experiences.

How the teacher responds to the information students bring back is crucial, as openness, creativity, continuity, and follow-up are all essential for deepening the process. Teachers can demonstrate interest in parents' wisdom and experiences by recording the stories brought back by the students, by inviting students to create classroom books with the stories they have collected, or simply by providing students with the time and space to share their stories with classmates. Teachers who do not speak children's home language can still invite their students to have conversations at home with parents in the home language, and invite students to share in the classroom what they have learned from their parents at home. What is important in this case is sensitivity, respect, and willingness to learn about students' culture. Our responses can serve to model respect for a diversity of experience and opinions.

There are many possibilities for generating curriculum activities from parents' contributions. When a group of parents in Windsor, California, was asked for the best advice they could offer their children, a father responded that he would tell his children, "We are here to create a better world." Teachers at the school decided to make a project based on this parent's words. In each classroom, teachers displayed a banner with the quote and asked each child to create a page for a classroom book on how we can all make a better world. Needless to say, a tangible sense of pride was generated in children with respect to their parents, and the response of the community as a whole was overwhelming.

Teachers looking for ideas on how to create their own conversation starters for parents and children, or for a ready-made program to implement, might want to review the Homeside Activities/Actividades Familiares program created by the Developmental Studies Center (1995). This program, which includes a Spanish-language parent video (1997), offers a simple way to begin validating children's families and communities at the school site by encouraging home conversations that serve as the basis for follow-up activities in the classroom.

Transformative Family Literacy: Parents and Children as Authors

In 1986, the *Proyecto de Literatura Infantil* [Children's Literature Project] was initiated by Alma Flor Ada, in coordination with the bilingual program of the Pájaro School District in northern California. This innovative project (Ada, 1988; see also Auerbach, 1989; Brown, 1993) was designed to work directly with parents to promote literacy practices and has led to a host of similar experiments in other locations.

The fundamental assumptions of this model include the following:

1. Parents are the first and most enduring teachers of their children. Regardless of literacy skills or level of formal education, they have a wealth of personal experience and family stories to share.

2. Parents' home language is a valuable resource for children's oral language and cognitive development. Children's home language also is connected to their sense of identity and community. Language also plays a key role in the transmission of history, culture, and values.

3. Parents are valuable resources for children's emotional and social growth and development. Sharing everyday experiences in a common language builds strong family ties and allows parents to guide and support their children as they grow into adolescence.

4. Parents are more inclined to read with their children if they themselves have been able to experience the pleasure and relevance of reading. When parents listen to a story and are invited to discuss its connections to their own lives, they are better able to share that experience with their children.

5. Picture books are an accessible medium for parents. Parents who are not literate are still able to retell the story to their children at home, using the illustrations as a support.

6. As parents and children are encouraged to share their own thinking, their own writing, and their own stories, their self-confidence grows in tangible and often surprising ways.

The format of the program consists of a series of monthly evening sessions during which parents meet in small groups to listen to and discuss selected children's literature. Parents are then given the book they have discussed to take home and share with their children. At each session, parents also are assisted in writing their own collective books and given blank books to take home for their own and their families' use. Each of these key elements is described more fully below. Educators wishing to implement this approach can find further information in the manual for this program (Zubizarreta, 1996).

The picture books chosen for the program are selected both for literary and artistic merit as well as for their potential for thought-provoking dialogue. Examples of books that have yielded excellent discussions include: *Frederick* (Leonni, 1982a), *Nadarín* (Leonni, 1982b), *La Conejita Marcela* (Tusquets, 1987), *Arturo y Clementina* (Turín, 1986a), *Rosa Caramelo* (Turín, 1986b), and *La Moneda de Oro* (Ada, 1993a). This methodology, inspired by Freire, is based on the premise that reading is an interactive process for the purpose of human growth and development (Ada & Campoy, 1997a; Freire, 1970).

Creative dialogue involves four phases. Questions in the *descriptive phase* invite participants to reflect on the actual content of the book, including the theme, principal characters, and major conflicts. In the *personal interpretative phase,* parents are invited to relate the story to their own life experiences. The *critical/multicultural phase* invites participants to offer their own perspectives, respond to the values presented in the book, discuss what aspects may or may not apply to their own culture, and examine other alternatives. During the final *creative transformation phase* the focus returns again to parents' own lives. Here, parents are invited to reflect on areas of potential growth and any insights gained through the reading and discussion.

Next, the facilitators help parents create their own collective book by posing a generative, open-ended question to the group. Each of the parents offers a contribution. Parents' words are recorded on chart paper, followed by the parent's full name. Entries are read aloud for possible corrections or additions. Afterward, the book is typed, duplicated, and bound, and copies made for all participants.

The collective books written by parents cover a wide range of topics. *From Yesterday to Tomorrow* is a collection of traditional sayings and proverbs; *Adivina, Adivinador* is a collection of riddles. Other titles include: *Celebrations of My Childhood, Our Grandparents, Our Dreams for Our Children and How We Can Help Them Come True, The Best Advice We Can Offer Our Children,* and *Things We Can Give That Can't Be Bought.* Sometimes facilitators may offer a simple sentence starter as a catalyst for parents' reflections, such as *Peace is . . . , Friendship is . . . , Family is . . . ,* and *Work is. . . .*

At the end of each session, parents are given blank books to take home. They can use these to create their own books and/or to encourage their children's writing. The number of parents with limited schooling who have chosen to create books by themselves or as family projects bears witness to the inspiration and energy generated by this simple, yet profound process. Often, the children write their own stories in the blank books. As parents bring these books back to share at subsequent meetings, the children are invited to read their stories aloud to the group, and the family is honored as a family of authors. Later, the books written by the children also are typed, duplicated, and sent home, along with the books collectively authored by the parents during the program sessions.

The results of this program and others like it have been overwhelmingly positive (Anaya, 1995; Gómez-Valdez, 1993; McCaleb, 1992; Murillo, 1987: Patrón, 1986: Reichmuth, 1981; Watts, 1988). Our ethnographic and participatory research has led us to conclude that parents who initially felt uncertain about their interactions with school personnel were able to establish a human, social relationship with them. In addition, they experienced their children's life at school firsthand. Once the gap they felt between home and school was bridged, parents were able to familiarize themselves with the contents of their children's education, regain trust in their own abilities, and take an active role in their children's and their family's literacy process. The group discussions helped parents develop or expand their contacts in their community. Over and over, parents expressed their appreciation for having had the opportunity at the meetings to form closer ties with other parents.

Teachers who participated in the meetings reported a greater understanding of their students, both in terms of the richness of their experiences and the challenges they face on a daily basis. As a result, they felt better equipped to serve the needs of each child. Teachers also reported that children who had the opportunity to see their parents recognized as authors appeared to gain a greater sense of self-esteem and a newfound appreciation for the wisdom of their parents' words, the variety of their parents' experiences, and the dignity of their parents' lives.

Parents also reported that they had gained a greater interest in books and reading. They reported that, in the course of sharing their thoughts with each other, they had come to realize that their own personal stories were at least as important as those found in books. Parents spoke about the usefulness of books for helping them reflect on their own lives and understanding themselves and the world with greater clarity. In these instances, parents were not only "reading the word," but "reading the world" (Freire, 1970).

The interest generated by the experience at Pájaro Valley has led to the replication of the project in many other sites under various names, including *Literatura Infantil* [Children's Literature], *Padres, Niños y Libros* [Parents, Children and Books], and *Padres y Niños Autores* [Parents and Children as Authors]. In California, the project thrived for several consecutive years at Glassbrook School in Hayward, at Marshall School in San Francisco, and at Project Even Start, at Windsor Elementary. As of this writing, the original program continues in Pájaro Valley as *Literatura Infantil y Familiar* [Literature for Children and Families] under the auspices of the Migrant Education Office. In Independence, Oregon, the *Padres Autores* [Parents as Authors] program brings in authors of children's books on a monthly basis to exchange ideas with parents. A duplicate of this model can be found in Beaverton, Oregon.

Conclusion

The purpose of this chapter was to show that, whether we work with children in the classroom or directly with parents, we can approach our work in ways that build upon and strengthen children's vital relationship to their families and communities. By inviting parents' experiences, reflections, and wisdom, we elicit their valuable contributions and help bridge the gap between them and their children, and between them and schools. By encouraging dialogue and communication at home in the home language, we support rather than destroy the existing social capital of the family.

As we recognize and build upon the strengths that Latino children bring to school, we help create truly supportive environments where learning can flourish. In doing this, we convey to children our deep respect for their families and communities and help fulfill this Latino mother's heartfelt wish.

Que los hijos no se avergüencen de sus padres porque no saben leer y escribir y por trabajar en el campo, y que les den su valor como padres.

[That our children not be ashamed of their parents because they don't know how to read and write, and because they work in the fields; and instead, continue to value and honor them as parents.]

Sra. Ortiz, McAllen, TX (1997)

References

Ada, A. F. (1988). The Pajaro Valley experience: Working with Spanish-speaking parents to develop children's reading and writing skills through the use of children's literature. In T. Skutnabb-Kangas & J. Cummins (Eds.), *Minority education: From shame to struggle* (pp. 223–238). Clevedon, Avon, England: Multilingual Matters.

Ada, A. F. (1993a). *La moneda de oro.* [Gold coins] Madrid: Editorial Everest.

Ada, A. F. (1993b). Mother-tongue literacy as a bridge between home and school cultures. In J. V. Tinajero & A. F. Ada (Eds.), *The power of two languages* (pp. 158–163). New York: Macmillan/McGraw-Hill.

Ada, A. F., & Campoy, F. I. (1997a). *Comprehensive language arts.* Cleveland, OH: Del Sol.

Ada, A. F., & Campoy, F. I. (1997b). *Parents, children and teachers as authors and protagonists.* Cleveland, OH: Del Sol.

Anaya, A. (1995). *Empowering minority parents through the use of dialogic retrospection and participatory research.* Unpublished doctoral dissertation, University of San Francisco.

Auerbach, E. (1989). Toward a social-contextual approach to family literacy. *Harvard Educational Review, 59*(2), 165–181.

Auerbach, E. (1990). *Making meaning, making change: A guide to participatory curriculum development for adult ESL and family literacy.* Boston: University of Massachusetts Press.

Brown, K. (1993). Balancing the tools of technology with our own humanity: The use of technology in building partnerships and communities. In J. V. Tinajero & A. F. Ada (Eds.), *The power of two languages* (pp. 178–198). New York: Macmillan/McGraw-Hill.

Coleman, J. S. (1991). *Policy perspectives: Parental involvement in education.* Washington, DC: U.S. Department of Education, Office of Educational Research and Improvement.

Comer, J. P. (1988). *Maggie's American dream: The life and times of a black family.* New York: Penguin Books.

Cummins, J. (1981). The role of primary language development in promoting educational success for language minority students. In California State Department of Education (Ed.), *Schooling and language-minority students: A theoretical framework* (pp. 3–49). Los Angeles: California State University, Education, Dissemination, and Assessment Center.

Delgado-Gaitán, C. (1994). Sociocultural change through literacy: Toward the empowerment of families. In B. M. Ferdman, R. M. Weber, & A. Ramirez (Eds.), *Literacy across languages and cultures* (pp. 143–170). Albany: State University of New York Press.

Developmental Studies Center. (1995). *Homeside activities: Conversations and activities that bring parents into children's schoolside learning* (Vols. K–6). Oakland: Author.

Developmental Studies Center. (1997). *Actividades familiares: Building on family strengths through conversations and activities in the home language* [12-minute Spanish-language video]. Oakland: Author.

Dolson, D. (1985). The effects of Spanish home language use on the scholastic performance of Hispanic pupils. *Journal of Multilingual and Multicultural Development, 6*(2), 135–156.

Freire, P. (1970). *Pedagogy of the oppressed.* New York: Continuum.

Gómez-Valdez, C. (1993). *The silent majority raise their voices: Reflections of Mexican parents on learning and schooling. A participatory research.* Unpublished doctoral dissertation, University of San Francisco.

Huerta-Macías, A., & Quintero, E. (1993). Teaching language and literacy in the context of family and community. In J. V. Tinajero & A. F. Ada (Eds.), *The power of two languages* (pp. 152–157). New York: Macmillan/McGraw-Hill.

Kerbow, D., & Bernhardt, A. (1993). Parental intervention in the school: The context of minority involvement. In B. Schneider & J. S. Coleman (Eds.), *Parents, their children, and schools* (pp. 115–146). Boulder, CO, and Oxford: Westview Press.

Leonni, L. (1982a). *Frederick.* Barcelona: Editorial Lumen.

Leonni, L. (1982b). *Nadarín.* Barcelona: Editorial Lumen.

McCaleb, S. P. (1992). *Parent involvement in education during early literacy development: A participatory study with Hispanic, African-American, and African parents through dialogue and co-authorship of books.* Unpublished doctoral dissertation, University of San Francisco.

McCaleb, S. P. (1994). *Building communities of learners: A collaboration among teachers, students, families and communities.* New York: St. Martin's Press.

Moles, O. C. (1993). Collaboration between schools and disadvantaged parents: Obstacles and openings. In N. Feyl Chavkin (Ed.), *Families and schools in a pluralistic society* (pp. 21–49). Albany: State University of New York Press.

Moll, L. C. (1990, April). *Community-mediated instruction: A qualitative approach.* Paper presented at the annual meeting of the American Educational Research Association, Chicago.

Montecel, M. R., Gallagher, A., Montemayor, A. M., Villarreal, A., Adame-Reyna, N., & Supik, J. (1993). *Hispanic families as valued partners: An educator's guide.* San Antonio: Intercultural Development Research Association.

Muller, C., & Kerbow, D. (1993). Parent involvement in the home, school, and community. In B. Schneider & J. S. Coleman (Eds.), *Parents, their children, and schools* (pp. 13–42). Boulder, CO, and Oxford: Westview Press.

Murillo, S. (1987). *Toward improved home–school interaction: A participatory dialogue with Hispanic parents in Berkeley, California.* Unpublished doctoral dissertation, University of San Francisco.

Nieto, S. (1992). *Affirming diversity: The sociopolitical context of multicultural education.* New York: Longman.

Patrón, R. L. (1986). *Promoting English literacy for Spanish-speaking students: A participatory study of Spanish-speaking parents, their children and school personnel, using an innovative intervention model in Spanish.* Unpublished doctoral dissertation, University of San Francisco.

Ramírez, J., & Douglas, D. (1989). *Language-minority parents and the school: Can home–school partnerships increase student success?* Sacramento: California State Department of Education, Bilingual Education Office.

Reichmuth, S. (1981). *Hispanic parent empowerment through critical dialogue and parent–child interaction within the school setting.* Unpublished doctoral dissertation, University of San Francisco.

Rodríguez, A., Rothstein, D., & Santana, L. (1994). What if parents were asking questions? Training for involving all parents. In D. Safran & E. Charlot (Eds.), *Families and schools: A global perspective for a multicultural society: Conference proceedings* (pp. 127–130). Orinda: John F. Kennedy University, Center for the Study of Parent Involvement.

Trueba, H. T. (1988). Culturally based explanations of minority students' academic achievement. *Anthropology & Education Quarterly, 19,* 270–287.

Turín, A. (1986a). *Arturo y Clementina* [Arthur and Clementine]. Barcelona: Editorial Lumen.

Turín, A. (1986b). *Rosa Caramelo.* Barcelona: Editorial Lumen.

Tusquets, E. (1987). *La conejita Marcela* [Marcela the Little Bunny]. Barcelona: Editorial Lumen.

Valdés, G. (1996). *Con respeto: Bridging the distances between culturally diverse families and schools: An ethnographic portrait.* New York: Teachers College Press.

Vygotsky, L. S. (1978). *Mind in society: The development of higher psychological process* (M. Cole, V. John-Steiner, S. Scribner, & E. Souberman, Trans. & Eds.). Cambridge, MA: Harvard University Press.

Watts, J. (1988). *A determination of parental expectations of and role in the educational process: Perspectives of African American parents.* Unpublished doctoral dissertation, University of San Francisco.

Zubizarreta, R. (1996). *Transformative family literacy: Engaging in meaningful dialogue with Spanish-speaking parents.* Cleveland, OH: Del Sol.

Afterword:

Re/constructing a New Reality

MARÍA DE LA LUZ REYES

A strong message emerging from these pages, pages written from insiders' perspectives, reveals the ongoing struggle to determine what is in the best interest of Latino children with respect to literacy instruction. For example, should Latino children have the right to use Spanish as a route to English literacy, or must they be forced to accept English as the primary or *only* route? The struggle to make this determination, however, is waged between two unequally matched opponents: members of the culture of power (Delpit, 1988) who control schools and establish policies and practices, and members of the Latino community, still a largely disenfranchised minority group.

Essentially, what's at stake is who has the right to define the world and others in it (Chapter 4, Halcón). The dominant majority wants Latinos to function as assimilated members of the larger "American" community, while Latinos refuse to "melt down," preferring to acculturate and thus retain their connections with their cultural identities. The positioning of others as "majority" and "minority" is, in reality, "socially and historically constructed, [and thus], they can be re/constructed" (Morgan, 1997, p. 1). In a small, but very real, way, this is what the authors of this book are doing: re/constructing a new reality of who Latinos are. They are debunking deficit myths regarding the so-called "disadvantages" of Latino students' language and culture. In its place, they are offering possibilities that can become realities in learning environments that respect and honor Latinos' ethnic and cultural identities.

As critical ethnographers and educators, these authors are interested in matters of class and ethnicity. And, as such, they are challenging the inequitable positioning of their children in schools, providing some examples of how nurturing and affirming cultural identities is the sound pedagogical path to critical literacy and other higher academic functions. Additionally, they are pointing out how, without realizing it, teachers can easily become

245

complicit with mainstream ideology and fail to acknowledge how their unexamined "habitudes" (Chapter 2, Diáz & Flores) lead to inequitable academic outcomes for Latinos.

The common thread running through this volume is a "Vygotskian pedagogy of hope" (Trueba, 1999; Vygotsky, 1978). This thread is intertwined with applications and understandings derived from Paulo Friere's (1970) theory of critical literacy. Although, as Luis Moll (Chapter 1) suggests, Vygotsky's work does not apply directly to the specific circumstances of Latino students, his theory provides a lens for dealing with diversity in schools because it is essentially "a theory of possibilities." The heart of Vygotsky's learning theory is that knowledge has its origins in sociocultural activity (Vygotsky, 1978; see also Moll, Chapter 1). To achieve higher psychological functions (i.e., critical thinking and critical literacy), the cultural and linguistic resources of learners must be acknowledged and incorporated in learning activities. The best way to mediate learning for children who speak a language other than English is to permit the use of their own language as a tool for learning.

Observations in schools suggest that educators have no problem understanding "culture with a small c," for example, the rules, values, and practices of a particular classroom, but they have greater difficulty understanding "culture with a capital C"—the cultural heritage of the students in the class. Teachers talk of creating a "cultural community" or a "community of learners" as a means of fostering students' learning potential. Yet, in too many cases, these same teachers are totally oblivious to ethnic and cultural differences among their students and to how these differences influence learning. There is still a dissonance, a disconcerting awkwardness, in dealing directly with this type of cultural diversity. It is not surprising, then, that many of the authors in this volume are still concerned with the rejection, omission, and/or undervaluing of Latino cultures.

This feeling of exclusion is exacerbated by xenophobic attitudes about the increasing number of "foreigners" in this country (with Latinos being the fastest-growing group). Many Latinos remain incredulous that the four California initiatives—making English the official language of California (Proposition 63), restricting immigration (Proposition 187), outlawing affirmative action (Proposition 209), and eliminating bilingual education (Proposition 227)—could pass in the most linguistically diverse state in the nation with the largest Spanish-speaking constituency outside of Latin America. "How was this possible?" they ask. There are numerous and varied answers to this question, too lengthy to consider here, but the point is that this negative social climate makes more difficult the task of persuading school administrators that supporting and incorporating the language and the culture of Latino students in schools is the most viable path to their academic success. And so, Latina and Latino teachers try to shield their students from the rejection and undervaluing that they know inevitably will come their way. As is evident from these readings, they put great efforts into making certain that their students are equipped with "survival strategies" by shifting the burden of teaching and learning from students' to teachers' shoulders.

With respect to conducting research, the academy trains scholars to "objectify" their topics and distance themselves from their "subjects" in order to produce credible intellectual work. Without apology, the educators in this volume reject this notion and embrace the belief that their daily experiences as Latinos provide "added value" to their academic work and their teaching. This position helps to reconcile their insider/outsider status with their subjective/objective stance. As researchers and teachers they refuse to treat their students and research participants as mere "others." On the contrary, they approach research *as praxis*, investing a great deal of time and energy in providing opportunities for improving conditions and uncovering insights that will have transformative value for members of those communities. It is not unusual to learn that many of these researchers are treated by their students and research participants as members of an extended family. The emergence of this inevitable bond exemplifies the integration of Vygotsky's theory of hope with Paulo Friere's (1970) critical literacy theory.

As advocates of critical literacy, they champion the oppressed and their causes. They understand the importance of "knowing the world and the word" (Freire, 1970; Freire & Macedo, 1987) and how these are critical factors in "the survival and adaptation" (Trueba, 1999, p. 592) of Latinos. These scholars are forging a literacy of liberation, one that allows their children to acquire critical literacy without forcing them to relinquish their ethnic and cultural identities. As Enrique "Henry" Trueba (1999) maintains, "break[ing] the cycle of underachievement and oppression and [moving] away from hegemonic instructional structures" (p. 592) requires not only Vygotsky's pedagogy of hope and Freire's critical literacy, but a deep understanding of how educators can move beyond this rhetoric, as the authors have demonstrated here.

References

Delpit, L. D. (1988). The silenced dialogue: Power and pedagogy in educating other people's children. *Harvard Educational Review, 58*(3), 280–298.

Freire, P. (1970). *Pedagogy of the oppressed.* New York: Continuum.

Freire, P., & Macedo, D. (1987). *Literacy: Reading the word and the world.* South Hadley, MA: Bergin & Garvey.

Morgan, W. (1997). *Critical literacy in the classroom.* New York: Routledge.

Trueba, E. T. (1999). Critical ethnography and a Vygotskian pedagogy of hope: The empowerment of Mexican immigrant children. *International Journal of Qualitative Studies in Education. 12*(6), 591–614.

Vygotsky, L. S. (1978). *Mind in society: The development of higher psychological process* (M. Cole, V. John-Steiner, S. Scribner, & E. Souberman, Trans. & Eds.). Cambridge, MA: Harvard University Press.

Index

About the Editors
and The Contributors

Alma Flor Ada is a Professor at the University of San Francisco where she teaches in the fields of multicultural and bilingual education. She is an award-winning author of children's books.

Héctor H. Alvarez is a research assistant, Ph.D. student, and teaching assistant in the Division of Urban Schooling, Graduate School of Education and Information Studies at the University of California at Los Angeles. His research examines the relationship between language, culture, and literacy learning; in particular, the discursive construction and representation of difference in literacy activities as it affects ethnic/racialized identity formation and academic engagement.

María V. Balderrama is an Assistant Professor in education at California State University, San Bernardino where she teaches courses, in bilingual/multicultural education. Her research interests focus on the education of Mexicano/Latino students.

Patricia Baquedano-López is an Assistant Professor in the Graduate School of Education at the University of California at Berkeley. Her research examines language socialization and literacy practices in urban schools and in after-school programs as they relate to the educational opportunities of Mexican immigrant students.

Lilia I. Bartolomé is an Associate Professor at the University of Massachusetts in Boston. Her research interests center on the educational experiences of Chicano/Mexicano students and other culturally and linguistically diverse students in U.S. schools. Her publications include: *Dancing with Bigotry: The Poisoning of Culture* (with D. Macedo, 2000), and *The Misteaching of Academic Discourses: The Politics of Language in the Classroom* (1998).

256

María Echiburu Berzins is a bilingual kindergarten teacher with the Mapleton Public Schools in Denver, Colorado. She is a strong advocate for bilingualism and biliteracy for Latino students.

Esteban Díaz is a Professor in the Department of Educational Psychology and Counseling in the College of Education at California State University at San Bernardino. His research interests examine the relationship between language, cognition, and literacy as they apply to bilingual learners and their teachers.

Bárbara Flores is Professor of Education at California State University at San Bernardino in the department of Language, Literacy, and Culture where she teaches in the Teacher Credential and Masters programs. She is a scholar activist and has conducted collaborative action research in schools with teachers and children.

María E. Fránquiz is an Assistant Professor in two program areas: Education, Equity, and Cultural Diversity Program, and Instruction and Curriculum in the Content Areas in the School of Education at the University of Colorado-Boulder. Her research examines Latino students' construction of academic identity and its effect on school achievement.

Kris D. Gutiérrez is a Professor in the Graduate School of Education at the University of California at Los Angeles where she teaches.

John J. Halcón is Professor of Education at the University of Northern Colorado, Greeley in the School for Study of Teaching and Teacher Education where he teaches foundations of education, bilingual/ESL, and multicultural education courses. His research interests are in the preparation of teachers for bilingual and culturally diverse students, and racism in higher education.

Bobbi Ciriza Houtchens teaches English and ESL at San Bernardino High School in California. She is a mother, an avid reader, and an outspoken advocate for children everywhere.

Robert T. Jiménez is an Associate Professor at the University of Illinois at Urbana Champaign. He teaches courses on qualitative research methods, second language literacy, and issues related to the education of Latina/o students. His research interests include how bilingual readers process and respond to texts, and the influence that literacy and identity have on one another.

Eloise Andrade Laliberty is a former classroom teacher and recipient of the Sallie Mae's One Hundred Most Outstanding First Year Teachers in the country. She is currently an elementary school principal with the Mapleton Public Schools in Denver, Colorado.

Alice E. López is a bilingual elementary teacher and bilingual education consultant. She is also the 1997 winner of the Milken Award for the Most Outstanding Teacher in Colorado. She has been an elementary teacher with the Mapleton Public Schools in Denver, Colorado since 1978.

Roberta Maldonado is a language arts/Title I Coordinator with the Boulder Valley Public School District. She is also a Ph.D. candidate in literacy at the University of Colorado–Boulder.

Carmen I. Mercado is an Associate Professor at Hunter College of the City University of New York where she teaches courses in language and literacy. Her most personally and professionally affecting experience has been that of collaborating with teachers, students, and families in constructing language together.

Luis C. Moll is a Professor in the College of Education, Department of Language, Reading and Culture at the University of Arizona at Tucson where he teaches. He is considered a leading expert in the application of Vygotskian theory in education.

Sonia Nieto is a Professor at the University of Massachusetts at Amherst. She writes in the area of multicultural education in which she is regarded as a leading expert.

María de la Luz Reyes is an Associate Professor in the School of Education at the University of Colorado–Boulder. Her research interests focus on Mexicano/Latino students' development of biliteracy in the elementary grades, and on racism in higher education.

Rosa Zubizarreta is an educator, writer, translator, staff developer, and consultant in the field of bilingual education. She also has worked as a bilingual classroom teacher.